DIGITAL SATIRE IN LATIN AMERICA

Reframing Media, Technology, and Culture in Latin/o America

Digital Satire in Latin America

Online Video Humor as Hybrid Alternative Media

Paul Alonso

Héctor Fernández L'Hoeste and Juan Carlos Rodríguez, Series Editors

UNIVERSITY OF FLORIDA PRESS

Gainesville

Publication of this work made possible by a Sustaining the Humanities through the American Rescue Plan grant from the National Endowment for the Humanities.

29 28 27 26 25 24   6 5 4 3 2 1

Library of Congress Cataloging-in-Publication Data
Names: Alonso, Paul, 1978– author.
Title: Digital satire in Latin America : online video humor as hybrid alternative media / Paul Alonso.
Description: Gainesville : University of Florida Press, 2024. | Series: Reframing media, technology, and culture in latin/o america | Includes bibliographical references and index. | Summary: "This book analyzes how digital-native audiovisual satire has become increasingly influential in national public debates within Latin America. Paul Alonso examines the role of online video creators in critiquing politics and society and amplifying public discourse, filling gaps left by traditional media and journalism" — Provided by publisher.
Identifiers: LCCN 2024017635 | ISBN 9781683404637 (hardback) | ISBN 9781683404750 (paperback) | ISBN 9781683404835 (pdf) | ISBN 9781683404941 (ebook)
Subjects: LCSH: Latin American wit and humor, Pictorial. | Digital media—Social aspects—South America. | BISAC: SOCIAL SCIENCE / Media Studies | HISTORY / Latin America / General
Classification: LCC NC1450 .A46 2024 | DDC 302.23/1098—dc23/eng/20240722
LC record available at https://lccn.loc.gov/2024017635

University of Florida Press
2046 NE Waldo Road
Suite 2100
Gainesville, FL 32609
http://upress.ufl.edu

UF PRESS
UNIVERSITY
OF FLORIDA

CONTENTS

FIGURES

ACKNOWLEDGMENTS

I would like to acknowledge the Ivan Allen College and the School of Modern Languages at the Georgia Institute of Technology for their continued support to my research and writing projects. I'd also like to thank all the satirists that generously allowed me to interview them for this book and other related publications (Guille Aquino, Maria Paulina Baena, Joanna Hausmann, Gerardo García, Jorge Ulloa, Ivana Szerman, Federico Simonetti, Jaime Ferraro, Pedro Saborido, Patricio Fernández, Ingrid Beck, Mariano Lucano, and Dario Adanti); Héctor Fernández-L'Hoeste for his comments on the first complete draft of this book; Neta Kanny for a first round of proofreading; and Stephanye Hunter, editor at the University of Florida Press, for her efficient work in the production of this book. Special thanks to Nina, Nicole, and Solange for laughing at my—often absurd—jokes.

1

Introduction

Audiovisual Satire in the Americas in the Time of the Internet

The beginning of the twenty-first century saw the global rise of satiric television as a powerful force in sociopolitical communication. In the context of 9/11, the Bush administration, the invasion of Iraq, the emergence of Fox News, and increasing public dissatisfaction with the news media, satiric US news shows such as *The Daily Show with Jon Stewart* and *The Colbert Report* (and later, during the Obama years, *Last Week Tonight with John Oliver*) became hugely popular and influential by criticizing the sociopolitical establishment and the role of the media in democracy. They had a transnational impact, and their formats were adapted in different parts of the world, with televised comedians reporting and commenting on the news in countries such as Egypt, Germany, and Mexico (Alonso, 2018; Baym & Jones, 2013). Meanwhile, from the emblematic *Saturday Night Live* to the transgressive *Da Ali G Show*, sketch comedy became edgier and increasingly political, and stand-up comedians—such as Dave Chappelle, Sarah Silverman, and Louis CK—became more vocal in questioning social prejudices. While many satiric television clips circulated globally via the internet, satiric shows of online origin or so-called digital-native shows were also becoming prominent by the 2010s. Before Donald Trump was elected, Barack Obama and Hillary Clinton appeared on the online satiric show *Between Two Ferns with Zach Galifianakis*, among other humorous venues. When Trump—an entertainer and media personality himself—became president, satirists on various platforms took an increasingly aggressive stance, ridiculing an administration that brought political spectacle to the center of power and that dismissed criticism by calling the oppositional media "fake news." At the same time, inspired by the boom of contemporary US satire, independent digital-native satiric shows began to flourish globally, expanding the options of critical humor beyond the regulations of corporate and commercial media.

In Latin America, a new wave of digital-native satire has become increasingly influential in national public debates, filling gaps in sociopolitical critique left by television and traditional media. In *Digital Satire in Latin America*, I analyze some of the most representative and influential satiric shows born on the internet and produced in the region, focusing on cases from Argentina, Colombia, Ecuador, Peru, and Mexico, as well as from the Latinx community in the United States. Most of these shows were pioneers in regularly producing for the internet original satiric content dealing with sociopolitical issues in their countries. Operating between 2010 and 2020, they obtained significant online viewership, recurrently participated in public debates, and were featured in other media outlets.[1] Exposing some of the prevalent cultural and sociopolitical tensions in the region, digital satire has become an increasingly relevant scene to question power and hegemonic values, and to discursively negotiate local and regional identities. Active on YouTube, Instagram, Facebook, TikTok, and Twitter (now X), young satirists rearticulate transnational media languages and critical entertainment formats, accumulating significant internet audiences, particularly among the millennial generation. Infused with a DIY (do-it-yourself) mentality, their shows reveal alternative models for the development of independent Latin American digital media. In an increasingly postnetwork era marked by the crisis of modern journalism and the rise of social media entertainment, this phenomenon has developed in a mediascape defined by hybridization and the emergence of new transgressive infotainment content. Latin American and Latinx satire on the internet, with its multilayered construction of meaning, can be seen as a unique type of subversive, "glocal" digital media produced by cultural globalization. At the same time, contemporary satiric media is a type of *critical metatainment*—a postmodern carnivalesque result of and a transgressive reaction to the process of tabloidization in the media spectacle era—not only because of its use of entertainment and humor to develop sociocultural and political critique, but also for its capacity to question the role of media in society and to deconstruct "news and entertainment genres through parody in order to challenge their claims of authority and/or moral consistency" (Alonso, 2018, p. 152).

While in my previous book, *Satiric TV in the Americas: Critical Metatainment as Negotiated Dissent* (2018), I focused on national and cable TV, I also devoted a chapter to Latin American digital humor. This book elaborates on those ideas regarding contemporary trends in audiovisual humor and their impact on sociopolitical communication. Drawing from theory on satire, infotainment, and cultural globalization, I examine the critical role that a new generation of online satiric TV shows has played in challenging the status quo, traditional journalism, and prevalent local media cultures. Considering the national and regional tensions and polarizations intensified during the Trump/COVID-19 era, this book maps, contextualizes, and analyzes relevant cases to understand the relation between political information, social and cultural dissent, critical humor, and entertainment in Latin(x) America. It also shows that as satiric formats travel to a particular national context, they are appropriated in different ways and adapted to local circumstances, thus having distinctive (subversive) implications. While the degree of popularity of these types of digital initiatives varies according to national restrictions, target (or niche) audience, level of irreverence, format, production quality, and ideological standpoint, they exemplify the many ways in which cultural globalization and hybridity operate in today's transnational entertainment and critical humor.

Digital Satire in Latin America seeks to illuminate the role of digital media in shaping changing notions of journalism and political communication in today's polarized democratic societies, the role of satire as resistance and negotiation in public discourse, and the role of critical entertainment in times of social crisis and confrontation. In this book, I argue that digital-native satire has become a unique type of *hybrid alternative media* that, in contexts of highly ideological polarization and sociopolitical crisis, is able to articulate critical, distinctive, and nonpartisan interpretations of reality, filling a gap left by traditional journalism and commercial entertainment. Using a combination of professional and nonmainstream practices, resources, and values, these satiric voices increasingly seek to dismantle fake news, elucidate social tensions, and establish new versions of "truth" with in-depth content that goes beyond the confrontational attack of polarized ideological or political views. They insert a much-needed, informed, reflexive, argumentative, and historically rooted perspective that amplifies democratic public discourse in saturated and discredited media environments, creating alternative—mostly young and liberal—online communities at the local and regional level, according to their own reports.[2] Adopting global formats and references, they also rearticulate local identities at the crossroads of their countries' sociopolitical and cultural tensions in relation to issues of race, gender, and social class while navigating the limits of political (in)correctness. To demonstrate these ideas, I address the following questions: What has been the role of digital satire as hybrid alternative media in today's political communication and national democracies?

How does contemporary digital satire address prevalent sociopolitical tensions and reflect the ideological polarization in Latin(x) American societies? What is the critical dialogue between contemporary digital satire and mainstream media/journalism? How are satiric discourses constructed to develop criticism and transgression and denounce discrimination while navigating political correctness? How does contemporary digital satire incorporate local and global referents to create new hybrid languages? And, what are the new business models for independent digital media production developed by popular digital satiric shows? Through a methodological analysis approach based on interviews and discourse/textual analysis of the shows and representative media contents, I answer these questions by offering three insights. First, I describe the cases in relation to the social, political, and cultural context to which they react. Second, I analyze the discourse and specific critiques developed by satirists, and their critical dialogue with local media culture, evaluating the cases' particularities and evolution. Third, I scrutinize the cultural role they have played in their societies, drawing conclusions based on their specific platforms and national contexts, and the way they circulate and resonate in other countries of the region. From a broader scope, I evaluate what we can learn about today's democracies and their contradictions through the analysis of satiric digital media while extending and refining the literature on contemporary satire, political communication, and cultural globalization in the time of the internet and social media networks. At the same time, this book contributes to the emerging field of Latin American digital humanities (Fernández L'Hoeste & Rodríguez, 2020), particularly in its critical exploration of cybercultures and the impact of digital technologies on the rearticulation of social identities.

Satire, Carnival, and Critical Metatainment

Satire, "a blend of wit and criticism, aimed particularly at political leaders and institutions" (Collins, 1996, p. 645), has taken an active role in contemporary critique of "dangerous religious, political, moral, or social standards" (Cuddon, 1991, p. 202). Connecting with Bakhtin's (1984) conceptualizations of the medieval carnival—a prevailing spirit of fun mixed with social criticism—contemporary satire has established itself as a transgressive space that captures and rearticulates the sharp humor of ordinary people as expressed in the unofficial spaces of popular culture where they can mock authority. Carnival behavior in the Middle Ages was considered transgressive (and for some critics, even revolutionary) because it inverted conventional oppositions (high and low, mind and body, the spiritual and the profane, culture and nature, male and female) and blurred the division between audience and performers. It was a space of freedom through laughter embodied in the figure of the court jester, the one who can speak truth to power without getting his head cut off. Carnival, nevertheless, was a licensed affair, a permissible and temporary rupture of a hegemonic social order that maintained its dominance by leaving room for the nondominant classes to enjoy a cultural space of their own (Hall, 1992; Stallybrass & White, 1997).

Critics of carnival maintain that it is not politically potent but rather serves the structural goals of the powerful: people have fun, temporarily reverse hierarchies to mock power, and then return to an unreflective daily life, thereby ending the potential for transgression (Eco, 1984). The modern turn degraded the carnival spirit and its radical character into a less challenging, more conservative "holiday mood" (Bakhtin, 1984, p. 33). Likewise, some characteristics of carnival culture (its embrace of bad taste, offensive and vulgar language, ritualistic degradation, parody, and excess) are typical of tabloid media (Glynn, 2000, p. 115), which tends to adopt a carnivalesque tone and styles to hold on to its authoritative status as the voice of the people while merely mimicking an attitude of transgression (Convoy, 2002). Furthermore, in contemporary media culture, transgression—defined as the (conscious) overstepping of boundaries that challenges written and unwritten social rules (Jenks, 2003)—"seems to be everywhere" (Hermes & Hill, 2021, p. 6), with populist leaders and politicians appropriating the symbolic impact of transgression with their outrageous behavior. While commercial media and politicians have domesticated the overstepping of boundaries and may make clever use of transgression for their own benefits, neither of them owns the countercultural power and unexpected social impacts of crossing limits to challenge the status quo (Hermes & Hill, 2021). In fact, since culture is increasingly uncertain and in flux, it is difficult to determine where boundaries now lie, and the limits are only found by crossing them (Bataille, 1985, 1987; Jenks, 2003). In other words, transgression is a fluid term and is in constant negotiation, as are its motivations, morals, and effects. Satire can be considered a front-runner in the negotiation of these limits in today's mediascape and public discourse.

From the psychoanalytic perspective, Freud (1960) considered humor to be a way to channel our aggression toward power, giving voice to unconscious desires and repressed feelings or anxieties. This humorous catharsis is produced by "a disjunction between the way things are and the way they are represented in a joke, between expectation and actuality. Humor defeats our expectations by producing a novel actuality, by changing the situation in which we find ourselves" (Critchley, 2002, p. 1). Satire's carnivalesque spirit of "potent, populist, critical inversion of all official worlds and hierarchies" (Stallybrass & White, 1997, p. 294) seeks to question the idea that the social order is a natural state instead of an exercise of power or, as Barthes (1972) put it, a myth. In other words, satiric humor offers a lens for realizing that a certain accepted "reality" is not a necessary condition, and not the only option. This humorous operation (and the consequential act of laughter) tends to be aggressive. Satire is a verbal attack that "passes judgment on the object of that attack, thereby enunciating a perceived breach in societal norms or values" (Gray et al., 2009, p. 12), while transforming chaotic human emotions (such as anger, indignation, or shame) into "a useful and artistic expression" (Test, 1991, p. 4). In this sense, satire's transgression "subversively challenge[s] universal notions by seeking to establish a deliberate sense of uncomfortableness as fundamental to our relations with the other and ourselves" (Black, 2021, p. 3). It "adeptly lends itself to a kind of spectral analysis of the workings of power, fueled by its own power as comedy" (Zupančič, 2016, p. 219). Contemporary satirists—like the ones analyzed in this book—come from this transgressive tradition, which in today's world targets not only the social, political, and cultural establishments but frequently also the media institutions that support them.

In a global mediascape saturated with television humor based on the constant repetition of jokes with prejudiced stereotypes, tabloid content, celebrities, and media spectacles, satire frequently runs the risk of not being funny or of being misunderstood. While laughter is certainly an important outcome for satire to have its full effect, it is not a necessary feature of the genre (Gray et al., 2009). Because of its unsettling nature, satire has always had difficulty making its way into mainstream mass media. This is true not only because satire has frequently targeted the values and practices of corporate media, but also because its transgressive nature risks alienating segments of broad audiences, thereby affecting potential advertising, a foundational method of support for commercial media. Furthermore, in contrast to most mass media content, satire does not offer easily digestible meanings; it requires a level of sophistication that places difficult demands on audiences, such as a sharp state of awareness, mental participation, and shared knowledge (Gray et al., 2009). Nevertheless, at the beginning of the century, in a context of declining readership of traditional journalism outlets and diminishing press credibility, the resurgence of political satire in the media—and particularly satiric infotainment, as a subgenre that parodies news and journalism—evidenced the possibility of the genre to become successful within commercial and cable television systems. In the United States, comedians Jon Stewart and Stephen Colbert were considered two of the country's most influential "journalists" during the 2000s, and their shows—*The Daily Show with Jon Stewart* and *The Colbert Report*—proved to be leading forces in US political debate (Amarasingam, 2011; Baym, 2010; Day, 2011; Jones, 2010). Later, *Last Week Tonight with John Oliver*, *Full Frontal with Samantha Bee*, and *The Daily Show with Trevor Noah*, among others, expanded the format, evidencing the need for more diverse voices in terms of gender, race, and nationality. Some critics even called these shows "neo-modern" journalism (Baym, 2005) or new types of public journalism (Faina, 2012). More recently, feminist satire has attracted increasing media and academic attention (Day, 2022, 2023; Day & Green, 2020; Finley, 2016; McAuliffe, 2023). While still significantly underexplored, contemporary Latin American satiric media (particularly in magazines, film, and television) has also been increasingly studied during recent years in relation to its sociopolitical communication role and its capacity to challenge the status quo and prevalent mainstream media practices and representations (Alonso, 2018, 2019; Burkart et al., 2021; Fraticelli, 2023; Poblete & Suárez, 2016).

At the same time, many contemporary satiric shows became part of a trend toward global infotainment, referring to a "cluster of program types that blur traditional distinctions between information-oriented and entertainment-based genres of television programming" (Baym, 2008). Infotainment has usually been framed negatively as a means of democratic political communication because it is related to "the globalization of US-style ratings-driven television journalism which privileges privatized soft news—about celebrities, crime, corruption and violence—and presents it as a form of spectacle, at the expense of news about political, civic and public affairs" (Thussu, 2007, p. 8). However, contemporary satire proves that it can also be a critical discourse to develop sociopolitical critique and question power. In times when the traditional journalism industry has experienced an economic and institutional crisis, contemporary satiric infotainment has added a subversive interpretation to the incessant stream of political images, exploiting leverage points—factual errors, logical contradictions, and incongruities—in both the establishment's political discourse and the media that disseminates it (Warner, 2007). Satire, then, has also become a tool to enforce accountability by pointing out falsehoods, inconsistencies, and irrelevant news blown out of proportion (Painter & Hodges, 2010). It challenges the legitimacy of dominant news and forces media professionals and the audience to think more responsibly about what journalism should look like (Feldman, 2007). Moreover, the debate over infotainment problematizes the idea of news, a social construct that means different things to different people (Bird, 2010). In this sense, infotainment is best understood as a phenomenon of border crossing that problematizes common assumptions that news is necessarily serious and that entertainment shows contain little in the way of sociopolitical significance (Brants, 1998; Delli Carpini & Williams, 1994, 2001). This tension exists in a global scenario where media content and public discourses have been increasingly shaped by hybridization: the cumulative melding of news, politics, popular culture, and marketing. Baym (2005, p. 262) calls this process "discursive integration," in which these once-differentiated discourses "have lost their distinctiveness and are being melded into previously unimagined combinations." While most of the cases analyzed in this book can be considered part of the hybrid subgenre of satiric infotainment dealing with the parody, deconstruction, or reframing of news, all of them question the role of the media in contemporary democracies from different perspectives.

These characteristics of today's satiric media have shaped it, as mentioned earlier, as a particular type of critical metatainment, a postmodern carnivalesque result of and a transgressive reaction to the process of tabloidization in the media spectacle era. As I have written elsewhere, "satiric media as critical metatainment are multilayered and complex discursive objects that use humor to develop a sociocultural and political critique, while at the same time questioning the role of media in society and deconstructing news and entertainment genres through parody in order to challenge their claims of authority and/or moral consistency" (Alonso, 2018, p. 152). In the case of critical metatainment broadcast via mainstream or commercial media outlets, satiric shows tend to negotiate their power to transgress within the limits of network regulations, interests, and editorial stands. In the case of digital-native satire, the internet offers different (arguably looser) parameters and restrictions, while also incorporating content producers within the framework of platform capitalism (Srnicek, 2017b),[3] as well as the "platformization" of cultural production (Nieborg & Poell, 2018; Poell et al., 2022).[4] The rise of social media entertainment—

understood as "an emerging proto-industry based on previously amateur creators professionalizing and engaging in content innovation and media entrepreneurship across multiple social media platforms to aggregate global fan communities and incubate their own media brands" (Cunningham & Craig, 2017, p. 71)—reflects this platform conditioning and has redefined the entertainment industry (Cunningham & Craig, 2016, 2019).[5] Within this scenario, digital satiric shows' dilemmas, concerns, and opportunities for subsistence and evolution relate to their predominant nature as hybrid alternative media enterprises.

Hybrid Alternative Media and Cultural Globalization

During the past few decades, an explosion of independent, digital-native outlets, home to content "born directly on the internet, without being the alter ego of any previous offline publication" (Salaverría et al., 2019, p. 232), has changed the global media landscape. Digitalization has caused profound structural changes in information systems and media industries as internet penetration has increased (although unevenly) all around the world (Dragomir & Thompson, 2014). In Latin America, a region marked by clientelist and patrimonial relationships between mainstream media and political and economic elites (Fox & Waisbord, 2002; Hallin & Papathanassopoulos, 2002; Waisbord, 2012), this phenomenon opened opportunities for a variety of entrepreneurial journalists and creators to launch start-up projects and thereby challenge official discourses, offer alternative perspectives and content, experiment with new business models, and fill the gaps left by traditional media (Harlow, 2022; Higgins Joyce, 2018; Salaverría et al., 2019; Schmitz Weiss et al., 2018). Within complex hybrid media systems of multiple modernities (Echeverria et al., 2022),[6] Latin American independent, digital media entrepreneurship—defined as the "creation and ownership of an enterprise whose activity adds an independent voice to the media marketplace" (Hoag, 2008, p. 74)—aligns with innovative types of alternative media shaped by the emergence of new digital technologies. Alternative media, nevertheless, is an ambiguous concept that has been used to refer to a variety of nonmainstream communication practices. Media scholars have noted that it is "a term so elastic as to be devoid of virtually any signification" (Abel, 1997, p. 79) or that alternative media is oxymoronic: "Everything is, at some point, alternative to something else" (Downing, 2001, p. ix). At a time when even the US alt-right has co-opted the "alternative" label, scholars have used many terms to elaborate further on these nonhegemonic media practices, such as *radical* (Downing, 2001), *citizens media* (Rodriguez, 2001), *advocacy* (Waisbord, 2009), *participatory/activist* (Waltz, 2005), and *grassroots autonomous media* (Jeppesen & Petrick, 2018).

Searching for common ground, Atton (2002, p. 4) defines alternative media as much by its capacity to generate nonstandard, often violational methods of creation, production, and distribution as by its content. In the case of the alternative press, it developed its own construction of news based on alternative values and frameworks of news gathering, sources, and access. Similarly, Hájek and Carpentier (2015) identify some essential characteristics of alternative media: a capacity to amplify marginalized voices and fill informative needs not met by mainstream media; levels of participation and pluralism in content and form; and noncorporate, horizontal, and noncommercial organization and funding. From a more activist perspective, O'Sullivan (1994, p. 10) notes that a primary goal of alternative media channels is to promote radical social change; they "avowedly reject or challenge established and institutionalized politics, in the sense that they all advocate change in society or at least a critical reassessment of traditional values."

While communication scholars in Latin America have tended to discuss the potential of alternative media as a counterbalance to unequal flows of information and cultural imperialism (Dorfman & Mattelart, 1975; Reyes Matta, 1983), these debates place alternative media as a rigid, marginal form that seeks the "construction of a new hegemony" (Reyes Matta, 1983, p. 52), usually aligned with left-wing, militant views. Rodriguez (2001, p. 11) criticizes this vision not only because of its narrow categories but also because "in this David versus Goliath scenario, alternative media is frequently declared a failure." Furthermore, the implementation of neoliberal policies in the 1990s reduced the control of the media by the state and increased the influence of the private sector (Lugo-Ocando, 2008). Given the need to democratize media in countries with highly concentrated, family-owned media companies historically aligned with business and political elites (Fox & Waisbord, 2002; Hughes & Lawson, 2005; Hughes & Prado, 2011; Martin-Barbero, 1993), the debate about the role and characteristics of alternative media has become more nuanced in recent years and has been further complicated by the digital revolution. As Harlow (2022, 2023) notes, many of today's Latin American digital-native sites are produced by professional journalists (not amateurs), many of whom left traditional mainstream media to conduct a different, more independent style of journalism. They tend to cover social movements and disenfranchised groups, and they often align themselves with causes such as justice, freedom of expression, and the fight against homophobia but do not associate themselves with the region's militant, activist press. While many extant studies focus on the case of journalism-oriented news sites (Alonso, 2022), they can easily be applied to most of the cases analyzed in this book.

In today's mediascape, very few independent, digital-native media projects meet all the revolutionary, counterhegemonic ideals expected from previous alternative militant media, and what is considered alternative at one point may be mainstream at another (Alonso, 2019; Bailey et al., 2008). Atton (2002) suggests that the radicality of an alternative publication might be interrogated in terms of its multidimensional character, a perspective that privileges the overlap and intersection of dimensions, evidencing that an alternative publication is, in the end, a hybrid product that includes mixed voices and discourses. This "crossover" might include "ideas, content, style, and not least, people between what might be termed the alternative and the mainstream" (Harcup, 2005, p. 370). Hájek and Carpentier (2015) suggest viewing such outlets as "alternative mainstream media." Harlow (2022) and I (Alonso, 2019) have used the phrases "hybrid popular media" and "hybrid alternative media," respectively, to refer to contemporary independent Latin American publications composed of a multilayered *mestizaje* (or blending) of professional practices, languages, and cultures. Connecting with the trend of "discursive integration" (Baym, 2005), this hybrid programming also results from globalization and has a potentially wide range of implications for public information, political communication, and democratic discourse.

Scholars have argued that globalization produces a variety of "hybrid," "creolized," or "glocal" phenomena, in which local elements are incorporated within globalized forms and in other combinations (Robertson, 1995). While hybridity and *mestizaje* are intrinsic characteristics of postcolonial societies, the production and consumption of cultural products represent a struggle for meaning between classes within countries, between high and popular cultures, and between local, national, and imported cultural traditions (García Canclini, 1995; Kraidy, 2005). For Martin-Barbero (1993), hybridity reveals the syncretic nature of popular culture, which both adopts and resists the dominant culture and also transforms it. In the internet era, Martin-Barbero (2007) warns about the potential of digital *mestizajes* to subvert the status quo, but also to legitimize current exclusionary practices. In this sense, hybridization describes a process in which elements of different cultures are synthesized together into new forms that reflect the original cultures but constitute distinct new ones (García Canclini, 1995).

In this scenario, global formats must tap into local culture to find audiences in new locations (Moran, 2009; Straubhaar, 2007). According to the notion of cultural proximity, audiences tend "to prefer and select local or national cultural content that is more proximate and relevant to them" (Straubhaar, 1991, p. 43). The consequential process of hybridization then becomes a negotiation between structure and culture, and its success partially depends on its ability to allow space for local specificities (Kraidy, 2005; Pieterse, 2009; Straubhaar, 2007). In terms of digital media, Taylor and Pitman (2007, p. 19) consider cyberspace, too, to be a "zone of negotiation" in which "Latin American practitioners are negotiating (temporary) spaces for the expression of localized identities." As part of this negotiation, Taylor and Pitman (2013, p. 22) find that online Latin American cultural practices engage with "a simultaneous tactical use of online fluidity and border-crossings, coupled with tactics of reterritorialization, reaffirmation of place, and reworkings of locality." While audience preference still largely depends on the cultural proximity of the local and the national (Straubhaar, 1991), regional programming also holds significance, highlighting the relevance of Latin America as a geolinguistic market (Sinclair, 2004). By adapting global formats (heavily influenced by the US versions), the Latin American satiric shows analyzed in this book are prevalent examples of hybrid products shaped by globalization and the phenomenon of discursive integration in media content.

Transgression, Political Correctness, and Polarization in the Trump/ COVID-19 Era

Because of its transgressive nature, carnivalesque satire that challenges hegemonic values and critiques power using controversial methods or by engaging with taboo topics has often been accused of being politically incorrect. Take, for example, the comedy of Sacha Baron Cohen, the Jewish comedian from London who created the satiric characters of Borat, Ali G, and Brüno. These exaggerated characters engaged in politically incorrect (sexist, anti-Semitic, homophobic, racist) behavior in order to expose society's bigotry, hidden prejudices, and tolerance of discrimination (Alonso, 2016, 2021). Baron Cohen's transgressive humor was subjected to criticism from both conservative and liberal sectors, and he was threatened by governments, associations, and individuals, suffered multiple investigations of obscenity and impropriety by media regulators, and provoked dozens of lawsuits. Similarly, satiric magazines such as *Charlie Hebdo* (France) and *Barcelona* (Argentina) have frequently been accused of being politically incorrect, and comedians such as Bill Maher have even used the term to label their own humor. It has become, nevertheless, an ambiguous and contradictory expression.

Many arguments against political correctness hold that "censorship and the notion that social norms dictating what is considered respectful, inclusive, and acceptable language would hinder productive discussion about difficult issues" (Gantt Shafer, 2017, p. 2), and some have presented valid concerns over who gets to decide what counts as politically correct language (Hughes, 2010). In parallel to criticisms of multiculturalism, immigration, and cultural diversity, attacks on political correctness remain prominent in debates about free speech and the autonomy of the individual (Paglia, 2018), and these attacks have proved to be politically popular (Esposito & Finley, 2019). At the same time, the term *politically correct* (or PC) has been used by conservatives to promote the idea of "a deep divide between the 'ordinary people' and the 'liberal elite,' who sought to control the speech and thoughts of regular folk. Opposition to political correctness also became a way to rebrand racism in ways that were politically acceptable in the post-civil-rights era" (Wegel, 2016).[7] While the PC debate is not as visible and widespread in Latin America as it is in the Anglo world (and might seem to be a foreign imposition), it has been increasingly present in academic and media controversies, reflecting a tension between the need to protect vulnerable populations from public discrimination and the limits of freedom of speech.

After the debate about policing speech reemerged in the context of Black Lives Matter and movements against sexual violence, Trump's electoral campaign and his election as the forty-fifth president of the United States inaugurated a new phase of (anti-)political correctness. Calling Mexican immigrants "rapists" and "criminals," and referring to women as "fat pigs," "dogs," "slobs," and "disgusting animals," Trump declared that "the big problem" of the United States was "being politically correct" (Fox News, 2015). His controversial policy proposals—deporting millions of undocumented immigrants, banning Muslims from entering the United States, and introducing unconstitutional stop and frisk—were accompanied by a rhetoric that played with conservative xenophobic fears. Trump capitalized on the Right's decades-long crusade against political correctness, blaming it for an array of social problems. Gantt Shafer (2017) notes that the term *political incorrectness* became in Trump's political context a means through which veiled or overt racism, sexism, and bigotry could be communicated to a white public through social media and political discourse, creating cathartic reactions. Trump's anti-PC rhetoric has been celebrated by his supporters as "telling it like it is" (Scatamburlo-D'Annibale, 2019), and he emerged in the conservative sphere as "a brash straight-shooter, a neoliberal truth-teller—the politically incorrect candidate that was going to get the things done" (Gantt Shafer, 2017, p. 2), with a strategy that has also been implemented by Latin American neopopulists. This approach has led the *Washington Post*, among many others, to the opinion that "Trump has killed satire" by becoming the "ultimate self-parody" (Von Drehle, 2020). While this exaggerated claim—political satire during the Trump administration did not die—was based on the dangerous caricature and reactionary comedic discourse and behavior of the president, the emergence of Trump and other similarly outrageous right-wing populist leaders around the world shifted the role of humor and irony in political communication. Reactionary and regressive jokes about race, gender, and class have long populated the entertainment mediascape, but across the past few decades scholars and cultural critics have devoted considerable energy to pointing out that conservatism and irony do not mix, highlighting the connections between satiric irony and progressive politics (Sienkiewicz & Marx, 2021). Scholars have asked, "Why is satire so liberal?" (Young et al., 2019), and articles in popular media have included titles such as "Why Conservatives Find Few Laughs on Late-Night Television" (Berr, 2018) and "Waiting for the Conservative Jon Stewart" (Morrison, 2015). Nevertheless, the Right is not devoid of comedy. Sienkiewicz and Marx (2021) have noted the rise of right-wing comedy in US media, with voices ranging from mainstream conservatism to the extremist, white nationalist alt-right. As a reaction, progressive political satirists have increasingly taken a more activist, participatory, and educational role with their humor (Becker, 2021; Jones et al., 2012; Kilby, 2018; Zekavat, 2021), a trend that we can also see in many of our Latin American cases.

The debate about the intentions, morals, and ideological leanings of satire is not new; after all, carnivalesque transgression has long had varied interpretations. Zupančič (2008) describes conservative comedy as false, stating that true comedy is by its nature subversive and deconstructs dominant ideologies. Critchley (2002) considers reactionary jokes intended to preserve the status quo to be the humor of the "untruth." Regarding the relation between political correctness and humor, Black (2021, p. 5) highlights how satire draws on taboo topics and subversive ideas, seeking to establish a deliberate sense of uncomfortableness in order to challenge traditional, conservative values regarding identity, sexuality, gender, race, and disability, among others, and says that "political correctness remains dependent upon its own inherent boundaries and forms of symbolic regulation." In this sense, in contrast to reactionary comedy, risqué, provocative, and irreverent humor seeks to "bypass the censorship of political correctness to be truly political" (Gherovici & Steinkoler, 2016, p. 13).

The appropriation of an anti–politically correct discourse by the Right can be seen as another symptom of the deepening political polarization across Western democracies. According to a 2020 report by the Pew Research Center, the United States is "exceptional" in its political divide (Dimock & Wike, 2020). The increasingly blatant disagreement between Democrats and Republicans on the economy, racial justice, climate change, law enforcement, and international engagement, among many other areas, was further highlighted in the 2020 presidential elections amid the COVID-19 pandemic. Supporters of Joe Biden and Trump believed that the differences between them were about more than just politics and policies; they were about "core American values" (Dimock & Wike, 2020). While polarization in the United States has been particularly noticeable since the political rise of Trump, it is not exceptional; it is symptomatic of a global trend. Other countries also exhibit a clear tendency toward deepening political fissures. Brexit polarized British politics, the rise of populist parties has disrupted political systems across Europe, and cultural conflicts have intensified divisions in many nations. Latin American democracies are "under extraordinary strain," and massive protests and other disruptive events all over the region have led international observers to "fear the escalation of divisive politics to the point of political rupture" (Carothers & Feldmann, 2021, p. 2).

While many of the Latin American political conflicts that have spurred polarization are rooted in historical socioeconomic inequalities, they also depict other fractures related to systemic corruption, conflicting sociocultural values, urban-rural divides, and long-standing ideological differences. In some places, the rise of illiberal populism threatens democratic norms for the sake of demagogic goals; in other places, destructive political fragmentation intensifies chronic conflicts with ever-shifting partisan actors (Carothers & Feldmann, 2021). The coronavirus pandemic, which in 2020 hit Latin America harder than any other region of the world, further agitated the already turbulent political landscape. The result has been not only an array of devastating health emergencies in the region, but also economic troubles. Many experts believe that Latin America faces a "lost decade" ahead as it recovers from the socioeconomic crises generated by the pandemic (Moreno, 2021). By hitting poor and marginalized citizens much harder than privileged sectors, the pandemic's effects have amplified the underlying inequalities between haves and have-nots. Furthermore, the stress created by the pandemic has "accelerated confrontational political dynamics, embodied by surging protests, deepening polarization, more populism, and a growing distrust in existing institutions" (Carothers & Feldmann, 2021, p. 34). Latin American digital satiric media reflects these tense and polarized realities, occupying a particularly revealing space of glocal discursive struggles. Its main sociopolitical critiques react to specific national and regional contexts, in which it performs the important function of saying what is otherwise unsaid in particularly chaotic circumstances. As Gray and colleagues (2009, p. 15) put it, "When historical reality presents periods of social and political rupture . . . , satire becomes a potent means for enunciating critiques and asserting unsettling truths that audiences may need or want to hear."

Furthermore, humor serves an important function for societies dealing with national tragedies and global crises. The United States, for example, saw the resurgence of televised political satire after 9/11 and the invasion of Iraq. In Latin America, satiric media has taken an active role within processes of social catharsis and collective healing after traumatic times, like bloody dictatorships or deep social crises (Alonso, 2018). Satiric magazines *The Clinic* and *Barcelona* acidly criticized the Pinochet dictatorship in Chile and the 2001 economic collapse in Argentina, respectively (Alonso, 2019). Brozo, *el payaso tenebroso* (The creepy clown), and his television show *El mañanero* (The early riser) became a satiric symbol of the opening of Mexico after the end of the seventy-one-year regime of the Institutional Revolutionary Party (PRI) (Alonso, 2015b). Similarly, *El francotirador* (The sniper) was a satiric television show that combined journalism and entertainment to confront political figures after the Fujimori dictatorship in Peru (Alonso, 2015a). Digital-native satire also highlights, as this book demonstrates, the importance of national and regional contexts to understanding the role of humorous critical metatainment in today's democratic societies.

Structure of the Book

Chapter 2 analyzes three key cases of the first wave of satiric Latin American YouTube, focusing on pioneering, DIY shows that became popular in their countries and later in the region. First up is *El Pulso de la República* (The beat of the republic), an online Mexican satiric news show à la *The Daily Show* created in 2012 by comedian Chumel Torres, who, after four years of producing his show independently on YouTube, transitioned to hosting a late-night show on HBO with regional reach. Next are the works from Malena Pichot, feminist Argentinean YouTube star: *La loca de mierda* (The crappy nutcase), a series of online videos about her breakup with her boyfriend that eventually made it to MTV; and *Cualca*, a satiric sketch show focused on gender issues. Last up is *Enchufe.tv*, an online comedy series satirizing Ecuadorian idiosyncrasies and local urban culture, which quickly became the most popular online television series in the country and a regional phenomenon in Latin America. In the contexts of the Televisa empire and the controversial election of Enrique Peña Nieto in Mexico, the #NiUnaMenos grassroots feminist movement in Argentina, and the tense relationship between Rafael Correa's government and the media in Ecuador, these shows questioned cultural stereotypes and sociopolitical norms while adapting and parodying transnational audiovisual formats and entertainment genres. These early cases not only revealed alternative models for the development of independent Latin American digital media, but also exemplified certain patterns of how cultural globalization and hybridity operate in today's transnational entertainment and commercial critical humor.

Chapter 3 examines how female YouTubers have reshaped journalism and gender discourse in postconflict Colombia, focusing on the cases of *La Pulla* (The Taunt) and *Las Igualadas* (The Equalized)—two video columns hosted by the newspaper *El Espectador*—which have successfully reached the millennial generation and reimagined the sociopolitical conversation of the country. *La Pulla* addresses some of the most complex, polarizing, and sensitive topics in Colombia, such as the long period of political violence involving guerrillas, paramilitaries, drug cartels, and the government, emphasizing the debates and consequences of the national peace process. *Las Igualadas*, conversely, focuses on gender issues, tackling problems such as sexual harassment, toxic relationships, and limitations to women's rights. This chapter examines the role of *La Pulla* and *Las Igualadas* within

Colombia's history of political and gender violence and the recurrent attacks on the press that once made the country one of the most dangerous places in the world for journalists. Treating these online television shows as representatives of new generational sensitivities against patriarchal structures of power and sexist/conservative media representations of political and gender issues, this chapter shows how these two online satiric shows have negotiated their space to develop independent critical infotainment and filled the informative gap left by traditional Colombian media. Finally, these online digital shows offer insight into a regional trend toward hybrid business models that combine traditional and alternative channels and resources.

Chapter 4 analyzes the case of *El Sketch*, created in 2016 by comedian Guille Aquino in Buenos Aires, as an example of digital satire in Argentina's deeply polarized society. From the 2001 economic crisis to the pandemic, a new wave of sociopolitical satire has captured the tensions and implications associated with this polarization, also known as *la grieta* (the crack or ideological gap). Combining foreign comedy referents with local humor and rock traditions, Aquino's short videos tackle some of the prevalent national tensions and ideological contradictions that contemporary Argentina inherited from Peronism. With millions of views on YouTube, Instagram, and Facebook, *El Sketch* has not only gone viral in Argentina, but also circulated among other urban centers in the region. While the show tackles the sociopolitical polarization in the country, it also exposes other global problems, such as discrimination, gentrification, bigotry, and global warming. Reflecting the complex scenario of Macrism and Kirchnerism in Argentina, *El Sketch* illuminates the role of satire in contemporary polarized democracies, the challenges to prevalent progressive and conservative views, and the way that multilayered satire navigates transgression and political correctness.

Chapter 5 turns to Peru. After the fall of Alberto Fujimori's authoritarian regime (1990–2000), which heavily controlled and co-opted mass media, newly recovered Peruvian democracy saw the rise of new irreverent television infotainment and satiric programs that challenged certain aspects of the sociopolitical establishment while also reproducing a variety of conservative values and stereotypes with high doses of sensationalism and tabloid practices. The increasing visibility of the blogosphere, new digital media outlets, and emerging YouTubers opened the path for more critical humor. New satiric digital shows not only offered new spaces for dissent but also targeted ingrained prejudices and biases disseminated by mainstream media's discourse. This chapter analyzes the cases of *Gente Como Uno* (People like us, *GCU*), a niche satiric show and an experimental intervention by the author (distributed by the portal Útero.pe) that caricaturized national television's right-wing prejudices, and El Cacash (The Poopie), a popular YouTuber who, in the guise of a gang member, hosts a satiric news show called *El Desinformado* (The Uninformed). The analysis of the first case introduces the notion of satiric literacy, while the second one illuminates the tensions of recent political instabilities—corruption scandals, presidential impeachments, and the polarized election during the pandemic—giving voice to the younger generation's saturation with traditional media. Through exaggerated or marginal personas, *GCU* and El Cacash are also interpreted as new DIY projects of transgressive satire that question a long tradition of prejudiced national comedy.

Focusing on Latinx digital humor in the United States and its constant question of identity, chapter 6 examines the case of Venezuelan American comedian Joanna Hausmann (host of *Joanna Rants*, a show on Flama, Univision's bilingual digital platform of 2014–16) in the context of President Trump's anti-immigration platform, racist/sexist comments, and incendiary rhetoric about the Latinx population. Warning about Mexican immigrants "bringing drugs" into the country and being "rapists," Trump intensified a tense and dangerous climate for many Latino communities and played into stereotypes historically disseminated by US media about Latinx people. The term *Latino* (now increasingly used in its gender-neutral form, Latinx) encompasses hugely diverse and multicultural communities and represents one of the nation's fastest growing populations.[8] Traditional Latinx/Hispanic media in the United States has conventionally tried to group these communities around ecstatic notions of *latinidad* to reach broader audiences, many times reinforcing the stereotypes disseminated by mainstream US media. During the past decade, nevertheless, a new wave of alternative Latinx media has challenged monolithic notions of Latinx identity, embracing its racial, cultural, linguistic, geographic, and generational diversity. This chapter analyzes *Joanna Rants* as a representative of contemporary popular digital comedy/satiric shows developed by and for a bilingual or English-speaking millennial Latinx generation that has embraced diversity as a central component of Latinx identities, a comedy trend that also includes Pero Like (Buzzfeed's project to create "content that resonates with English-speaking Latinxs" [Wang, 2016]), and Mitú (a large multichannel network that describes itself in terms of "the 200%—youth who are 100% American and 100% Latino" [Mitú, n.d.]).

This chapter illustrates the new ways in which the issue of identity is approached (and contested) by a new generation of Latinx creators. Framing the discussion within the evolution of Latinx media, entertainment, and ethnic comedy in the United States, this chapter also illuminates current ideological tensions within Latinx communities and offers insight into a time in which the Latinx vote for Trump significantly increased in the 2020 election.

Finally, in chapter 7, I detail my conclusions, circling back to the questions posed earlier in this introduction. Considering digital satiric shows as a recently established form of hybrid alternative media that challenges prevalent media discourses and sociocultural contradictions in polarized societies, I answer these questions by summarizing the analysis of the cases presented in the book. I illuminate similarities and differences in the cases while highlighting their unique characteristics shaped by their sociopolitical and cultural environments. The conclusions emphasize the local implications of the global trend toward multimedia infotainment and political humor, locating multilayered satire at a privileged intersection between transgression and media norms. Connecting the notion of critical metatainment with subversive cultural globalization, *Digital Satire in Latin America* shows how digital satiric discourses are negotiated in a clickbait mediascape that exists within diverse sociopolitical and cultural tensions, offering a new language to narrate, understand, and contest the pandemic and postpandemic world. Finally, it problematizes the challenges and limitations of contemporary satire in today's broken or damaged sociopolitical systems.

Notes

1 An exception to these criteria is one of the cases of chapter 5, which is included as a hyperalternative experiment and firsthand intervention by the author to gain wider insight about the production, circulation, and interpretation of digital satire and to introduce the concept of satiric literacy.

2 Because of the lack of audience research about satire and entertainment in the region, most audience references included in the book rely on the producers' reports from their own social media accounts, which are general and not specific. Most of them primarily reported millennial audiences.

3 The concept of platform capitalism denotes the operations of companies—such as Google, Facebook, Uber, Amazon, Apple, and Airbnb—that provide the hardware and software foundation for others to operate on (Srnicek, 2017b). In terms of social media platforms (such as YouTube), these companies bring together advertisers,

content creators, and users. Debates about the political, economic, and cultural effects of platform capitalism have become central for contemporary democracies. According to Srnicek (2017a), "the platform business model is predicated upon a voracious appetite for data that can only be sated by disregard for privacy (and often workers' rights) and constant outward expansion."

4 Nieborg and Poell (2018, p. 4276) define platformization as "the penetration of economic, governmental, and infrastructural extensions of digital platforms into the web and app ecosystems, fundamentally affecting the operations of the cultural industries." Poell (2020, p. 650) argues that the platformization of digital cultures presents three main interrelated challenges: "First, platformization complicates the question of media concentration, as platform corporations integrate highly diverse businesses, not only hosting and curating media content, but also functioning as advertising networks, data intermediaries, and so on. Second, it thwarts the regulation of media content, as platforms channel vast amounts of heterogeneous materials, shared by a broad range of users, making it extremely difficult to maintain oversight. Third, the growing dominance of platform corporations over the cultural domain makes it vital, but also difficult, to develop and sustain online public service media and alternative noncommercial platforms."

5 Traced to soon after the acquisition of YouTube by Google in 2006, the formats of social media entertainment "differ sharply from established film and television, and are constituted from intrinsically interactive audience-centricity and appeals to authenticity and community in a commercializing space" (Cunningham & Craig, 2017, p. 72).

6 Based on Hallin and Mancini's (2004, 2007, 2012) work on models of media systems and their relationship with Western democratization processes, many scholars have viewed Latin American media systems as hybrid ones that present characteristics of polarized pluralistic countries as well as several liberal traits (Hallin et al., 2021). Echeverria and colleagues (2022, p. 4) describe how Latin American "multiple modernities," based on "the appropriation, adaptation, or rejection of certain elements of Western institutions, ideals and values," have developed certain media system consequences: "persistent clientelism and state instrumentalization even within democratic regimes, competing journalistic cultures with more than one ethos, constant state interference in media differentiation processes, and the existence of distinct subnational systems."

7 Hughes (2010) traces the use of "politically correct" to the 1930s—both to Mao Zedong, chairman of the Chinese Soviet Republic and to American communist publications of the time—referring to the proper ways of adhering to the party line. Other genealogies locate the origins of the phrase's more widespread use in the feminist movement, Black Power movement, and leftist circles of the 1960s and 1970s (most likely as an ironic borrowing from Mao), where it was a kind of in-joke to criticize excessive orthodoxy and self-righteousness within the Left (Wegel, 2016). Today defined in most dictionaries as the avoidance of forms of expression or action that are perceived to exclude, marginalize, or insult groups of people who are socially disadvantaged or discriminated against, "political correctness" entered the popular lexi-

con in the United States in the late 1980s due to public debates on college campuses (Hughes, 2010) and became popularized in the 1990s when a wave of stories began to appear in newspapers and magazines. The term was appropriated and rebranded by the Right. Conservative journalists and scholars have called political correctness a "purely totalitarian concept" (Drucker, 1998) hiding "radical agendas" driven by "liberal fascism" (Bernstein, 1990), and compared politically correct "thought police" to Stalinists, McCarthyites, Hitler Youth, Christian fundamentalists, Maoists, and Marxists (Wegel, 2016).

8 A controversial term, *Latinx* has generated significant debate about its politics, implications, and uses (Milian, 2017). Chapter 6 discusses different approaches to the issue of naming and conceptualizing *latinidad* in the United States.

References

Abel, R. (1997). An alternative press, why? *Publishing Research Quarterly, 12*(4), 78–84.

Alonso, P. (2015a). The impact of media spectacle on Peruvian politics: The case of Jaime Bayly's *El francotirador*. *Journal of Iberian and Latin American Studies, 21*(3), 165–186.

Alonso, P. (2015b). Infoentretenimiento satírico en México: El caso de Brozo, el payaso tenebroso. *Cuadernos.Info, 37,* 77–90.

Alonso, P. (2016). Sacha Baron Cohen and *Da Ali G Show*: A critique on identity in times of satiric infotainment. *Journal of Popular Culture, 49*(3), 582–603.

Alonso, P. (2018). *Satiric TV in the Americas: Critical metatainment as negotiated dissent.* Oxford University Press.

Alonso, P. (2019). Satiric magazines as hybrid alternative media in Latin America. *Latin American Research Review, 54*(4), 944–957.

Alonso, P. (2021). Sacha Baron Cohen: Agent Provocateur mit Mission. In G. Dachs (Ed.), *Konsens Dissens* (pp. 86–98). Suhrkamp Verlag.

Alonso, P. (2022). Hybrid alternative digital-native media in Latin America during the pandemic: Two Peruvian cases of entrepreneurial journalism hosted from Spain. *Journal of Latin American Communication Research, 9*(1–2), 3–28.

Amarasingam, A. (Ed.) (2011). *The Stewart/Colbert effect: Essays on the real impacts of fake news.* McFarland.

Atton, C. (2002). *Alternative media.* Sage.

Bailey, O., Cammarts, B., & Carpentier, N. (2008). *Understanding alternative media.* McGraw Hill.

Bakhtin, M. (1984). *Rabelais and his world.* Indiana University Press.

Barthes, R. (1972). *Mythologies.* Paladin.

Bataille, G. (1985). *Literature and evil.* Marion Boyers.

Bataille, G. (1987). *Eroticism.* Marion Boyers.

Baym, G. (2005). *The Daily Show*: Discursive integration and the reinvention of political journalism. *Political Communication, 22*(3), 259–276.

Baym, G. (2008). Infotainment. In W. Donsbach (Ed.), *The international encyclopedia of communication*. Wiley. https://doi.org/10.1002/9781405186407.wbieci031

Baym, G. (2010). *From Cronkite to Colbert: The evolution of broadcast news*. Paradigm.

Baym, G., & Jones, J. (Eds.) (2013). *News parody and political satire across the globe*. Routledge.

Becker, A. B. (2021). Stephen Colbert takes on Election 2020: #betterknowaballot, voter mobilization, and the return to playful participatory satire. *Journal of Information Technology & Politics, 18*(4), 417–429.

Bernstein, R. (1990, October 28). Ideas and trends: The rising hegemony of the politically correct. *New York Times*.

Berr, J. (2018, July 31). Why conservatives find few laughs on late-night television. *Forbes*.

Bird, S. E. (Ed.) (2010). *The anthropology of news and journalism: Global perspectives*. Indiana University Press.

Black, J. (2021). *Race, racism, and political correctness in comedy*. Routledge.

Brants, K. (1998). Who's afraid of infotainment? *European Journal of Communication, 13*(3), 315–335.

Burkart, M., Fraticelli, D., & Várnagy, T. (Eds.) (2021). *Arruinando chistes: Panorama de los estudios del humor y de lo cómico*. Editorial Teseo.

Carothers, T., & Feldmann, A. (Eds.) (2021). *Divisive politics and democratic dangers in Latin America*. Carnegie Endowment for International Peace.

Collins, R. (1996). A battle for humor: Satire and censorship in *Le Bavard*. *Journalism and Mass Communication Quarterly, 73*(3), 645–656.

Convoy, M. (2002). *The press and popular culture*. Sage.

Critchley, S. (2002). *On humour*. Routledge.

Cuddon, J. A. (1991). *The Penguin dictionary of literary terms and literary theory*. Penguin Books.

Cunningham, S., & Craig, D. (2016). Online entertainment: A new wave of media globalization? *International Journal of Communication, 10*, 5409–5425.

Cunningham, S., & Craig, D. (2017). Being "really real" on YouTube: Authenticity, community and brand culture in social media entertainment. *Media International Australia, 164*(1), 71–81.

Cunningham, S., & Craig, D. (2019). *Social media entertainment: The new intersection of Hollywood and Silicon Valley*. New York University Press.

Day, A. (2011). *Satire and dissent*. Indiana University Press.

Day, A. (2022). Mothers and whores: Female performers and comedic controversies. *Studies in American Humor, 8*(1), 32–50.

Day, A. (2023). Gender and genre in Hannah Gadsby's *Nanette*. *Television & New Media*. Advance online publication. https://doi.org/10.1177/15274764231201966

Day, A., & Green, V. (2020). Asking for it: Rape myths, satire, and feminist lacunae. *Journal of Women in Culture and Society, 45*(2), 449–472.

Delli Carpini, M. X., & Williams, B. A. (1994). "Fictional" and "non-fictional" television celebrates Earth Day: Or, politics is comedy plus pretense. *Cultural Studies, 8*(1), 74–98.

Delli Carpini, M. X., & Williams, B. A. (2001). Let us infotain you: Politics in the new media environment. In W. L. Bennett & R. M. Entman (Eds.), *Mediated politics: Communication in the future of democracy* (pp. 160–181). Cambridge University Press.

Dimock, M., & Wike, R. (2020, November 13). America is exceptional in the nature of its political divide. *Pew Research Center.* https://www.pewresearch.org/fact-tank/2020/11/13/america

Dorfman, A., & Mattelart, A. (1975). *How to read Donald Duck: Imperialist ideology in the Disney comic.* International General.

Downing, J. (2001). *Radical media: Rebellious communication and social movements.* Sage.

Dragomir, M., & Thompson, M. (Eds.) (2014). *Mapping digital media: Global findings.* Open Society Foundation.

Drucker, P. F. (1998). Political correctness and American academe. *Society, 35,* 380–385.

Echeverria, M., González, R. A., & Reyna, V. H. (2022). Bringing history back into media systems theory: Multiple modernities and institutional legacies in Latin America. *International Journal of Press/Politics.* Advance online publication. https://doi.org/10.1177/19401612221141315

Eco, U. (1984). The frames of comic "freedom." In T. Sebeok (Ed.), *Carnival!* (pp. 1–10). Mouton.

Esposito, L., & Finley, L. (Eds.) (2019). *Political correctness in the era of Trump.* Cambridge Scholars.

Faina, J. (2012). Public journalism is a joke: The case of Jon Stewart and Stephen Colbert. *Journalism, 14*(4), 541–555.

Feldman, L. (2007). The news about comedy: Young audiences, *The Daily Show*, and evolving notions of journalism. *Journalism, 8*(4), 406–427.

Fernández L'Hoeste, H., & Rodríguez, J. C. (Eds.) (2020). *Digital humanities in Latin America.* University of Florida Press.

Finley, J. (2016). Black women's satire as (Black) postmodern performance. *Studies in American Humor, 2*(2), 236–265.

Fox, E., & Waisbord, S. R. (2002). *Latin politics, global media.* University of Texas Press.

Fox News. (2015, August 6). *I think the big problem this country has is being politically correct.* [Video]. Facebook. https://www.facebook.com/watch/?v=10153545049191336

Fraticelli, D. (2023). *El humor hipermediático: Una nueva era de la mediatización reidera.* Teseo.

Freud, S. (1960). *Jokes and their relation to the unconscious.* Hogarth.

Gantt Shafer, J. (2017, September 28). Donald Trump's "political incorrectness": Neoliberalism as frontstage racism on social media. *Social Media + Society.* https://doi.org/10.1177/2056305117733226

García Canclini, N. (1995). *Hybrid culture: Strategies for entering and leaving modernity.* University of Minnesota Press.

Gherovici, P., & Steinkoler, M. (Eds.) (2016). *Lacan, psychoanalysis, and comedy.* Cambridge University Press.

Glynn, G. (2000). *Tabloid culture: Trash taste, popular power, and the transformation of American television*. Duke University Press.

Gray, J., Jones, J., & Thompson, E. (Eds.) (2009). *Satire TV: Politics and comedy in the post-network era*. New York University Press.

Hájek, R., & Carpentier, N. (2015). Alternative mainstream media in the Czech Republic: Beyond the dichotomy of alternative and mainstream media. *Continuum, 29*(3), 365–382.

Hall, S. (1992). Cultural studies and its theoretical legacies. In L. Grossberg, C. Nelson, & P. Treichler (Eds.), *Cultural studies* (pp. 277–286). Routledge.

Hallin, D. C., & Mancini, P. (2004). *Comparing media systems: Three models of media and politics*. Cambridge University Press.

Hallin, D. C., & Mancini, P. (2007). Un estudio comparado de los medios en América Latina. In B. Díaz (Ed.), *Medios de comunicación: El escenario Iberoamericano* (pp. 91–94). Fundación Telefónica.

Hallin, D. C., & Mancini, P. (2012). *Comparing media systems beyond the Western world*. Cambridge University Press.

Hallin, D. C., Mellado, C., & Mancini, P. (2021). The concept of hybridity in journalism studies. *International Journal of Press/Politics, 28*(1), 219–237.

Hallin, D. C., & Papathanassopoulos, S. (2002). Political clientelism and the media: Southern Europe and Latin America in comparative perspective. *Media, Culture & Society, 24*(2), 175–196.

Harcup, T. (2005). "I'm doing this to change the world": Journalism in alternative and mainstream media. *Journalism Studies, 6*(3), 361–374.

Harlow, S. (2022). A new people's press? Understanding digital-native news sites in Latin America as alternative media. *Digital Journalism, 10*(8), 1322–1341.

Harlow, S. (2023). *Digital-native news and the remaking of Latin American mainstream and alternative journalism*. Routledge.

Hermes, J., & Hill, A. (2021). Transgression in contemporary media culture. *International Journal of Cultural Studies, 24*(1), 3–14.

Higgins Joyce, V. M. (2018). Independent voices of entrepreneurial news: Setting a new agenda in Latin America. *Palabra clave, 21*(3), 710–739.

Hoag, A. (2008). Measuring media entrepreneurship. *International Journal on Media Management, 10*(2), 74–80.

Hughes, G. (2010). *Political correctness: A history of semantics and culture*. Wiley-Blackwell.

Hughes, S., & Lawson, C. (2005). The barriers to media opening in Latin America. *Political Communication, 22*(1), 9–25.

Hughes, S., & Prado, P. (2011). Media diversity and social inequality in Latin America. In M. Blofield (Ed.), *The great gap* (pp. 109–146). Pennsylvania State University Press.

Jenks, C. (2003). *Transgression*. Routledge.

Jeppesen, S., & Petrick, K. (2018). Toward an intersectional political economy of autonomous media resources. *Interface: A Journal for and about Social Movements, 10*(1–2), 8–37.

Jones, J. (2010). *Entertaining politics: Satiric television and political engagement.* Rowman and Littlefield.

Jones, J., Baym, G., & Day, A. (2012). Mr. Stewart and Mr. Colbert go to Washington: Television satirists outside the box. *Social Research, 79*(1), 33–60.

Kilby, A. (2018). Provoking the citizen: Re-examining the role of TV satire in the Trump era. *Journalism Studies, 19*(13), 1934–1944.

Kraidy, M. (2005). *Hybridity or the cultural logic of globalization.* Temple University Press.

Lugo-Ocando, J. (2008). *The media in Latin America.* McGraw Hill Education.

Martin-Barbero, J. (1993). *Communications, culture and hegemony: From the media to the mediations.* Sage.

Martin-Barbero, J. (2007). Latin American cyberliterature: From the lettered city to the creativity of its citizens. In C. Taylor & T. Pitman (Eds.), *Latin American cyberculture and cyberliterature* (pp. xi–xv). Liverpool University Press.

McAuliffe, J. (2023). How to feminist affect: Feminist comedy and post-truth politics. *Philosophy and Social Criticism, 49*(2), 230–242.

Milian, C. (2017). Theorizing Latinx [Special issue]. *Cultural Dynamics, 29*(3).

Mitú. (n.d.) *About Mitú.* https://wearemitu.com/about-mitu/

Moran, A. (2009). Global franchising, local customizing: The cultural economy of TV program formats. *Continuum: Journal of Media & Cultural Studies, 23*(2), 115–125.

Moreno, L. A. (2021, January/February). Latin America's lost decades. *Foreign Affairs, 100*(1).

Morrison, O. (2015, February 14). Waiting for the conservative Jon Stewart. *Atlantic.*

Nieborg, D., & Poell, T. (2018). The platformization of cultural production: Theorizing the contingent cultural commodity. *New Media & Society, 20*(11), 4275–4292.

O'Sullivan, T. (1994). Alternative media. In T. O'Sullivan, J. Hartley, D. Saunders, M. Montgomery, & M. Fiske (Eds.), *Key concepts in communication and cultural studies* (2nd ed., p. 10). Routledge.

Paglia, C. (2018). *Provocations: Collected essays.* Knopf Doubleday.

Painter, C., & Hodges, L. (2010). Mocking the news: How *The Daily Show* with Jon Stewart holds traditional broadcast news accountable. *Journal of Mass Media Ethics, 25*(4), 257–274.

Pieterse, J. N. (2009). *Globalization and culture: Global mélange* (2nd ed.). Rowman and Littlefield.

Poblete, J., & Suárez, J. (Eds.) (2016). *Humor in Latin American cinema.* Palgrave Macmillan.

Poell, T. (2020). Three challenges for media studies in the age of platforms. *Television & New Media, 21*(6), 650–657.

Poell, T., Nieborg, D., & Duffy, B. E. (2022). *Platforms and cultural production.* Polity Press.

Reyes Matta, F. (Ed.) (1983). *Comunicación alternativa y búsquedas democráticas.* Fundación Friedrich Ebert and Instituto Latinoamericano de Estudios Transnacionales.

Robertson, R. (1995). Glocalization: Time-space and homogeneity-heterogeneity. In M. Featherstone, S. Lash, & R. Robertson (Eds.), *Global modernities* (pp. 25–44). Sage.

Rodriguez, C. (2001). *Fissures in the mediascape*. Hampton Press.

Salaverría, R., Sádaba, C., Breiner, J., & Warner, J. (2019). A brave new digital journalism in Latin America. In M. Túñez-López (Ed.), *Communication: Innovation & quality* (pp. 229–247). Springer International.

Scatamburlo-D'Annibale, V. (2019). The "culture wars" reloaded: Trump, anti-political correctness and the Right's "free speech" hypocrisy. *Journal for Critical Education Policy Studies, 17*(1), 69–119.

Schmitz Weiss, A., Higgins Joyce, V., Harlow, S., & Alves, R. (2018). Innovation and sustainability: A relation examined among Latin American enterprenurial news organizations. *Cuadernos.Info, 42*, 87–100.

Sienkiewicz, M., & Marx, N. (2021). Appropriating irony: Conservative comedy, Trump-era satire, and the politics of television humor. *JCMS: Journal of Cinema and Media Studies, 60*(4), 85–108.

Sinclair, J. (2004). Geo-linguistic region as global space: The case of Latin America. In R. Allen & A. Hill (Eds.), *The television studies reader* (pp. 130–138). Routledge.

Srnicek, N. (2017a, September 20). The challenges of platform capitalism: Understanding the logic of a new business model. *Institute for Public Policy Research.* https://www.ippr.org/the-challenges-of-platform-capitalism

Srnicek, N. (2017b). *Platform capitalism*. Polity Press.

Stallybrass, P., & White, A. (1997). From carnival to transgression. In K. Gelder & S. Thorton (Eds.), *The subcultures reader* (pp. 293–301). Routledge.

Straubhaar, J. (1991). Beyond media imperialism: Asymmetrical interdependence and cultural proximity. *Critical Studies in Mass Communication, 8*, 39–59.

Straubhaar, J. (2007). *World television: From global to local*. Sage.

Taylor, C., & Pitman, T. (Eds.) (2007). *Latin American cyberculture and cyberliterature*. Liverpool University Press.

Taylor, C., & Pitman, T. (2013). *Latin American identity in online cultural production*. Routledge.

Test, G. (1991). *Satire: Spirit and art*. University of South Florida Press.

Thussu, D. K. (2007). *News as entertainment: The rise of global infotainment*. Sage.

Von Drehle, D. (2020, July 14). Trump has killed satire. *Washington Post.*

Waisbord, S. (2009). Advocacy journalism in a global context. In K. Wahl-Jorgensen & T. Hanitzsch (Eds.), *The handbook of journalism studies* (pp. 371–385). Routledge.

Waisbord, S. (2012). Political communication in Latin America. In H. Semetko & M. Scammell (Eds.), *The SAGE handbook of political communication* (pp. 437–449). Sage.

Waltz, M. (2005). *Alternative and activist media*. Edinburgh University Press.

Wang, S. (2016, February 12). BuzzFeed launches Pero Like, a distributed project for the "English-speaking Latinx" community. *Nieman Lab.* https://www.niemanlab.org/2016/02/buzzfeed-launches

Warner, J. (2007). Political culture jamming: The dissident humor of *The Daily Show with Jon Stewart. Popular Communication, 5*(1), 17–36.

Wegel, M. (2016, November 30). Political correctness: How the Right invented a phantom enemy. *Guardian.*

Young, D. G., Bagozzi, B., Goldring, A., Poulsen, S., & Drouin, E. (2019). Psychology, political ideology, and humor appreciation: Why is satire so liberal? *Psychology of Popular Media Culture, 8*(2), 134–147.

Zekavat, M. (2021). Employing satire and humor in facing a pandemic. *HUMOR, 34*(2), 283–304.

Zupančič, A. (2008). *The odd one in: On comedy.* MIT Press.

Zupančič, A. (2016). Power in the closet (and its coming out). In P. Gherovici & M. Steinkoler (Eds.), *Lacan, psychoanalysis, and comedy* (pp. 219–234). Cambridge University Press.

2

Pioneers of Latin American Digital Humor as Cultural Globalization

El Pulso de la República (Mexico), Malena Pichot (Argentina), *Enchufe.tv* (Ecuador)

In February 2022, a news report accused the eldest son of the Mexican left-wing president Andrés Manuel López Obrador (AMLO) of living a luxurious lifestyle in Houston, Texas, at direct odds with his father's austerity discourse (Olmos et al., 2022). In response, popular YouTuber Chumel Torres released a segment of his online satiric news show *El Pulso de la República* (The beat of the republic, *EPR*), in which he showed a clip of Senator Bertha Caraveo expressing her support for AMLO's son. Torres mocked the senator as "stupid" and called her a "bootlicker" (El Pulso de la República, 2022b). Caraveo decided to legally denounce Torres for gender violence, and the Mexican attorney general's office opened an investigation against the vlogger (Salmerón, 2022). It was not the first time that Torres, who for a short time went from being an independent YouTuber to the host of a late-night show on HBO Latin America, was involved in this type of controversy. Accused of using a racial slur against AMLO's son, Torres had seen his HBO show suspended by the network in 2020 (Blanck, 2020). The tension between the president and the satirist has since made many headlines, and AMLO has referred to the YouTuber as an "ideologue of conservatism" (Pérez Quintana, 2022). How did a former engineer from Chihuahua who created a DIY YouTube channel in 2012 become one of the most visible critics of the Mexican president?

This chapter analyzes *El Pulso de la República* as a representative case of the first wave of satiric Latin American YouTube, channels and creators with a DIY mentality that became popular in their countries and later in the region during the 2010s. It also examines the case of Malena Pichot, an Argentinean feminist YouTube star who became famous for *La loca de mierda* (The crappy nutcase) (a series of homemade online videos about a breakup with her boyfriend that made it to MTV) and *Cualca* (a satiric sketch show focused on gender issues); and the case of *Enchufe.tv*, an online comedy series satirizing Ecuadorian idiosyncrasies and local urban culture, which became the most popular online television series in the country and a regional phenomenon in Latin America. In the contexts of the Televisa empire and the controversial election of Enrique Peña Nieto in Mexico, the #NiUnaMenos grassroots feminist movement in Argentina, and the tense relationship between Rafael Correa's government and the media in Ecuador, this chapter shows how these satirists questioned sociopolitical and cultural norms while adapting and parodying transnational audiovisual formats and entertainment genres. These early cases are paradigmatic examples of a trend of independent Latin American digital humor born on the web that became popular first as alternative entertainment and then negotiated its place in mainstream media, reaching regional or international recognition. While the popularity of these types of digital initiatives varies according to the target (or niche) audience, levels of irreverence, format, production quality, and ideological stand, these early manifestations of sociopolitical digital satire exemplify how cultural globalization and hybridity operate in contemporary transnational entertainment and commercial critical humor.

El Pulso de la República (*EPR*): YouTube Political News Satire in Mexico

El Pulso de la República, a humorous political news show on YouTube, was created in Mexico City in 2012 by Chumel Torres, a mechanical engineer in his early thirties from the northern city of Chihuahua. Torres has frequently referred to *EPR* as inspired by the satiric work of his American heroes Jon Stewart and Stephen Colbert and has declared that he wants to be "the Mexican Seth MacFarlane" (A. Ramos, 2014). *EPR* closely follows the format of *The Daily Show*, *The Colbert Report*, and *Saturday Night Live*'s Weekend Update (a comedian host dressed in a dark, serious suit delivers sardonic monologues about political news accompanied with images and videos that ironically illustrate his critical points), using Mexican slang and references to local popular culture. By 2022, *EPR*'s YouTube channel had more than 2.7 million subscribers, with millions more following Torres on other social media networks. Before becoming a media celebrity, Torres worked for seven years in a *maquila*, a border factory that assembles goods for sale in the United States. He made a name for himself as a "tuitstar" (a

Figure 1. Mexican comedian Chumel Torres created *El Pulso de la República*, a satiric news YouTube channel inspired by US political humor shows, as an alternative to the country's concentrated media. Film still.

star on Twitter) due to his tongue-in-cheek tweets leading up to the 2012 presidential elections, with an especially controversial tweet about candidate Andrés Manuel López Obrador. Because of his social media influence, Torres was offered a weekly column on a political blog and then hired as an editor for a digital newspaper in Mexico City, where the idea of creating a satiric news show took shape:

> I wrote columns that were scripts of *EPR* but without a camera. It occurred to me that we could convert them into videos. I began recording myself with an iPhone. I created different takes because I didn't know if it'd be better to do a left-wing or right-wing character, or Muppets, or a woman. I decided that later. Then I met Durden (co-writer of *EPR*), we talked, and we began to write. (Torres, quoted in Mulato, 2016)[1]

Torres had already written several pilots in Chihuahua before he partnered with Durden (José Alberto Sánchez Montiel, a social media specialist and Mexican tuitstar), and then together they wrote a "superpilot" for CNN. However, the news company took too long to edit it, so Torres decided to do it himself and release the show on YouTube (see figure 1). He has described the early stages of the project before it became a success:

We did it with a webcam and edited it in iMovie, very low quality. But the script was good, and we already had our followers on Twitter, so we did not begin from zero. Then Yayo [a YouTuber with more than 1.7 million subscribers] published our shows on his channel. We had 18,000 views, but after he published our show on his channel, we reached 250,000. Then we took off. (quoted in Mulato, 2016)[2]

EPR consolidated its style in the coming years with videos that were consistently uploaded once or twice a week. The show remained low budget, with only a small crew. Torres described *EPR*'s production style as like *Wayne's World*: "We are three dudes in a small room doing a good show" (quoted in Mulato, 2016).[3] The main focus was on developing a solid script that balanced entertainment and sociopolitical critique:

In the beginning, we argued a lot because, for example, I am more pop in my criteria to choose stories, and Durden is more serious. I could choose the story of Justin Bieber taking his dick out at the beach, and he would choose a story about the community self-defense groups in Michoacán. But in three years, we learned to balance comedy and journalism. (Torres, quoted in Mulato, 2016)[4]

This negotiation of approaches and topics occurred within a national context shaped by corruption, violence, and concentration of media ownership. For over seven decades (1929–2000), the Institutional Revolutionary Party (PRI) held an authoritarian regime in Mexico disguised as a democracy. Called "a perfect dictatorship," the system was sustained with the help of political repression, institutionalized corruption, electoral fraud, control of workers unions, and a corrupt press. During the PRI's regime, it was common for reporters to receive payolas (known as *embutes*, *chayos*, or *chayotes*) from officials or politicians to cover their versions of the news, while media owners received payments disguised as political ads, subsidies, and other fiscal benefits (Alves, 2005). During this period, media concentration in Mexico was also incentivized through a tacit alliance between the PRI and the media, particularly Televisa, the largest media conglomerate in the country and a chief participant in the entertainment industry worldwide (Calleja, 2012; Fernández, 1982; Sosa & Gómez, 2013; Trejo, 1985; Villamil, 2010). Thanks to this relationship, Televisa and TV Azteca (the other major media conglomerate, owned by the powerful Salinas family) operated as a de facto duopoly for decades. Televisa's owner and founder, Emilio "el Tigre" Azcárraga Milmo, considered himself "a soldier of the PRI." After the end of the Cold War, the implementation of neoliberal economic policies, and the wave of democratization in Latin America during the 1990s, the PRI's regime began to crumble under the weight of corruption. When 1997 electoral reforms allowed new political parties to purchase airtime from media groups for their electoral campaigns, Emilio Azcárraga Jean, Azcárraga Milmo's son, was already saying that democracy was "good business." The victory of the National Action Party (PAN) in the presidential election of 2000 brought Vicente Fox to power and put an end to the PRI's seventy-one years of political dominance. During Fox's administration, discussion of drafting a law to put media at the service of democratic efforts began; however, this resulted in the scandalous "Televisa Law" of 2006 (crafted in marathon, daylong sessions and approved in fewer than two weeks), which evidently favored the media giant (Gaytán & Fregoso, 2006).[5]

After the polarizing presidential election of 2006, which concluded in a virtual tie, Felipe Calderón (the PAN candidate) ascended to power, facing protests from thousands of followers of AMLO (at the time representing the Party of the Democratic Revolution [PRD]), who questioned the results of the election. During this political crisis, Calderón's administration launched an unprecedented war against drug trafficking. The initiative led to a countrywide bloodbath—more than 121,000 people were killed during Calderón's six years in power ("Más de 121," 2013)—without any practical results. In this violent scenario, Mexico became one of the most dangerous countries for journalists in the world. From 2000 to 2014, Mexico's National Human Rights Commission documented the deaths of eighty-eight journalists or media workers who were allegedly killed for reasons related to their work. Eighty-nine percent of the attacks against journalists in Mexico at this time went unpunished (Badgen, 2014).

Despite some efforts to limit media concentration and Televisa's power, Calderón ended up succumbing to the private media networks. A "factual (or de facto) power" because of its influence on the public agenda and political decisions (Lay, 2013), Televisa supported the PRI during the presidential election of 2012. The network's partisan coverage was for many a decisive factor in the electoral success of the PRI's candidate, Enrique Peña Nieto, the former governor of the State of Mexico. The electoral results sparked a wave of criticisms and protests against the media, specifically Televisa, for misinforming its audience and not playing its democratic role in the elections (Parish Flannery, 2012). One consequence was the creation of the citizens movement Yo Soy 132, initially formed by Mexican students calling for the democratization of mass media and the repudiation of the mediatic imposition of Peña Nieto as the president of Mexico. It was during this time that *El Pulso de la República* became an alternative political news source that resonated with a young generation fed up with the monolithic power of media conglomerates and their overwhelming influence on national politics. *EPR's* Durden explained:

> Young people who voted for the first time in 2012 were deflowered electorally by one of the worst elections in memory. Downtrodden, denigrated, and humiliated, we did the shameful walk from the voting booths to our homes, more disgusted with the news, polls, and politics than ever. Friendships ended because of political differences, families fought, and, worst of all, a generation was lost because nobody really cared. And in that moment, when everything was unpopular, when people hated everything related to politics and news, we launched our show. ("La historia," 2017)[6]

Amid this polarization and disenchantment, *EPR* played a cathartic function in relation to the general (and generational) discontent with the national sociopolitical climate. It covered the most prominent issues of the news agenda from a critical perspective rarely seen in mainstream media, focusing on the Peña Nieto administration.[7] In fact, *EPR's* most popular video (with around 2.5 million views as of 2023) focuses on corruption accusations and conflicts of interest in relation to the contractors that built the president's house, allegedly bought by his wife, telenovela actress Angélica Rivera (El Pulso de la República, 2014a). In the video, Torres caustically reframes the First Lady's responses to the accusations and explanations of her contributions while mocking the soap opera star's affected, solemn tone. Another popular *EPR* episode is about Mexican businessman Carlos Slim, the second-richest man in the world in 2014, and Telmex, his telecommunications monopoly (El Pulso de la República, 2014b). After contextualizing the power that Slim has in Mexico, Torres explains the abusive practices of Telmex. He recounts the company's reputation for poor service, its economic role in the country, and its impact on Mexican families' budgets, and compares its practices with those of telecommunications companies in other countries. Through jokes, Torres explains the history of Telmex and its questionable privatization to highlight the influence that the telecommunications monopoly has had on freedom of expression and citizens' lives.

While Torres has declared that he avoids stories about organized crime because he "loves the fact that he has his head attached to his shoulders" (Tuckman, 2015), he has criticized the inefficacy of the government in its efforts to pacify the country. One of his most popular videos is about the capture of the Mexican drug lord Joaquín "El Chapo" Guzmán Loera in 2014 (El Pulso de la República, 2014e). After questioning the competence of the Mexican intelligence system, Torres not only mocks how Peña Nieto's government cited the military accomplishment for political gains, but also warns that El Chapo has escaped before and could do it again. In the episode, Torres even mockingly created a game for viewers to bet on how long El Chapo would stay in jail before becoming a fugitive again. Months later, in 2015, El Chapo scandalously escaped from a maximum security prison, creating one of the biggest political crises of Peña Nieto's administration.[8] *EPR* videos also covered other important sociopolitical issues in Mexico, including inequality (El Pulso de la República, 2014c), political links between the PRI and networks of prostitution (2014d), public protests and deaths in Oaxaca generated by educational reforms (2016f), censorship against journalist Carmen Aristegui (2015a), the impact of drug trafficking in the lives of Guerrero's peasants (2016d), and the disappearance of forty-three students in Ayotzinapa (2016a). When center-left AMLO, now representing the National Regeneration Movement (Morena) party, took power in 2018, Torres continued with his critical coverage, evidencing a nonpartisan perspective in his humorous approach and questioning the incongruities of AMLO's political project, the so-called fourth transformation of Mexican society. Episodes satirizing AMLO's propaganda mechanisms (El Pulso de la República, 2022a, 2022c), increasing anticonstitutional and authoritarian traits (2019b), and attacks on freedom of expression (2019a) created a tense relationship with the president, who frequently referred to Torres as "an ideologue of conservatism," without further explanation of what he meant (Pérez Quintana, 2022). *EPR* has also covered international issues, creating connections to explain their impact for Mexican viewers: Donald Trump's presidential campaign (El Pulso de la República, 2015d), Britain's exit from the European Union (2016b), the massacre in Orlando's gay nightclub Pulse (2016c), the scandal regarding fiscal havens known as the Panama Papers (2016e), and, of course, the COVID-19 pandemic and its global and local implications (2020, 2021). Special episodes on high-profile Mexican cases that have made it to the international news have also remained a priority, such as one on Genaro García Luna, erstwhile top security official and public face of Mexico's war on drugs, who was prosecuted in the United States for taking millions in bribes from cartels (El Pulso de la República, 2023). Under the umbrella of the *El Pulso de la República* brand, Torres also produced *Encerrados pero Informados* (Locked but informed), a podcast created in March 2020 to analyze the pandemic context with other Mexican humorists and commentators, as well as *Se dice y no pasa nada* (There is talk but nothing happens), a weekly podcast on topical issues. Since pandemic restrictions were lifted, Torres, who has also dabbled in the national stand-up comedy circuit, has increasingly experimented with real-time streaming with studio audiences. Throughout, he has been part of innovating and diversifying the traditional satiric news format, a trend that seems to have intensified in the postpandemic world.

For Torres, the goal of his show is to translate news into an appealing format and to inform people about news that has already been published, but that the audience might not have read or understood. Despite its news coverage, he has described his show as political entertainment and distinguished his satiric take from journalism:

> We are not a news channel; we analyze what has already happened, with journalistic rigor, because I don't lie. In other words, *EPR* has never been a show about current news. . . . I do not want to have breaking stories, because we are not protected by any huge network or television station. We try to do a show that responds to what you have already seen. (quoted in A. Ramos, 2014)[9]

The distinction between political entertainment and journalism is an important one. On the one hand, it's the same take as his US satiric models (Jon Stewart made similar remarks during his early years to protect his editorial freedom from legal and ethical accusations). On the other hand, it also speaks to the kind of leverage and legal support that an institution demands to be able to break news in Mexico. While the show has been critical of how power works in the country, Torres rejects the suggestion that he has any type of partisan political stand, bears activist intentions, or is a militant of any social movement (A. Ramos, 2014). Torres considers YouTube to be the most democratic platform to develop digital projects while maintaining ideological independence, and he treasures the freedom of expression the online medium offers: "On *El Pulso de la República* I can say whatever the fuck I want without anybody wagging a finger at me," he said to the *Guardian* (Tuckman, 2015). The internet also proved to be the perfect medium to reach his target millennial audience, viewers between the ages of fourteen and thirty-four when he got started, who "either don't watch the news or are sick of watching the news" (Tuckman, 2015).[10] Torres believes that the internet has much better content than mainstream television and is the ideal platform for the dissemination of relevant public information. For Torres, television has become obsolete: "Television treated us like idiots, and we just got sick of it, so we started making something we would watch. They are paying for their sins," he said to the *Guardian* (Tuckman, 2015). The comedian has repeated his perspectives on media in several interviews and conferences, taking a DIY message to young people who are frustrated with the coverage of politics by the major media: "If the newspaper doesn't like you, doesn't listen to you, doesn't give you any money, doesn't offer any opportunities, well then, create your own project. Anybody can shoot a video or record a radio program and upload it to the web. The only limitation is what you have in your head" (quoted in Breiner, 2014).

In many ways, *EPR* was a reaction to mainstream media and its coverage of the news, particularly to Televisa, which has traditionally aligned with the political ruling class and has become a de facto power in the country. "For 50 years, they have been censoring the news and stomping on the truth. It's a news source that nobody believes. My target audience doesn't watch it. It's on the point of dying, if not economically, then because of its content," said Torres (quoted in Breiner, 2014). Despite his critical attitude toward mainstream television, *EPR*'s growing audience brought Torres offers to migrate his show to major channels, including Televisa. In the same article, Torres said that he rejected the offers and that his response to the media giant was, "You're the enemy, man." He explained that he would not have the editorial control he wants even if the media conglomerate were to offer it. "On national television nobody mucks with the President," he said to the *Guardian* (Tuckman, 2015). Nevertheless, he agreed to do a series of *cápsulas* (short videos) for Televisa during the World Cup in Brazil, which prompted a major backlash. "It was a really dark time for us. I had around 1,000 tweets a day saying, 'You fucking sold out, how could you do this?' I will never ever ever ever ever do it again," Torres told the *Guardian* (Tuckman, 2015). This episode evidenced one of the prevalent tensions between independent satirists and the mainstream media: how to deal with attempts at co-optation while also developing a sustainable career and media project, when legitimacy is built on being an alternative to corrupt or biased commercial television. In the case of Torres, the answer was provisionally found on regional cable.

In 2016, HBO Latin America hired Torres to write and host *Chumel con Chumel Torres*, a weekly late-night show à la *Last Week Tonight with John Oliver* targeting Latin American audiences. The comedian explained his decision to work with HBO in an internet promo: "I feel HBO focuses more on the content instead of on getting along with sponsors and people." At HBO, Torres did in-depth pieces on issues affecting Latin American societies and Latinx communities in the United States, such as sexism, corruption, discrimination, identity politics, and immigration. Nevertheless, in 2020, HBO decided to put the show on hold after Torres was accused of using a racial slur against the son of the president.[11] It was a bizarre cancelation case. The National Council to Prevent Discrimination (CONAPRED), the government agency dedicated to preventing discrimination, had announced that it would be holding a forum on racism and classism in Mexico. Torres was among the invited participants. Later that day, Beatriz Gutiérrez Müller, wife of AMLO, criticized CONAPRED via Twitter for inviting Torres to the event, referring to a radio episode in which Torres had mocked her son with allegedly racist connotations (Torres had called him "chocoflan," referring to a dessert that has light and dark colors).[12] Within days of the First Lady's tweet, CONAPRED canceled the forum on racism and classism, the director of the institution announced her resignation, and HBO Latin America "temporarily suspended" Torres's show. While many condemn the alleged misogynistic or racist implications of Torres's humor, critics have also pointed out how political elites have used political correctness and "cancel culture" to silence the critical infotainer and attack his freedom of expression (Blanck, 2020; Salmerón, 2022). This episode can be seen as an example of how political correctness has been shrewdly appropriated by Latin American politicians when it works to their benefit, mastering a hypocritical game—just like in the United States. Interestingly, after Torres's HBO show was canceled, *EPR* continued as a local satiric infotainment show on YouTube (and on the radio) that dealt primarily with Mexico's national news agenda and aggressively critiqued the president. The glocalization process of this case is noteworthy: *EPR* adapted a global format, creating a unique hybrid product primarily targeting a national audience, and then, after significant success, the satiric show was elaborated for a macroregional audience. When the transnational show at HBO was canceled because of pressures on the network by a political correctness scandal that offended powerful people, the original online platform remained available as a safety valve and direct line to the comedian's national audience.

Cualca: The Feminist Humor of Malena Pichot in Argentina

Before becoming a feminist icon of the millennial generation in Argentina, Malena Pichot, a liberal arts student in her early twenties from Buenos Aires who worked as a proofreader in a publishing house, broke up with her boyfriend. It was 2008. Her way of dealing with the separation was to upload a series of humorous videos on YouTube under the label *La loca de mierda*.[13] The series was based on monologues of an overwrought, depressed woman going through heartbreak while questioning several clichés about women and their relationships with men. She explained her motivations to *El País*: "The problem that women have is that we get defined by the guy we are with. I felt so embarrassed that it happened to me; it was so humiliating for me that I took it to the extreme, doing the videos" (quoted in Suárez, 2015).[14] "I felt like the typical *concheta* [upper-class girl] without problems, who gets depressed because a guy does not love her; and it wasn't that terrible; I was just an unsatisfied bougie girl," she added to *La Nación* (Pizarro, 2011).[15] *La loca de mierda* became an online success and was acquired by MTV for a second season of twenty-nine episodes in 2009. From there, Pichot's media career took off across radio, television, and film. She has described her popularity in those early stages as a "different famous" (a way to imply "YouTube famous" in contrast to "television famous"), to which she attributes her close connection with her audience (Mascardi, 2022). While making a name for herself as a stand-up comedian and radio and television personality, she has most often turned to the internet to showcase her work. Pichot was a pioneer in Argentina in using social media not only to launch her comedy career, but also to become a public feminist figure.

While she has described herself as a *cheta* (posh) from Belgrano, an upper-middle-class neighborhood in Buenos Aires, her satiric humor frequently targets the prejudices of this social class (Garófalo, 2012). In 2012, Pichot created *Cualca*, a series of satiric television sketches that criticized sexism, racism, homophobia, and other social prejudices through surreal, absurd, and visceral humor (see figure 2). The name *Cualca* comes from a colloquialism that loosely means "whatever" (Zavaley, 2012). While *Cualca* was initially a segment of the television show *Duro de domar* (Hard to tame, Channel 9), its viral videos (of around five minutes) became especially successful online, through its Vimeo and YouTube accounts. *Cualca* was written and acted by Pichot and four other comedians that she brought together and described to *Rolling Stone* as "the most talented young actors

Figure 2. Malena Pichot became an iconic feminist comedian with her show *Cualca*, in the context of the #NiUnaMenos grassroots feminist movement in Argentina. Film still.

from Argentina": Julián Kartun, Julián Lucero, Julián Doregger, and Charo López (Zavaley, 2012).

"Piropos" (Flirtatious remarks) is one of the most popular *Cualca* videos (Pichot, 2014d).[16] In this sketch, Pichot acerbically criticizes street harassment against women. She enumerates types of this sexist behavior and then presents the experience from the point of view of a woman who reacts violently, killing the men that harass her on the streets. She ends the sketch by saying, "We want to be clear that we are against murdering people. But society does not seem to care that you show me your dick or that you tell me that you want to fuck me in the ass. So, keep doing it. Maybe one day you might even rape me."[17] Other *Cualca* videos that deal critically with issues of gender are "Negación" (Negation), about women who live in denial as a strategy to cope with gender norms, beauty canons, sexual harassment, and domestic violence (Pichot, 2014c); and "Chicas inseguras" (Insecure gals), in which she satirizes the behavior of young women trying to get attention from self-absorbed men while at the same time mocking the teen entertainment industry (Pichot, 2014a). In "Entrevistando al enemigo" (Interviewing the enemy), Pichot parodies a television talk show host who interviews an anti-abortion activist and a rugby player (characters played by other actors), who are presented as examples of the Argentinean Right (Pichot, 2014b). She confronts the conservatism of these characters, revealing some of their most dreadful moral values and prejudices, especially in relation to gender. In a "teaser" for the second season of the show, Pichot plays herself receiving instructions from a television producer in advance of the new season (Pichot, 2014e). For example, the new theme is "Three girls over thirty that still can." Malena asks, "Can what?" The producer responds: "Have children, be happy, have a purpose in life." Another request for the new season is that she needs to show more skin, "taking advantage of the fact that she still has a few years of physical validity left." Finally, the producer asks her not to do scatological jokes; those should be left to male actors. The sketch ends with Malena farting on the producer's face. This satiric video connects with a constant preoccupation of Pichot's humor: the way women are portrayed in the media, and the expectations and limits established for female performers. "It upsets me that society educates women to be dumbasses, to show their ass, and appear in *Big Brother*," she said to *La Nación* (Pizarro, 2011).[18]

At the beginning of her media exposure with *La loca de mierda*, Pichot did not define herself as a feminist, and she playfully answered questions about her militancy: "I shave, I want to have brand-name clothes, I'm within the system. I don't hate men, I don't say that they are all sons of bitches; I just say that my ex is a son of a bitch," she said to *La Nación* (Pizarro, 2011).[19] She explained later that when she came of age in the 1990s, Argentinean women were not widely using the term *feminist*: "It was the internet. I watched many female comedians from the United States who were talking about feminism. And I respected it, but I thought that to be a feminist one needed to be militant and part of an armed struggle. I did not call myself a feminist," she said to *Jot Down* (Mascardi, 2022).[20] In a similar vein, Pichot has also rejected the label *female humor* for her work:

> The category of *female humor* only exists because men cannot identify with a woman. Female humor does not exist because there is no male humor. There is only humor; sometimes it's done by men and sometimes by women. But because the hegemonic discourse is male, women have to identify with men, but it's hard for men to identify with a woman. Men need the category of female humor because women are always the otherness, the distinct, the different. ("Malena Pichot: 'Hago humor,'" 2013)[21]

Pichot's rise to fame happened at a time when sexism and violence against women were being highly discussed in Argentina, as part of an initiative that reached its peak with #NiUnaMenos (Not One Less), an antifemicide protest movement that was born out of a massive public demonstration at the Congressional Plaza in Buenos Aires, on June 3, 2015. This demonstration, publicly supported by several television personalities through media campaigns, was attended by nearly three hundred thousand people and backed by women's rights groups, unions, political organizations, and even the Catholic Church. The #NiUnaMenos movement has since spread through Argentina and Latin America. As part of this movement, Pichot has frequently participated in public debates about feminism in Argentina and has strongly reacted to sexist remarks by public figures. When Argentina's former president Mauricio Macri said that "women like to be catcalled, even if you tell them 'What a nice ass you have,'"[22] Pichot reacted in a column:

> No woman is going to die because someone says, "What a nice ass you have to be fucked to pieces," but neither the president nor 90 percent of society understand that it is wrong. And that which we all know is wrong has to do with the fact that many were killed because they were Black, fat, homosexual, or Jewish, and many women were mistreated and killed because they were women. (Pichot, 2014f)[23]

When rock star Gustavo Cordera, former front man of the legendary Argentine band Bersuit Vergarabat, defended the rape of underage women by saying on a public show that "there are women who need to be raped," Pichot was clear in her accusation: "A person who says women need to be raped does so because he himself has raped women" ("Malena Pichot: 'una persona,'" 2016). Similarly, she has publicly questioned the way the media portrays cases of violence against women, confronted conservative voices such as a journalist and political scientist who linked feminism with pedophilia ("La increíble discusión," 2016), and debated other female public figures on the "correct" use of the label *feminism* ("Malena Pichot le pidió disculpas,'" 2022; Mascardi, 2022). With the same critical tone, Pichot, who doesn't like to be labeled an actress and considers herself primarily a scriptwriter, has frequently reflected on the state of comedy in Latin America:

> In Latin America, comedy is very underdeveloped, because the trajectory of humor is misogynistic and simplistic. I'm not saying that everything is shit; there are exceptions, but at the popular level, it is all shit. There is not a social consciousness in any sense, and I think that is the main problem of Latin American stand-up comedy and humor in general. (quoted in Suárez, 2015)[24]

Pichot has frequently described the humor that she enjoys as uncomfortable, politically incorrect, and visceral. She has revealed that most of her comedic referents are American, mentioning names such as Jerry Seinfeld, Sarah Silverman, Amy Schumer, Kristen Schaal, Maria Bamford, Dave Chappelle, and Louis CK; and series such as *Will and Grace*, *Friends*, *Arrested Development*, *Cheers*, *Curb Your Enthusiasm*, and *Girls*. As for comedy in Spanish, she includes shows such as *Muchachada Nui* (from Spain) and the Argentine *Cha cha cha*, as well as the works of Antonio Gasalla and Juana Molina. Nevertheless, the comedian has stated that she considers most Argentine humor of the nineties to be "deplorable" ("Malena Pichot: 'Hago humor,'" 2013), and many of her critiques about the sexist component of the entertainment industry in Argentina deal with the type of commercial television that was produced during that decade and that is still prevalent. This is why Pichot has rejected certain offers to work in mainstream media: she wants to keep control of her creative work and does not want to be restricted in the type of content she is allowed to produce. In this sense, the internet has remained her preferred platform.

When *Cualca*'s season on *Duro de domar* ended in December 2013 after forty-six episodes, Pichot took her comedy back to the web. *Cualca*'s acting group developed an online crowdfunding campaign (#ojalavuelvaCualca) to independently fund the show's second season. They had a goal of US$22,995 that was exceeded by more than $5,000 through fan donations. The second (and last) season had ten episodes, and the last video was posted on January 16, 2015. Pichot explained to *La Capital* the reasons for the end of the show: "*Cualca* was a very expensive product; it had a lot of production costs. It looked very cute and was very well done. But the truth is that there is no money for that. We worked almost for free for a year, but we cannot do it anymore" ("Malena Pichot: 'Hago humor,'" 2013).[25] In fact, *Cualca*'s videos have been described as "unprecedented in Argentina" (Garófalo, 2012) because of their high production quality. This slick quality has also marked Pichot's other comedic projects, including *Por ahora* (For now, 2013; a comedy series for Cosmopolitan TV that was described as *Cualca*'s spin-off),[26] *Mundillo* (Little world, 2015), *Tarde Baby* (Late baby, 2018), and *Chalet* (2023), all increasingly long audiovisual pieces following the sitcom format, in contrast to the shorter, more prevalent TikTok styles.[27] She has pointed out that with these independent (or coproduced) works released online she does not seek to appeal to massive audiences; her goal is just to reach enough people to be able to produce her content with "a decent budget" (Majlin, 2022). In 2015, Pichot took her stand-up show to Spain, and in 2018, Netflix released her comedy special *Estupidez compleja* (Complex stupidity), in which she expands on topics such as gender, language, and abortion (Netflix Latinoamérica, 2018). In collaboration with part of *Cualca*'s cast, Pichot was also a protagonist in *Finde* (Weekend, 2021), a horror comedy indie movie that was born out of the pandemic's tensions and frustrations and that was released online. Combining influences of Austrian film director Michael Haneke (who explores social issues through characters estranged from modern society) and the new wave of American horror comedy, the movie also aimed to address the nostalgia and problems of Argentina's millennial generation. These last examples of Pichot's work—international stand-up shows, a Netflix comedy special, longer digital generational sitcoms, and an online horror movie—evidence her attempts to reach (niche) global Hispanic audiences with her multilayered feminist comedy, influenced by global media culture and rooted in Argentine experiences relatable to other realities.

Enchufe.tv: Hollywood at the Service of Ecuadorian Idiosyncrasies

In 2021, amid the pandemic, *Enchufe.tv*—a pioneer Ecuadorian YouTube comedy channel—celebrated its tenth anniversary. It was already an established brand in the Latin American digital environment, with more than twenty-five million subscribers. *Enchufe.tv* was created in 2011 by a group of young Ecuadorian filmmakers (Leonardo Robalino, Christian Moya, Martín Domínguez, and Jorge Ulloa), who were critical of the country's audiovisual production and were seeking to renovate Ecuadorian audiovisual culture. Produced by Touché Films in Quito, the humorous and satiric skits featured Ecuadorian idiosyncrasies and, according to the creators and producers, were based on personal experiences, popular sayings, Ecuadorian traditions, and family and romantic relationships, among other topics that were relatable to their young audiences:

> The premise was to do something to be criticized and not to criticize from the outside. As audiovisual producers, we wanted to do something similar to what we would like to see. . . . One of our premises for renovating the audiovisual culture in Ecuador was to take this to a new level and professionalize all aspects of media production. Our objective was to be the Latino *CollegeHumor*. . . . A professor of ours said that *Enchufe.tv* is the US audiovisual tradition at the service of Latin American idiosyncrasies. (J. Ulloa, personal interview, 2014)[28]

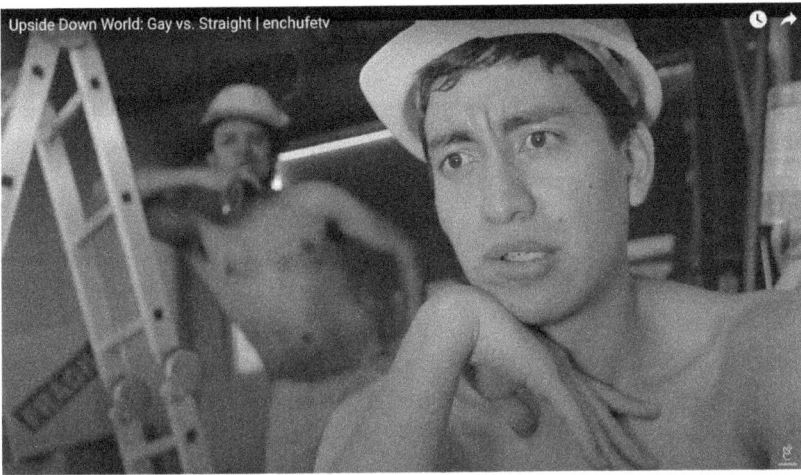

Figure 3. *Enchufe.tv*, an online comedy series satirizing Ecuadorian idiosyncrasies and local urban culture, became popular during a time of tensions between Rafael Correa's government and the media. Film still.

From the beginning of their project, *Enchufe.tv* creators decided that the internet would be their primary outlet because they would enjoy fewer restrictions (such as on the use of colloquial language, swear words, slang, and controversial topics) than in traditional media outlets. On November 13, 2011, the first sketch, "El peor casting" (The worst casting) was uploaded to their newly created YouTube channel (Enchufetv, 2011). During their first season, four- to five-minute sketches were uploaded every Sunday, with teasers and short promotional videos released during the week. After a few months, their videos went viral, receiving millions of views. Some of the most popular videos of this initial period were "Visión Carnaval" (Carnaval vision), "Me gusta" (I like it), and "Compra Condones" (Buying condoms). This last remains one of *Enchufe.tv*'s most popular videos, with almost sixty million views as of 2023 (Enchufetv, 2012a). By July 2012, *Enchufe.tv* was ranked as the most popular Ecuadorian YouTube channel on the web. Viewership came primarily from Ecuador, but soon Mexico became its main market, accounting for around 30 percent of viewers and channel subscribers. Colombia, Peru, and the United States soon became additional principal markets for *Enchufe.tv*'s content (A. Centeno, personal interview, 2014). In September 2013, *Enchufe.tv* released a compilation of its first season of videos on Ecuavisa, a national television station. At a time when television penetration in Ecuador was 97 percent and internet penetration was only 57 percent, national television allowed the producers to reach a broader national audience. Its videos have also aired on international networks and cable stations, such as Estrella TV and TNT. Nevertheless, the web remains *Enchufe.tv*'s main platform, and its social media team stays active on Facebook, Twitter (now X), Instagram, and TikTok (see figure 3).

Enchufe.tv's business model is an interesting example of entrepreneurial efforts to make an independent web project sustainable: a production company (Touché Films) produces a comedy series of high audiovisual quality as a showcase of its talent and potential in order to find new advertising clients. The production company funds the project until it becomes sustainable (through sponsors and advertising), which, for *Enchufe.tv*, happened in its third year. By 2015, the company employed more than thirty people across the creative team, production, postproduction, acting, digital and multimedia operations, and management. The intention was to shoot content in international locations, countries that had the potential not only for large audiences but also for new business partners. In 2013, *Enchufe.tv* was ranked globally as forty-ninth for number of subscribers to a YouTube channel. That same year, *Enchufe.tv* received a Golden Play Button, awarded to YouTube channels with over one million subscribers. In 2014, *Enchufe.tv* won Show of the Year at the Streamy Awards (the so-called Oscars of the web). By its tenth anniversary, the YouTube channel had reached almost twenty-five million subscribers, and there were an additional fifty million followers on social media. With all this local and regional popularity, *Enchufe.tv* became a breakthrough for audiovisual culture in Ecuador, a country where the media operated in a tense political climate.

Ecuadorian Media and Satire under Correa's Government

After a period of political instability in which Ecuador had seven presidents in ten years, Rafael Correa's leftist government was inaugurated in 2007 and reelected for a third term in 2013 (he stayed in power until 2017). A popular president with high approval ratings during his first terms, Correa changed the constitution, increased public spending, defaulted on foreign loans, and clashed with the United States on several issues. According to the World Bank, poverty levels and inequality in Ecuador dropped significantly between 2006 and 2013 ("Profile," 2013). When the price of oil—Correa's main source of funding for his "revolution"—plummeted, government spending and his approval ratings both dropped. While many considered him to be a progressive, Correa, who described himself as part of the "Christian Left," was opposed to abortion (even in cases of rape) and called gay marriage "barbarism" (Miroff, 2014). He was also increasingly accused of authoritarianism, corruption, and attacks on freedom of expression.[29]

The relationship between the media and Correa's government was tense. The president referred to the private media as his "greatest enemy." While protecting WikiLeaks founder Julian Assange in Ecuador's embassy in London, Correa undertook measures against the private media comparable to those of Hugo Chávez in Venezuela. Both presidents, for example, repeatedly harassed the private media on accusations of serving the conservative elites, used government advertising and economic incentives to induce positive reporting, imposed legal sanctions and other forms of "soft censorship" to limit press scrutiny, expanded state-run broadcasting, and became media figures through the use of airtime on national television (Boas, 2012; Frajman, 2014; Kellam & Stein, 2016). In Ecuador, where media ownership has been described as oligarchic, mostly resting with a small number of rich families, Correa's policies were justified as "state activism" to reduce the traditional privileges that the private media has held in the country and to put the media at the service of citizens (I. Ramos, 2012, 2013). Nevertheless, Correa created the "largest media empire in Latin America in the hands of government" by nationalizing media outlets, controlling dailies and news agencies, and seizing television and radio stations from former bankers (Lara, 2013).

In June 2013, the controversial Organic Law on Communications was approved in Ecuador. President Correa considered the law to be an initiative to democratize the media, strengthen freedom of expression, and promote "a good press" in the country (Martínez, 2013). However, several private media outlets in Ecuador and international organizations saw it as an attempt to silence the media and punish any criticism of the government. The law created state-mandated ethical guidelines and defined social communication as a "public service," making it susceptible to state regulation. As an ironic result, with 174 documented aggressive acts against media outlets, journalists, and citizens, 2013 became the most hostile year against freedom of expression in Ecuador ("El Silencio asfixiante," 2014).[30]

The government's attacks against freedom of expression in Ecuador were also aimed at satire and political humor. Political cartoonist Xavier "Bonil" Bonilla, from the newspaper *El Universo* (The universe), was sanctioned twice for his satiric work (Freedom House, 2015). Similarly, Correa targeted digital and social media. In 2013, the Ecuadorian government proposed penalizing individuals who expressed opinions that could be considered defamatory on social media (Fundamedios, 2013). At the same time, the president recruited "trolls" among his followers to fight critical and satiric voices against him and his government online (Constante, 2015).

This is the political context in which *Enchufe.tv* appeared and evolved. When it became popular and massively successful, the project interested not only new advertising clients (big companies such as supermarket chain Supermaxi and telecommunications providers Movistar and Claro) but also the government. According to the magazine *Soho*, "There is a presidential document that evidences a US$11,000 contract for social communication services with Touché Films. It's dated December 2012. This led to many problems and accusations that they were sellouts to the government" (Varas, 2014).[31] Andrés Centeno, executive producer of Touché Films, accepted that Touché Films had among its clients two government ministries, but held that this was not a reflection on *Enchufe.tv* (Varas, 2014).[32] Criticism increased that same year when a video by *EnchafoTV* (a parody of *Enchufe.tv*) appeared mocking Guillermo Lasso, an oppositional leader and presidential candidate (who would become president in 2021). Some former members of Touché Films participated in the production of the video. After these tensions, the creators and producers of *Enchufe.tv* tried to clarify that they did not make political humor but are rather "apolitical" ("Jorge Ulloa," 2020).

Enchufe.tv's Sociocultural Critiques and the Commercial Manufacturing of Hybridity

Enchufe.tv's producers have repeatedly claimed that their humor is independent of the political sphere and its tensions (Alonso, 2018). By distancing themselves from explicit sociopolitical critique and focusing on the aesthetic and commercial aspects of their products, *Enchufe.tv*'s producers flourished in a heavily controlled media environment. Nevertheless, many of their videos have a clear carnivalesque component, and some exhibit social satire. An example of this is *Mundo al revés* (World upside down), a series of videos from *Enchufe.tv* that turn predominant views about sociocultural stereotypes upside down.[33] It is a carnivalesque world in which inverted values ridicule social and cultural prejudices embedded in stereotypes, a process with political implications. For example, in the sketch "Gringos y Latinos," working- and middle-class Americans immigrate to Latin America in harsh conditions, searching for a better life (Enchufetv, 2013a). Many of them (the poorest ones) cross the border without documents in search of the Latin American dream. A border official shoots them while calling them *malditos ilegales* (damned illegals), and he spits on the floor, the smoking rifle in his hand. When they arrive, the US immigrants face constant discrimination and challenges in finding work because of their undocumented status and poor language skills. They are stereotyped as ignorant people, potential criminals, or terrorists, generating paranoia in the local community. At the same time, immigrant women are exoticized as sensual objects and good dancers, because "they have the rhythm in their blood." The satiric strategy is similar in the sketch "Gays y heteros," which criticizes homophobia (Enchufetv, 2013b). In this sketch, heteronormative values are inverted, and heterosexuality is presented as deviance. By positioning homosexuality as hegemonic and heterosexuality as marginal, the sketch emphasizes the absurdity of misconceptions and prejudices based on sexual orientation. At the same time, it not only satirizes the arguments against same-sex marriage (a controversial topic in the country) but also, with the final scene, suggests the decadence of marriage as an institution in a predominantly Catholic society where the president, a self-declared Christian Leftist, opposes same-sex marriage.

Other *Mundo al revés* videos include "Hombres y mujeres" (Men and women), "Sexismo" (Sexism), and "Belleza" (Beauty) (Enchufetv, 2012b, 2014a). Taking a perspective opposite to the dominant ideology, these videos ridicule stereotypes and sociocultural prejudices (such as xenophobia, sexism, homophobia, and canonical notions of beauty), evidencing the absurd and arbitrary system of values embedded in society. In this sense, *Mundo al revés* questioned static identities and promoted understanding of difference, of the Other. This critical humor transgressed certain norms of the country's television and media culture (e.g., norms of language and topic), but its critical and transgressive spirit seemed restricted by the sociopolitical context of the country and the show's own commercial nature. In other words, *Enchufe.tv*'s satire criticized homophobia, xenophobia, sexism, and other social vices without risking its commercial development, because these topics resonated positively with the target millennial audience and did not cross the limits set by the government's policing. This does not mean that *Enchufe.tv* has not been controversial. Some of its content has indeed generated controversy abroad, which could be seen as a noteworthy transnational strategy to reach audiences in other countries of the region.

On July 6, 2014, *Enchufe.tv* uploaded a parody trailer of a fake movie spin-off based on *El Chavo del Ocho* (The kid from number eight), a Mexican television sitcom widely broadcast since 1971 in Latin America as well as many other countries (Enchufetv, 2014b). Created by Mexican comedian Roberto Gómez Bolaños, also known as Chespirito (a diminutive hispanization of "Shakespeare"), *El Chavo del Ocho* tells of the adventures and misfortunes of a poor orphan (nicknamed "el Chavo") and other inhabitants of the *vecindad* (neighborhood), a fictional low-income housing complex in Mexico. At the peak of its popularity, during the mid-1970s, *El Chavo del Ocho* was the most watched show on Mexican television and had a Latin American audience of 350 million viewers. The show continues to be immensely popular as an emblematic comedy of "clean" humor for the entire family. Very different from *El Chavo del Ocho*, *Enchufe.tv*'s parody (titled *El Chico del Barril* [The kid from the barrel]) includes a similar plot to *The Da Vinci Code* and copies the style of Christopher Nolan's action movies. It features two agents, one American and the other Middle Eastern, who are searching for the real name of "el Chavo." The trailer shows a dark, violent, and sexual configuration of the beloved sitcom characters. Parodies of the most famous characters of *El Chavo del Ocho* appear in *El Chico del Barril*, making twisted reference to their popular catchphrases. The trailer ends with the US agent discovering the classic squeaky hammer of the Chapulín Colorado (Red Grasshopper, another character created by Chespirito) in the desert. A few hours after the YouTube video was uploaded, the controversy began. Mexican radio and television (and later diverse Latin American media) disseminated the news. Actors from *El Chavo del Ocho* publicly accused *Enchufe.tv*'s parody of distorting and twisting their creations and of profiting from them through shocking images. Televisa, the Mexican television station that owns the rights to *El Chavo del Ocho*, asked YouTube to take the video down. While the video was taken down for a few hours, *Enchufe.tv*'s producers defended their product as an original tribute to the iconic show. The video became public again, and the controversy ended when Roberto Gómez Bolaños's son praised *Enchufe.tv*'s work, accepting the tribute to his father ("Los de EnchufeTV," 2014). Within a few days, the video had millions of views, and *Enchufe.tv*'s audience had grown by 700 percent in Mexico (Varas, 2014).

Enchufe.tv's parody of *El Chavo del Ocho* exemplifies the producers' intentions of blending Hollywood (or the American audiovisual tradition) with Latin American popular culture, as they have repeatedly stated. The parody is also an example of the show's hybrid and glocal manufacturing. As a parody, it already implies a combination, dialogue, and juxtaposition of different texts in order to create a new one. In the case of *El Chico del*

Barril, it is a double parody, playing on the local/regional tradition and the global one. It is a tribute to one of the most important referents of Latin American popular humor, developed through the trailer format of a Hollywood action movie. The objects of parody are also revealing. On the one hand, *El Chavo del Ocho*, a symbol of noncontroversial and innocuous comedy, is not only a Mexican referent but also a popular icon for most Latin American countries; several generations watched daily reruns of the show on national television for decades. On the other hand, the movie *The Da Vinci Code* and filmmaker Christopher Nolan's style are representative of effects-driven and commercial Hollywood action films. The two objects of parody are connected by their huge commercial success. The parody of both audiovisual products is based on the transgression of codes and themes of their respective genres. In the case of *El Chavo del Ocho*, *Enchufe.tv*'s parody distorts the configuration of the original naive characters (children played by adults): they carry guns, have blood on their clothes, and have erotic encounters while maintaining traits and dress codes of their original models. In relation to *The Da Vinci Code* and Nolan's movies, the focus is on the formal aspect: the parody adopts the visual narrative strategies of Hollywood action movie trailers while evidencing the artificial and spectacular techniques employed to catch the audience's attention in the service of an absurd plot. In this sense, the parody works at the content and formal level. From another perspective, the film *The Da Vinci Code* is in itself an interpretation of a previous mass culture product: the best-selling novel by Dan Brown, which has the same title and has motivated the creation of a variety of literary and audiovisual parodies itself. At the same time, Nolan's style also has an intertextual dimension, which is manifested in his reboot of the Batman film franchise (a successful trilogy itself fed by Frank Miller's graphic novels of the 1980s and *The Long Halloween* by Jeph Loeb and Tim Sale). Chespirito's work also has a parody aspect, especially concerning his character Chapulín Colorado. Embodying many aspects of Latin American and Mexican culture, the Chapulín is a critique of American cultural hegemony and the unrealistic image of American superheroes.[34] In contrast to Superman or Captain America, the Chapulín is imperfect, clumsy, and timid, but he is good hearted and succeeds at the end of his adventures (most of the time by good luck). The final text involved in the parody is a nonexistent one: the movie that the trailer promotes. In this sense, *Enchufe.tv*'s trailer parody becomes an intertextual and metatextual object with several layers of parody that reflect its hybrid discursive universe. Combining diverse cultural traditions, audiovisual genres, and levels of reality, *Enchufe.tv*'s discourse appeals to varied audiences that can relate to any (or many) of the layers at the local, regional, and global levels. Consequently, it also reveals the manufactured condition of its carnivalesque hybridity as a commercially successful strategy for independent digital media that seeks a transnational audience. While the parody of *El Chavo del Ocho* became popular in many Latin American countries, it targeted Mexico, where *Enchufe.tv* developed its biggest audience. The producers' plans to shoot new content in different Latin American countries with local talent (or to import talent from other countries to Ecuador) highlight a similar strategy of increasingly glocalizing their audiovisual production in the region. A recent example of this strategy is *Enchufe.tv*'s movie *Misfit* (2021), a teenage comedy produced in Ecuador with talent from Ecuador, Mexico, Argentina, Peru, Colombia, the United States, and Spain.[35]

Conclusion

In the 2010s, when traditional media felt distant, reactionary, or corrupt, a wave of digital satire shows revealed successful models for independent media production, attracting young millennial audiences. Through their online content, these shows developed, consolidated, and negotiated their place in relation to mainstream media and public debate. Their formula involved producing innovative, risqué, and high-quality audiovisual humor that filled gaps left by national mainstream television. These online shows dealt critically with sociocultural and political issues and were especially appealing to digital urban audiences eager for new content aligned with international (usually US) media production, but with a local flavor. While heavily influenced by the US comedy tradition (political satire such as *The Daily Show* or *The Colbert Report* for *EPR*, contemporary US stand-up comedy and series such as *Seinfeld* and *Girls* for *Cualca*, and *CollegeHumor* and Hollywood formats for *Enchufe.tv*), all the cases outlined here successfully digested their foreign influences and adapted them to the local culture, creating a unique glocal voice that tapped into particular national tensions (the audience's frustration with the media's coverage of the 2012 electoral campaign and the politically imbricated role of Televisa in Mexico; the responsibility of entertainment and advertising in reproducing sexist values in Argentina, a country with high rates of femicide and growing social movements for women's rights; and the conflictive relation between private media and Correa's government, affecting freedom of expression in Ecuador).

As part of their core critiques, these satirists and their shows have been openly critical of national television. After becoming popular on the web with millions of subscribers, followers, and viewers on social media platforms, they negotiated their relationships with national mainstream television (Chumel Torres rejected the offer to take *EPR* to Televisa, but agreed to do a series of videos during the World Cup for the media giant before transitioning to a transnational media outlet; Malena Pichot's *La loca de mierda* made its second season on MTV, her *Cualca* was originally developed as a segment for a national TV show, and she became a recurrent radio and television personality; and *Enchufe.tv* released its videos on television, reaching new national and regional audiences while creating transnational partnerships). Nevertheless, all cases maintained the internet as their main platform, frequently citing creative freedom as their primary reason and the possibility of reaching loyal audiences at any moment as a close second. It is important to note here their initial adaptability to new social media platforms. While all three cases initially became popular on YouTube, they also tailored their presences on Facebook, Instagram, and Twitter for different audiences, languages, and uses. Nevertheless, at some point they limited their presence on trendy new platforms, such as TikTok. In this sense, the evolution of their presence on social media also reflects how internationalization is constantly negotiated via different platforms and communications technologies.

As part of their evolution, these online satirists and their shows obtained regional or international reach. Chumel Torres expanded the political satire of *EPR* by focusing on broader Latin American issues with his late-night show on HBO, targeting a regional audience. Malena Pichot, whose feminist videos are already famous in various Latin American cities, has intensively promoted her humorous work through shows in Spain and released a stand-up comedy special on Netflix. As an independent and commercial production company, Touché Films has developed strategies to reach Latin American audiences with *Enchufe.tv* by developing content that dialogues with different countries' traditions of popular culture and working with local talent from those countries. This internationalization marks an interesting stage in these cases' relationship with cultural globalization: while the cases first adapted international referents to create a unique voice at the local/national level, they then adapted this voice to reach wider regional or geolinguistic audiences, creating a new layer in their hybrid process.

Notes

This chapter is an updated version of my previous work on the cases of *El Pulso de la República*, Malena Pichot, and *Enchufe.tv* (Alonso, 2018, 2020). I include them in this book because of their foundational importance for the region's development of audiovisual digital satire in the YouTube era.

1 "Escribía columnas que básicamente eran guiones de *El pulso* pero sin cámara. Se me ocurrió que podíamos convertirlos en videos y ya. Empecé a grabarme con el iPhone y hacía diferentes *takes* (tomas) porque no sabía si era mejor hacer un personaje de izquierda o de derecha, o *muppets* o una mujer, eso lo decidí después. Luego conocí a Durden (co-escritor de *El pulso de la República*), platicamos y comenzamos a escribir."

2 "Lo hacíamos con una *webcam* y editábamos con *iMovie*, todo chafa. Pero el guión estaba padre y ya teníamos nuestros *followers* en Twitter, entonces no empezamos de cero. Luego Yayo, creador de 'No me revientes' (canal de YouTube que nació en 2010 y que cuenta con más de 1.700.000 suscriptores) publicó en su espacio nuestros programas. Teníamos 18.000 vistas, pero después de que publicó en su canal ya teníamos 250.000, ahí despegamos."

3 "Somos tres güeyes en un pinche cuartito haciendo un buen *show*."

4 "Antes nos peleábamos mucho porque, por ejemplo, yo soy más pop en mi manera de escoger notas y Durden, más serio. Yo podía escoger la nota de Justin Bieber sacándose el pito en la playa y él la de las autodefensas de Michoacán. Está cabrón, pero en tres años aprendimos a hacer un balance entre comicidad y periodismo."

5 The Federal Law of Radio and Television, also known as the Televisa Law, conceded to Televisa and TV Azteca the free use of the national digital frequency spectrum, a public good, among other privileges.

6 "Jóvenes que votaron por primera vez aquel 2012 vieron que eran desvirgados electoralmente por uno de los peores comicios de los que se tenga memoria. Manoseados, vilipendiados y con los tacones en la mano emprendimos la caminata de la vergüenza de las urnas a nuestras casas más asqueados de las noticias, las encuestas y la política que nunca. Amigos se perdieron por diferencias políticas, familias se pelearon y lo peor de todo, una generación se perdió porque realmente a nadie le importaba. Y en ese momento en el que todo era impopular, en el que la gente odiaba todo lo que tuviera que ver con la política y las noticias, a dos locos se les ocurre sacar un programa que giraba en torno a eso."

7 An important figure of satiric infotainment in Mexico is the Brozo, *el payaso tenebroso* (the shady clown), a fictional character created by comedian and journalist Victor Trujillo. Brozo was a coarse and marginal clown who angrily and subversively commented on the news and criticized political and economic elites. After being critical of Televisa, Brozo was hired by the media giant and negotiated his ability to transgress certain media norms from within the company (Alonso, 2015, 2018; Ruggiero 2007).

8 *EPR* also covered the escape of El Chapo and its implications (El Pulso de la República, 2015b, 2015c).

9 "No somos un canal de noticias, somos un canal de análisis de lo que ya pasó con rigor periodístico porque no digo mentiras. Es decir, *El Pulso de la República* nunca ha sido un noticiero coyuntural, no maneja noticias nuevas. . . . No quiero tener exclusivas de nada porque no nos protege ningún tipo de aparato de noticias, canal o un network gigante. Tratamos de hacer un programa que sea como réplica de lo que ya viste."

10 Durden, cocreator of *EPR*, has described his millennial audience as "one of the most difficult *pokemon* to catch for many sectors of power (who, by the way, do not know what a pokemon is), such as businesses, marketing companies, and political elites. The word *millennial* is the most repeated one in advertising meetings, as well as in electoral campaigns. It's the biggest and most influential generation. And most importantly, it does not play with the same rules of the past, mainly because of the internet and social media" ("La historia," 2017).

11 Since the cancellation of the HBO show, videos of it are no longer available online.

12 The allusion to chocoflan, a flan flavored with chocolate, hints at the fact that AMLO is darker skinned while his partner is white, and, thus, the son is biracial. Though this sort of observation of an interracial couple might be common in the United States, it is not common in Mexico and many other Latin American countries to speak of racial mixing explicitly; this is because it is generally considered a result of the colonial heritage of the social caste system.

13 The first *La loca de mierda* video was uploaded on August 30, 2008 (Pichot, 2008).

14 "El problema que tenemos las mujeres es que nos define el tipo con el que estamos. A mí me dio tanta vergüenza que me pasara eso, para mí fue tan humillante y tan vergonzoso, que lo llevé al extremo haciendo los videos."

15 "Me sentía la clásica concheta sin problemas que se deprime porque un pibe no la quiere, y no era tan terrible, sólo una burguesa insatisfecha."

16 Similar ideas to "Piropos" have been developed by Spaniard Alicia Murillo, and in media campaigns against sexism, like *10 Hours of Walking in NYC as a Woman* (Bliss, 2014).

17 "Queremos dejar en claro que nosotros estamos absolutamente en contra del asesinato. La sociedad no está de acuerdo con matar gente. Pero a la sociedad no parece importarle que me muestres la pija o que me digas que me quieres romper el orto. Así que seguí haciéndolo, por ahí que un día te animás y me violas."

18 "Me angustia que la sociedad eduque a las mujeres para que sean pelotudas. La media es mostrar el culo y salir en Gran Hermano."

19 "Me depilo, quiero tener la ropa de moda: estoy adentro del sistema. . . . No odio a los hombres, no digo que son todos unos hijos de puta, digo que mi ex es un hijo de puta."

20 "Lo que me pasó fue por internet. . . . Yo veía muchas comediantes mujeres en Estados Unidos que sí hablaban de feminismo. Y me pasaba que respetaba mucho el feminismo y a las feministas, pero creía que para ser feminista había que militar en

una horda con armas, había que formar parte de la lucha armada. No me decía a mí misma feminista."

21 "La categoría 'humor femenino' existe porque los hombres no pueden identificarse con una mujer. No existe un humor femenino porque no existe un humor masculino. Existe el humor, a veces lo hacen hombres y a veces lo hacen mujeres. Como el discurso hegemónico es masculino, la mujer puede identificarse con el hombre pero al hombre le cuesta identificarse con una mujer. El hombre necesita crear la categoría de 'humor femenino' porque la mujer es siempre la otredad, lo distinto, lo diferente."

22 "A las mujeres les gustan los piropos, aunque les digan qué lindo culo tenés."

23 "Ninguna mujer se va a morir porque le digan 'que hermoso culo que tenés para rompértelo todo' pero ni el jefe de gobierno ni el 90% de la sociedad entienden que está mal. Y aquello que todos sabemos que está mal tiene que ver con que es real que muchos se murieron cagados a palos por ser negros, gorditos, putos o judíos y a muchas mujeres las violentaron realmente y las mataron por ser mujeres."

24 "En América, la comedia está muy atrasada porque tenemos una trayectoria misógina y simplista del humor. No quiero que parezca que digo que todo es una mierda, hay excepciones, pero sí creo que a nivel popular es una mierda. No hay conciencia de nada, no hay conciencia social en ningún sentido y creo que ese es el problema mayor del stand up y del humor en general en Latinoamérica."

25 "*Cualca* era un producto muy caro, tenía mucha producción. Se veía muy lindo y estaba muy bien realizado. Pero la verdad es que no hay guita para eso. Nosotros trabajamos un año casi por amor al arte, pero ya no podemos hacerlo más."

26 *Por ahora* involved the same group of actors as *Cualca*. It was ironic that Cosmopolitan TV in Latin America broadcast the series, since *Cosmopolitan* magazine reinforces female stereotypes. In contrast to *Cualca*, the episodes of *Por ahora* were around thirty minutes long and focused more on the problems of a group of thirty-something friends (relationships, immaturity, insecurities) than on social issues.

27 Pichot has not significantly participated in platforms such as TikTok or Twitch. "I've stayed behind," she said about the use of new digital platforms to deliver her stories (Mascardi, 2022).

28 "La premisa fue hacer algo para ser criticados y no criticar desde afuera. Como productores de audiovisuales, queríamos hacer algo como lo que nos gustaría ver. . . . Una de nuestras premisas para renovar el audiovisual ecuatoriano fue llevar esto a otro nivel y profesionalizar todos los aspectos del medio. Nuestro objetivo era ser el 'College Humor' latino. . . . Un maestro nuestro decía que Enchufe.tv es la tradición audiovisual gringa al servicio de la idiosincrasia de América Latina."

29 In 2020, Correa was sentenced in absentia to eight years in prison for bribery. He was living in Belgium, where he had requested asylum. In 2022, Ecuador's National Court of Justice requested his extradition ("Ecuador begins effort," 2022).

30 According to the report "The stifling silence" by Fundamedios ("El Silencio asfixiante," 2014), the year 2013 in Ecuadorian media was characterized by the country's controversial new communications law, an increase in censorship, and public offi-

cials' hostility toward the press. The most aggressive acts came from public officials, followed by the government in the form of administrative or legal measures.

31 "Existe un documento de la Presidencia de la República que evidencia un contrato de 11 mil dólares, por servicios de comunicación social, con Touché Films. Está fechado en diciembre de 2012. Esto trajo muchos problemas en su momento y las acusaciones de haberse vendido al Gobierno se multiplicaron por redes sociales."

32 Jorge Ulloa, who declared an initial sympathy for Correa, later recalled about this period: "All audiovisual producers of the time worked for the government." That is, government advertising and its budget for audiovisual propaganda became the main source of income for many producing companies ("Jorge Ulloa," 2020).

33 The trope of the world turned upside down can be traced to the Middle Ages (Donaldson, 1970) and is a central component of carnival culture. Connected to the tradition of Menippean satire, it seeks to offer an inverted (and perhaps clearer) perspective on reality in order to test the "solidity" of our conventional ideological beliefs (Chiang, 2004). The observation of the normal world from this unconventional viewpoint forces us to rethink our most common assumptions.

34 In fact, Chespirito's work has a strong element of critique toward the United States. One of his villains is called Super Sam, a parody of Uncle Sam. Additionally, El Chavo's vicinity is a type of *conventillo* or *quinta*, which embodies a rejection of the urban spatial order promoted by US-style urbanization.

35 In 2018, 2btube, a Spanish company with offices in the United States, Mexico, and Spain, acquired 51 percent of Touché Films. The whole operation was rebranded in 2021 as 2bLatam (Meléndez, 2022).

References

Alonso, P. (2015). Infoentretenimiento satírico en México: El caso de Brozo, el payaso tenebroso. *Cuadernos.Info, 37,* 77–90.

Alonso, P. (2018). *Satiric TV in the Americas: Critical metatainment as negotiated dissent.* Oxford University Press.

Alonso, P. (2020). Carnival, hybridity, and Latin American digital humor: The Ecuadorian case of Enchufe.tv. In H. Fernandez L'Hoeste & J. C. Rodriguez (Eds.), *Digital humanities in Latin America* (pp. 177–193). University Press of Florida.

Alves, R. (2005). From lapdog to watchdog: The role of the press in Latin America's democratization. In H. de Burgh (Ed.), *Making journalists* (pp. 181–202). Routledge.

Badgen, S. (2014, April 21). 89% de ataques contra periodistas mexicanos siguen impunes, según comisión de derechos humanos. *LatAm Journalism Review.* https://latamjournalismreview.org/es/articles/89-de

Blanck, N. (2020, June 23). Here's why HBO suspended Mexican comedian Chumel Torres's show. *Remezcla.* https://remezcla.com/film/chumel-torres

Bliss, R. (2014, October 28). *10 hours of walking in NYC as a woman* [Video]. YouTube. https://www.youtube.com/watch?v=b1XGPvbWn0A

Boas, T. C. (2012). Mass media and politics in Latin America. In J. I. Domínguez & M. Shifter (Eds.), *Constructing democratic governance in Latin America* (4th ed., pp. 48–77). Johns Hopkins University Press.

Breiner, J. (2014, March 12). Mexican blogger builds a business out of political satire. *News Entrepreneurs.* http://newsentrepreneurs.blogspot.mx/2014/03/mexican -blogger-builds-business-out-of.html

Calleja, A. (2012). La concentración mediática en México. *Café político.* chrome -extension://efaidnbmnnnibpcajpcglclefindmkaj/https://mx.boell.org/sites/ default/files/aleida2mediatica.pdf

Chiang, H.-c. (2004). The trope of an upside-down world: Carnival and Menippean satire in Richard Brome's *The Antipodes. Concentric: Literary and cultural studies, 30*(2), 55–72.

Constante, S. (2015, February 4). Correa recibe de su propia medicina en las redes sociales. *El País.* https://elpais.com/internacional/2015/02/04/actualidad/1423076927 _196128.html

Donaldson, I. (1970). *The world upside down.* Oxford University Press.

Ecuador begins effort to extradite Rafael Correa from Belgium. (2022, April 22). *Al Jazeera.*

El Pulso de la República. (2014a, November 19). *Angélica Rivera responde: La Casa Blanca* [Video]. YouTube. https://www.youtube.com/watch?v=z74G7AuCVKc

El Pulso de la República. (2014b, April 21). *Carlos Slim Shady* [Video]. YouTube. https:// www.youtube.com/watch?v=BoP9q-j5FhQ

El Pulso de la República. (2014c, March 24). *México: Los más ricos y los más tontos* [Video]. YouTube. https://www.youtube.com/watch?v=xZEN8LhUXaU

El Pulso de la República. (2014d, April 7). *PRIstitución* [Video]. YouTube. https://www .youtube.com/watch?v=mogkSrlv8UU

El Pulso de la República. (2014e, February 24). *¡Se escapó el Chapo! (Anteriormente)* [Video]. YouTube. https://www.youtube.com/watch?v=CIsosUPetwU

El Pulso de la República. (2015a, March 16). *Carmen Aristegui y el Pulso de los 70* [Video]. YouTube. https://www.youtube.com/watch?v=DF9febPq0Xo

El Pulso de la República. (2015b, July 14). *#Noerapenal de máxima seguridad* [Video]. YouTube. https://www.youtube.com/watch?v=uFTN0XVpB7Y

El Pulso de la República. (2015c, July 12). *Se escapó el Chapo (Ahora si)* [Video]. You-Tube. https://www.youtube.com/watch?v=ZVyWV5Gc7Fc

El Pulso de la República. (2015d, June 25). *Y Trump mamá también* [Video]. YouTube. https://www.youtube.com/watch?v=MQ3WWj5h59A

El Pulso de la República. (2016a, May 2). *Ayotzinapa: ¿Capítulo final?* [Video]. YouTube. https://www.youtube.com/watch?v=64ajZUssYQI

El Pulso de la República. (2016b, June 27). *Brexítame* [Video]. YouTube. https://www .youtube.com/watch?v=724hvmhnYIA

El Pulso de la República. (2016c, June 16). *El Pulse de Orlando* [Video]. YouTube. https:// www.youtube.com/watch?v=xrUgURj-vFk

El Pulso de la República. (2016d, May 5). *Narcopulco* [Video]. YouTube. https://www .youtube.com/watch?v=z0KapGuJ1a0

El Pulso de la República. (2016e, April 7). *Panamá pay-per-view* [Video]. YouTube. https://www.youtube.com/watch?v=URR4FB72FRs

El Pulso de la República. (2016f, June 23). *¿Qué pasó en Oaxaca?* [Video]. YouTube. https://www.youtube.com/watch?v=RQLGDNrafbE

El Pulso de la República. (2019a, May 16) *AMLO: From Brozo with love* [Video]. YouTube. https://www.youtube.com/watch?v=_FJ21EnzSaI

El Pulso de la República. (2019b, January 29). *AMLO (ma) maduro* [Video]. YouTube. https://www.youtube.com/watch?v=MxEkCV3JbKc

El Pulso de la República. (2020, March 2). *¡Ya llegó el Coronavirus!* [Video]. YouTube. https://www.youtube.com/watch?v=e_S0mhxRmQU&t

El Pulso de la República. (2021, January 28). *¡Détente, Covid Enemigo!* [Video]. YouTube. https://www.youtube.com/watch?v=1ZS1mt1mqDo&t

El Pulso de la República. (2022a, February 21). *¿AMLO no estás sólo?* [Video]. YouTube. https://www.youtube.com/watch?v=MwtJ0L6oWZI

El Pulso de la República. (2022b, February 17). *Duelo de Betitos* [Video]. YouTube. https://www.youtube.com/watch?v=OI2HyCxGJAU

El Pulso de la República. (2022c, March 3). *La 4t se Belinda* [Video]. YouTube. https://www.youtube.com/watch?v=hBjt7hYdSZ0

El Pulso de la República. (2023, February 13). *Especial: García Luna* [Video]. YouTube. https://www.youtube.com/watch?v=zaTSYrlqy0c&t

El Silencio asfixiante: La libertad de expresión en el Ecuador durante el 2013. (2014, January 22). *Fundamedios*. http://www.fundamedios.org.ec/articulos/el-silencio-asfixiante-la-libertad-de-expresion-en-el-ecuador-durante-el-2013

Enchufetv. (2011, November 13). *The Worst Casting Session* [Video]. YouTube. https://www.youtube.com/watch?v=TyiMl5doLwU

Enchufetv. (2012a, October 8). *Cordones, te dije cordones* [Video]. YouTube. https://www.youtube.com/watch?v=BtmlRE4Iy5Y

Enchufetv. (2012b, September 9). *Mundo al revés: Hombres y mujeres* [Video]. YouTube. https://www.youtube.com/watch?v=ZU8zS-l45ZA

Enchufetv. (2013a, February 3). *Mundo al revés: Gringos y latinos* [Video]. YouTube. https://www.youtube.com/watch?v=n2ISkJZC6DI

Enchufetv. (2013b, June 23). *Upside down world: Gay vs. straight* [Video]. YouTube. https://www.youtube.com/watch?v=3at_j5JtDik

Enchufetv. (2014a, November 2). *Mundo al revés: Belleza* [Video]. YouTube. https://www.youtube.com/watch?v=h7aSEuxaRjo

Enchufetv. (2014b, July 6). *Trailer del Chavo (La película)* [Video]. YouTube. https://www.youtube.com/watch?v=pQFzVr2YUGM

Fernández, F. (1982). *Los medios de comunicación masiva en México*. Juan Pablos.

Frajman, E. (2014). Broadcasting populist leadership: Hugo Chávez and Aló Presidente. *Journal of Latin American Studies*, 46(3), 501–526.

Freedom House. (2015, February 8). *Gobierno Ecuatoriano continúa persecución contra caricaturista* [Press release]. https://freedomhouse.org/article/gobierno-ecuatoriano-continua-persecucion-contra-caricaturista

Fundamedios. (2013, September 3). Gobierno ecuatoriano pide que se penalice la opinión en redes sociales. *IFEX*. https://ifex.org/es/gobierno-ecuatoriano-pide

Garófalo, L. (2012, July 6). Malena Pichot, no cualquiera. *Los Inrockuptibles*. https://medium.com/los-inrockuptibles/malena-pichot-no-cualquiera-9cc55c846623

Gaytán, F., & Fregoso, J. (2006). La ley Televisa de México. *Revista Chasqui, 94*, 40–45.

Jorge Ulloa: "Somos un país en donde todo está por hacer." (2020, December 8). *Plan V*. https://www.planv.com.ec/historias/perfiles/jorge-ulloa-somos-un-pais-donde-todo-esta-hacer

Kellam, M., & Stein, E. (2016). Silencing critics: Why and how presidents restrict media freedom in democracies. *Comparative Political Studies, 49*(1), 36–77.

La historia del Pulso de la República, según Durden. (2017, April 4). *Esquire*. https://www.esquirelat.com/lifestyle/la-historia-del-pulso-de-la-republica-segun-durden/

La increíble discusión entre Malena Pichot y un periodista que vinculó al feminismo con la pedofilia. (2016, August 12). *El Destape*. http://www.eldestapeweb.com/la-increible-discusion-malena-pichot-y-un-periodista-que-vinculo-al-feminismo-la-pedofilia-n19867

Lara, T. (2013, June 13). Ecuadorian legislators approve new communications law. *LatAm Journalism Review*. https://latamjournalismreview.org/articles/ecuadorian-legislators

Lay, I. (2013). Medios electrónicos de comunicación, poderes fácticos y su impacto en la democracia de México. *Revista Mexicana de Ciencias Políticas y Sociales, 217*, 253–268.

"Los de EnchufeTV son talentosos," afirma el hijo de "Chespirito." (2014, July 11). *El Comercio*. http://www.elcomercio.com/tendencias/youtube-enchufetv-televisa

Majlin, B. (2022, October 19). Malena Pichot: "El hater no está en la vida real; en la calle nunca nadie te putea." *Montevideo Portal*. https://www.montevideo.com.uy/Noticias/Malena-Pichot—El-hater-no-esta-en-la-vida-real-en-la-calle-nunca-nadie-te-putea—uc835694

Malena Pichot: "Hago humor para molestar un poco." (2013, April 7). *La Capital*. http://www.lacapital.com.ar/malena-pichot-hago-humor-molestar-un-poco-n437053.html

Malena Pichot le pidió disculpas a Mónica Farro: "No creí que pudiera ofenderla." (2022, September 28). *Infobae*. https://www.infobae.com/teleshow/2022/09/28/malena-pichot-le-pidio-disculpas-a-monica-farro-no-crei-que-pudiera-ofenderla/

Malena Pichot: "una persona que dice que a las minas hay que violarlas es porque violó." (2016, August 14). *El Patagonico*. http://www.elpatagonico.com/malena-pichot-una-persona-que-dice-que-las-minas-hay-que-violarlas-es-porque-violo-n1503739

Martínez, A. (2013, June 20). Ecuador's controversial Communications Law in 8 points. *LatAm Journalism Review*. https://latamjournalismreview.org/articles/ecuadors-controversial-communications-law-in-8-points/

Mascardi, J. (2022, April). Malena Pichot: "Se puede hacer cualquier chiste, pero no lo puede hacer todo el mundo." *Jot Down*. https://www.jotdown.es/2022/04/malena-pichot/

Más de 121 mil muertos, el saldo de la narcoguerra de Calderón: Inegi. (2013, July 30). *Proceso.* https://www.proceso.com.mx/nacional/2013/7/30/mas-de-121-mil -muertos-el-saldo-de-la-narcoguerra-de-calderon-inegi-121510.html

Meléndez, A. (2022, May 16). Enchufe.tv: la historia de la millonaria apuesta del cine ecuatoriano. *Bloomberg Línea.* https://www.bloomberglinea.com/2022/05/16/ enchufetv-la-apuesta-de-humor-ecuatoriano-que-se-hizo-universal/

Miroff, N. (2014, March 15). Ecuador's popular, powerful president Rafael Correa is a study in contradictions. *Washington Post.*

Mulato, A. (2016, February 6). Chumel Torres: "El Pulso de la república no es un noticiario. Somos pizza, chelas y muchas risas." *El País.* https://verne.elpais.com /verne/2015/12/28/articulo/1451341987_641339.html

Netflix Latinoamérica. (2018, March 2). *Malena Pichot: Estupidez compleja* [Video]. YouTube. https://www.youtube.com/watch?v=tg-4sLzqv6M

Olmos, R., Ayala, V., & Gutiérrez Vega, M. (2022, January 27). Así vive en Houston el hijo mayor de AMLO. *Mexicanos Contra la Corrupción.* https://contralacorrupcion .mx/asi-vive

Parish Flannery, N. (2012, September 14). Mexico's media monopoly vs. the people. *Fortune.* http://fortune.com/2012/09/14/mexicos-media-monopoly-vs-the-people/

Pérez Quintana, E. (2022, March 17). Chumel Torres, el comediante que se ha vuelto la nueva obsesión de AMLO. *Yahoo!* https://es-us.noticias.yahoo.com/chumel -torres-el-comediante-que-se-ha-vuelto-la-nueva-obsesion-de-amlo-174648267 .html

Pichot, M. (2008, August 30). *La loca de mierda* [Video]. YouTube. https://www.youtube .com/watch?v=yK5fhmOsnx8

Pichot, M. (2014a, November 27). *Cualca: Chicas inseguras* [Video]. YouTube. https:// www.youtube.com/watch?v=xS0DVNPJivg

Pichot, M. (2014b, June 1). *Cualca – Entrevistando al enemigo II* [Video]. YouTube. https://www.youtube.com/watch?v=vxFv3Vf4JlQ

Pichot, M. (2014c, June 3). *Cualca – Negación* [Video]. YouTube. https://www.youtube .com/watch?v=gOk7IsFziK4

Pichot, M. (2014d, April 26). *Cualca – Piropos* [Video]. YouTube. https://www.youtube .com/watch?v=nXsEVOar6TA

Pichot, M. (2014e, October 29). *Cualca teaser!* [Video]. YouTube. https://www.youtube .com/watch?v=HsCnWiB_37A

Pichot, M. (2014f, April 25). Mauricio y la violencia de todos los días. *Telam.* http://www .telam.com.ar/notas/201404/60768-malena-pichot-macri-piropos.html

Pizarro, E. (2011, February 20). Loca pero no tanto. *La Nación.* https://www.lanacion .com.ar/lifestyle/loca-pero-no-tanto-nid1351193/

Profile: Ecuador's Rafael Correa. (2013, February 27). *BBC.* http://www.bbc.com/news/ world-latin-america-11449110

Ramos, A. (2014, November 12). Me gustaría convertirme en el Seth MacFarlane mexicano. *Hora Cero.* http://horacerotam.com/espectaculos/gustaria-convertirme

Ramos, I. (2012). La contienda política entre los medios privados y el gobierno de Rafael Correa. *Utopia y Praxis Latinoamericana, 17*(58), 65–76.

Ramos, I. (2013). Trayectorias de democratización y desdemocratización de la comunicación en Ecuador. *Iconos—Revista de Ciencias Sociales, 45*, 67–82.

Ruggiero, T. E. (2007). Televisa's Brozo: The jester as subversive humorist. *Journal of Latino-Latin American Studies, 2*(3), 1–15.

Salmerón, C. (2022, March 21). El discurso misógino de Chumel y el privilegio del acceso directo a la justicia. *Washington Post*.

Sosa, G., & Gómez, R. (2013). En el país Televisa. In O. Rincón (Ed.), *Zapping TV: El paisaje de la tele latina* (pp. 83–97). Fundación Friedrich Ebert.

Suárez, R. (2015, October 23). Malena Pichot: La loca de mierda quiere conquistar España. *El País*. https://elpais.com/elpais/2015/10/21/tentaciones/1445424424 _962719.html

Trejo, R. (Ed.). (1985). *Televisa: El quinto poder*. Claves Latinoamericanas.

Tuckman, J. (2015, August 28). El Pulso de la Republica: Meet Chumel Torres, Mexico's answer to Jon Stewart. *Guardian*.

Varas, E. (2014, September 16). Enchufe TV, fenómeno ecuatoriano en Internet. *Revista Soho*.

Villamil, J. (2010). *El sexenio de Televisa*. Grijalbo.

Zavaley, E. (2012, August 7). Cualquierismo en TV abierta. *Rolling Stone*. https://www .lanacion.com.ar/espectaculos/cualquierismo-en-tv-abierta-nid1497143/

3

How Female YouTubers Reshaped Journalism and Gender Discourse in Postconflict Colombia

La Pulla and *Las Igualadas*

The mass protests that began in Colombia in April 2021, amid the pandemic, evidenced decades of sociopolitical tensions and economic inequalities. While the protests were ignited by an unpopular tax reform proposed by the government of conservative president Iván Duque, thousands of protesters—including students, teachers, health-care workers, farmers, Indigenous communities, and many others—took to the streets, widening their demands for the government to address long-standing problems related to education, health care, poverty, police violence, and other social issues (Turkewitz, 2021). International organizations and observers confirmed the use of excessive force by the police during the demonstrations, resulting in dozens of deaths and widespread reports of sexual abuse against women (Foggin, 2021), while the president blamed dissident leftist fighters for much of the violence ("Colombian forces," 2021). This turbulent national context condensed many of the main topics that *La Pulla* (The taunt), a popular Colombian YouTube satiric news show, has covered since 2016.[1] "If you watch some of our early episodes from six years ago, most of the arguments (with some worse statistics) still stand for Colombia," said Maria Paulina Baena, host of *La Pulla*. "And it is similar for other countries of the region, because we Latin Americans are united by deeply ingrained corruption and violence" (personal interview, 2022).[2]

Hosted as a video column at *El Espectador* (Spectator), Colombia's oldest newspaper, *La Pulla* addresses some of the most complex, polarizing, and highly sensitive topics in the country, such as the long period of political violence involving guerrillas, paramilitaries, drug cartels, and the government, and emphasizes the debates and consequences of the national peace process. It employs a John Oliver–esque style of in-depth analysis in two- to eight-minute videos. It has become influential in national political debates, especially for millennials (80 percent of its followers were between the ages of eighteen and thirty-four during its first few years), with its YouTube channel counting more than one million subscribers as of 2023 and some of its videos obtaining more than three million views. This success has also translated into professional recognition. In 2016, *La Pulla*'s coverage of same-sex couples' right to adopt children was awarded the highly prestigious Simón Bolívar National Journalism Award, and more recently, in 2022, Baena received the One Young World Journalist of the Year Award. While being associated with *El Espectador*, *La Pulla* seeks to remain independent from the traditional newspaper by fundraising for its own salaries, equipment, and expenses, thus becoming part of a new generation of entrepreneurial digital business models for online journalism.

Similar to *La Pulla* and also distributed by *El Espectador*, *Las Igualadas* is a video column hosted by journalist Mariángela Urbina (twenty-five years old when the show began). It focuses on gender issues in Colombia but also converses with feminist debates in other Latin American countries and Spain. The name takes ownership of a colloquialism used to describe women who are deemed disrespectful or ignorant of authority. With colloquial and humorous language, *Las Igualadas* videos tackle issues such as sexual harassment, toxic relationships, and women's rights over their bodies, reaching mostly a young female audience (60 percent of their audience are women under twenty-five). The videos have resulted in a backlash of sexist aggression, with anonymous rape and death threats, evidencing the harassment that many Colombian women face in their daily lives. In a time when women's groups have reported that violence against women has increased since the 2016 peace accords were signed, *Las Igualadas* aligns with a regional trend toward online feminist voices virally confronting patriarchal structures in the media. It also connects with an increasing international visibility and reach of female comedians and feminist satire (Day, 2022, 2023; Day & Green, 2020; Finley, 2016; McAuliffe, 2023), and their role as "hot spots" in "wider culture wars, a site of battle over conflicting conceptualizations of gender, race, power, and public space" (Day, 2022, p. 33).

This chapter examines the role of *La Pulla* and *Las Igualadas* within the country's history of political and gender violence perpetrated by guerrillas, paramilitaries, and drug traffickers, as well as recurrent attacks against the press that made Colombia one of the most dangerous places in the world for journalists. Through content analysis of videos and interviews, it shows how these online satiric programs have negotiated their space in Colombia's mediascape by filling a nonpartisan informational gap for the country's millennial generation, particularly in relation to the long period of political violence and the polarization produced by the peace process. I argue that by embracing a hybrid business model that combines traditional and alternative channels and resources, these satiric infotainment shows became representatives of new generational sensitivities against violence, corruption, patriarchal structures of power, and sexist/conservative media representations of political and gender issues. They also resumed a legacy of irreverent Colombian political humor in the media, which was deeply affected by comedian Jaime Garzón Forero's assassination in 1999.

Political Violence, Journalism, and Humor in Colombia

Between 1964 and 2016 (when controversial peace accords were signed), Colombia was home to the longest-running civil war in the Western hemisphere. The complex armed conflict involved many actors (the government, left-wing guerrillas right-wing paramilitaries, and drug trafficking cartels). Political actions, economic interests, illegal economies, class alliances, and social movements overlapped, intersected, and diverged in different periods and regions of the country, resulting in the normalization of violence in civilian communities (Rodriguez, 2011). While the conflict's roots can be found in the inequalities established in colonial times, its republican origins date back to a ten-year civil war known as La Violencia (1948–58) that confronted liberals and conservatives and claimed the lives of more than 200,000 people. The conflict took a new direction in the 1960s with the formation of guerrilla groups, such as the Revolutionary Armed Forces of Colombia (Fuerzas Armadas Revolucionarias de Colombia, FARC), the National Liberation Army (Ejército de Liberación Nacional, ELN), and, later, the less radical M-19. The subsequent formation of right-wing paramilitary forces to fight against the guerrillas took national violence even further. In the 1980s, the spread of the illegal drug trade, the growth of drug cartels, and the US-backed war on drugs—known as Plan Colombia—increased the intensity of the conflict. For over half a century, the violence affected the lives of all citizens (especially the most vulnerable). The conflict left as many as 220,000 dead (most of them civilians), 25,000 disappeared, and 5.7 million displaced (Klobucista & Renwick, 2017). The evolution of this conflict and its impact on Colombian society were detailed in a report by the National Center for Historical Memory (Sánchez, 2013).

Journalism and freedom of expression became casualties of the political violence and national conflict (Caballero, 2000; Gómez, 2001; Gómez-Giraldo & Hernández-Rodriguez, 2009; Lauria, 2004). Colombia, the oldest democracy in the region, was declared in 1998 by the Inter American Press Association to be the world's most dangerous place for the press. During the late 1980s and the early 1990s, drug cartels and armed groups kidnapped and killed many journalists (such as Guillermo Cano Isaza, editor and publisher of the daily *El Espectador*, who was gunned down in front of his paper's office in 1986). Investigative teams inspired by the Watergate era at the end of the 1970s began to disintegrate. When drug cartels were dismantled, smaller criminal organizations stepped in to take their place. They also attacked the press. A report by the Committee to Protect Journalists stated that the decentralization of drug-smuggling operations made journalism even more dangerous (Otis, 2018). It became difficult to tell who the journalists' enemies were, because local traffickers formed alliances with political elites and organizations, from state governors to guerrillas and right-wing paramilitary groups, leading many reporters to self-censorship (Caballero, 2000).

A shocking attack on freedom of expression, and particularly relevant to this chapter, was the assassination of political satirist Jaime Garzón Forero in 1999. A journalist, comedian, and peace activist, Garzón was murdered in his car in Bogotá by right-wing paramilitary forces (the United Self-Defense Forces of Colombia), in alliance with state agents (Higuera, 2020). The murderers perceived him as an ally of the guerrillas because of his activist work toward peace in the country (he was a negotiator in the release of the FARC's hostages). More than two decades later, the case remains open, and not all culprits have been prosecuted ("21 años," 2020).

Garzón's murder shocked the nation. He was popular on Colombian television during the 1990s for his political comedy shows *Zoociedad* (1990–93) and *Quac: El noticero* (Quac: The newscast, 1995–97), a pioneering satiric news program à la *The Daily Show*. Through his particular blend of humor and sociopolitical commentary, Garzón questioned the deadly nexus of violent actors in the country while criticizing corruption and neoliberal policies (Hide, 2019; Mora, 2016). He lampooned presidents, politicians, priests, paramilitaries, narco bosses, guerrilla commanders, journalists, celebrities, and other personalities of Colombia. His cast of fictional characters included Quemando Central (an ultraright military chief), Compañero John Lennin (a radical leftist always against something), Godofredo Cínico Caspa (an ultraconservative political pundit), Emerson de

Francisco (a cynical and inept newscaster), and Dioselina Tibaná (a house-keeper in the president's quarters), among others. But his most memorable character was Heriberto de la Calle, a *lustrabotas* (shoeshiner) who called out politicians and celebrities alike. In the tradition of transgressive, mar-ginal satiric personas (like the ones created by British comedian Sacha Baron Cohen), Heriberto de la Calle interviewed Colombian personali-ties while polishing their shoes. With a confrontational attitude that ques-tioned power, he asked poignant questions, becoming for many the voice of the unheard nation. Twenty-two years after Garzón's murder, people still gather at the place where his car was left by his killers to remember him. Every year on the anniversary of his death, his name becomes a national trending topic on Twitter (now X). Garzón's murder became a symbol of the trauma generated by the ubiquitous violence as well as the limits of freedom of expression in Colombia. It might also explain the dearth of sig-nificant transgressive satire or sociopolitical humor in the country's media. The cases analyzed here have attempted to fill this gap. They not only offer uncensored information about sensitive topics but also reintroduce an ir-reverent satiric infotainment language for a new generation.

Peace Negotiations and the Media in a Polarized Country

Many Colombian governments tried to develop peace talks but failed in their attempts. On June 23, 2016, President Juan Manuel Santos signed a historic cease-fire deal with the FARC rebels. A national referendum was held a few months later to ratify the agreement. The approval of the ref-erendum was taken for granted based on opinion polls, but 50.2 percent of voters opposed it. While progressives saw the deal as a hopeful early stage of demobilization and sustainable peace, conservatives felt that the peace deal was too lenient on guerrillas. A revised peace deal was signed and then approved by Congress on November 30, 2016, but the country was already intensely polarized (Miranda, 2016). Many critics have pointed at the media and misinformation campaigns for fueling this polarization (García-Marrugo, 2013; Gómez-Giraldo et al., 2010; Prager & Hameleers, 2021).

Colombian mainstream media has shown biases in the coverage of the conflict. With the exception of *El Espectador* (of independent liberal lean-ing), most of Colombia's newspapers have historically been linked to po-litical and economic powerhouses.[3] The daily *El Tiempo* was owned for a long time by the Santos family and since 2012 has been owned by Luis

Carlos Sarmiento Angulo, Colombia's wealthiest man ("Estos son los valores," 2021; Moreno Quevedo, 2023). The weekly *Semana*, owned since 2020 by the Gilinski Group, was edited for decades by Alejandro Santos (Juan Manuel Santos's nephew), while the conservative *El Colombiano* has long been controlled by the Hernández and Gómez families—the former accused of promoting right-wing ideologies, and the latter sentenced for dispossessing farmers of their land (Alsema, 2019). The two main commercial television networks, RCN and Caracol, are respectively in the hands of the Ardila Lülle and the Santo Domingo families (Arroyave Cabrera, n.d.), which own some of the country's most powerful corporations and have both been accused of sponsoring paramilitary groups (Alsema, 2019).

Studies on the influence of the media coverage of the conflict on Colombia's public perception found that the language of the traditional press tended to lessen or omit the responsibility of paramilitaries in the violence and stress that of the guerrillas (García, 2016; García-Marrugo, 2013). Reporters would also often mainly relate the point of view of the military and ignore that of rural Colombians (who suffered most in the war), focusing on urban incidents such as kidnappings of public figures and attacks against government buildings (Daniels, 2018). Further, self-censorship was prevalent among journalists as a result of professional pressures, editorial restrictions, harassment, and threats (Barrios & Miller, 2021; Cancino-Borbón et al., 2022; Garcés-Prettel et al., 2019). Possibly because of the persistent bias, a majority of Colombians said in a poll that the paramilitaries were "a necessary evil" (Alsema, 2016; "La gran encuesta," 2007). As an alternative to traditional media coverage, independent news websites (Pacifista, Colombia 2020, and La Silla Vacía, among others) have attempted to include new perspectives on peace, offer a voice to marginalized groups, and expose political corruption. From the perspective of satiric infotainment, *La Pulla* and *Las Igualadas* are part of this wave of digital media, reshaping the country's sociopolitical communication with argumentative, informed, and verifiable information and nonpartisan analysis.

Despite an initial overall decline in violence after the peace deal, conflict-related attacks at the hands of former guerrillas and paramilitary successor groups continued (Human Rights Watch, 2020). According to a United Nations report, Colombia had the highest number of murders of social activists and human rights defenders in Latin America in 2020. When Donald Trump was elected in the United States and Iván Duque—the conservative political heir of former right-wing president Álvaro Uribe—took office in Colombia, both leaders undermined the pact's prospects of success (Fattal, 2019). And while there was a significant decrease in indiscriminate violence against civilians after the accords were signed, journalists and media professionals became selectively targeted. Many of these attacks were developed through virtual platforms, and there was a noticeable uptick in online harassment via social media, emails, and comments. Politicians, who have increasingly used Twitter or X to express their opinions and engage with their followers, generate new risk scenarios for reporters (Barrios et al., 2019). An example is a controversial confrontation between former president Uribe and journalist and satirist Daniel Samper Ospina. Reacting to a critical column by Samper Ospina, Uribe called him a "child rapist" without any evidence, making him a national trending topic on Twitter and exposing the journalist to a series of attacks (Uprimny, 2017). Similarly, the cartoonist Matador (Julio César González) was forced to stop using social media due to death threats from a citizen who claimed his drawings were offensive to the president (Otis, 2018). Such reactions occur in a country where millions of people get their news (and fake news) via WhatsApp and other social media, where misinformation campaigns prevail (Ávila, 2019; Becerra, 2019). In postconflict Colombia, self-censorship, online harassment, and misinformation are increasing threats to freedom of expression. *La Pulla* can be seen as a direct reaction to this mediascape.

La Pulla: Enraged Political Satire for a Frustrated Generation

Created by a small group of young journalists for the newspaper *El Espectador*, *La Pulla* began in 2016 as a two- to eight-minute "video column." Inspired by American satiric shows like *The Daily Show with Jon Stewart* and *Last Week Tonight with John Oliver*, the producers had also followed the emergence of YouTubers and were trying to attract young audiences to the analysis/opinion section of the publication. Maria Paulina Baena, a twenty-five-year-old former intern at the paper who had been recently hired to cover environmental issues auditioned to be in front of the camera and was selected to be the host of the show. In the tradition of Jaime Garzón's political satire (which Baena acknowledges as an influence), the team tried to show the absurdities and contradictions of the sociopolitical reality through humor. But the concept wasn't just a combination of humor, investigation, and in-depth analysis. *La Pulla* expressed rage and exasperation with the political establishment, corruption, and violence. "We began as a rabid video column in which we complained about the world and the country that we lived in," Baena, a political science and communication student at the time, said. She continued: "We soon found a more sarcastic, cynical, and explicative tone to keep complaining about the reality that we inherited, but always backed up with arguments, facts, numbers, and reporting" (personal interview, 2022).[4] She considered it important to communicate the generational anger and frustration. "It's like putting all my energy into a character, putting all my rage. . . . Furious, indignant, with a very strong tone, we are getting this from the young people," she told the Knight Center for Journalism in the Americas (Baddour, 2018). And that's how her character materialized: a frankly irritated woman, dressed in a dark suit jacket and a tie, delivering abrasive journalistic reports while waving her arms with a tone of frustration. In contrast to many other newscasts and similar satiric shows of the region, *La Pulla* was hosted by a woman who broke prevalent female stereotypes reproduced on television and in popular culture (see figure 4). Baena's character is an angry and assertive woman who doesn't care about pleasing or seducing, but harshly criticizes the sociopolitical reality of the country.[5]

La Pulla's first video, about a scandal involving sexual abuse by police officers, launched in April 2016 and went viral (La Pulla, 2016c). The second video, about the energy crisis during Santos's government, got even more views (and a response from the presidency, which legitimated it as a recognized political communication format) (El Gran Electrón, 2016). Since then, *La Pulla* has published regular videos (more than 330 by 2022), gathering millions of visits on Facebook and YouTube. With a team of between three and five people, the videos were initially filmed with minimal resources in the office of the publisher (*El Espectador*'s publisher is Fidel Cano Correa, nephew of the assassinated editor Guillermo Cano Isaza).

For some years, *El Espectador* had been trying to reach younger audiences without success (Martinez, 2018). *La Pulla* changed all that: its YouTube channel has more than one million subscribers (compared to *El Espectador*'s five hundred thousand) as of 2022 (YouTube, n.d.a, n.d.b), and some of *La Pulla*'s videos have nearly three million views on YouTube (and more than five million on Facebook), while the newspaper tends to have significantly less online engagement. More importantly, 80 percent of *La Pulla*'s followers in its first few years were between the ages of eighteen and thirty-four (Martinez, 2018). This success was partially due to a reorganization of newsroom hierarchies, foregrounding younger journalists more

Figure 4. *La Pulla*, a satiric video column hosted by Maria Paulina Baena at the newspaper *El Espectador*, has addressed some of the most polarizing and sensitive topics in postconflict Colombia. Film still.

attuned with social media platforms and languages over the "old guard" editors who traditionally call the shots. As part of this innovation, *La Pulla* also implemented an original business model that does not depend on advertising. In order to maintain the show's independence, *La Pulla*'s team found other ways of funding, such as seeking grants from foundations and nonprofit organizations. It won a grant from the Open Society Foundations to produce episodes on violence in Latin America. German foundation Friedrich-Ebert-Stiftung financed episodes on housekeepers, multinational corporations, a Bogotá slum, and cyberactivism. The team also earns money by giving public talks and workshops at universities, organizations, and schools. The funds cover the team's salaries, equipment, and expenses, so that the producers can work on *La Pulla* full time (Martinez, 2018). "We have never been censored at *El Espectador*," Baena said. "But since the newspaper is part of a bigger media conglomerate that might have conflicting interests, we are protected by having our own funding. It shields us" (personal interview, 2022).[6]

Journalistic investigation is a central aspect of *La Pulla*'s work. The producers spend a week or more digging into every story and many hours working individually and together on the script (La Pulla, 2016b; Páramo, 2016). Baena described the process to *Revista Semana*: "Every fifteen days we have a general meeting to define the topics for the show and develop a timeline for the investigation. Then, we all work on the script. At the end of the process, Fidel Cano revises the text and gives the final touches" ("Nos emberracamos," 2016).[7] "We are like *El Espectador*'s child," Baena added to the Nieman Foundation. "When someone calls to complain, they call Fidel, they don't call us" (Martinez, 2018). It's revealing how the process combines the work of the young creative team with the supervision of an experienced editor. It not only highlights the importance of intergenerational collaboration, but also functions as a defense mechanism against liability. Baena highlights the exceptionality of *El Espectador* as an "editorial umbrella":

> I do not think we could have done *La Pulla* in any other Colombia media outlet. There are many [corporate] filters for producing journalistic content. *El Espectador* has always been characterized by its freedom and independence (and professionalism). It's one of the few media outlets in Colombia that has not kneeled before power. Despite being part of a wider media conglomerate, it is a newspaper that values and battles for freedom of expression above anything else. (personal interview, 2022)[8]

Because of its visceral and irreverent tone, *La Pulla* has been criticized for lacking objectivity. However, Baena clarifies that the show is not "balanced journalism," but opinion based on arguments and evidence. "We take a position. We criticize everyone [all the different political groups] without taking sides. And we do not agree with the accusation that, in this time of postconflict and reconciliation, we are polarizing. . . . *La Pulla* is barely the beginning of a deeper conversation," she said to *Revista Semana* ("Nos emberracamos," 2016).[9] From this perspective, *La Pulla* has targeted the corruption and failures of the political class and its responsibility in the history of violence in the country. One of the most popular videos—"¿Por qué nadie se mete con Álvaro Uribe?" (Why is everyone afraid of Álvaro Uribe?)—profiles the former president of Colombia (2002–10), his links with paramilitaries and drug trafficking, and his role in violations against human rights, highlighting the possible reasons for the impunity of one of the most powerful men in Colombia (La Pulla, 2018d). In "This Is How Uribe Silences His Critics," Baena recaps the history of violence in the country, leading to the political strategies that the conservative leader uses to evade accountability: stigmatizing his critics as "guerrilleros" while promoting polarization in the country (La Pulla, 2017f). The video ends with the host seriously addressing the camera: "Here is a message for Mr. Uribe and all who are watching our show. We hate the guerrillas. We hate the paramilitaries. Our only weapons are our words and this camera. You know why we need to say this? So, we don't get killed."[10] With this dramatic statement reflecting the reaction of many journalists after seeing so many of their colleagues killed over the past decades, *La Pulla* addresses a central problem for Colombian journalists: the history of violence against critical voices in the country.[11] This issue is further explicated in the video "10 Steps to Be Assassinated in Colombia," in which the show denounces the systematic killing of social leaders and critical voices in Colombia during the postconflict era while framing the horrific news in the context of President Santos receiving the Nobel Peace Prize in Norway (La Pulla, 2017a). The fear and dejection reflected in *La Pulla*'s coverage of the violence frequently devolve into frustration. "I'm already tired of doing episodes of *La Pulla* counting the deaths," Baena said. "We can help make the issue more visible, but we don't know how to stop it" (personal interview, 2022).[12]

La Pulla's general (and generational) repudiation of violence carries over into its coverage of the political class and particularly its coverage of the national elections, in which the show criticizes all political camps. The video "Ivan Duque Is the Worst Candidate to the Presidence [*sic*] (or That's What We Think)" addresses the contradictions of the conservative candidate in some of the main areas of the national agenda: economic policies, the restructuring of the justice system, national security, drug trafficking, health care, and the peace process (La Pulla, 2018b). After analyzing Duque's ideas, the host interprets Duque's relationship with Uribe and explains why it might be fair to think that if Duque wins, the former president would be the real power in the shadows. However, *La Pulla* does not only criticize the Right. In "Gustavo Petro NO merece ser presidente" (Gustavo Petro does NOT deserve to be president), the host profiles the former mayor of Bogotá and left-wing presidential candidate (and the person who would become president in 2022) (La Pulla, 2018a). After pointing out the falsehoods disseminated about Petro, *La Pulla* analyzes the real reasons that make him a questionable leader: his egocentrism and pride, his despotic political decisions, his incapacity to receive criticism, his shady political allies, his negative financial decisions as mayor, and the ways in which he manipulated the statistics to exaggerate his accomplishments. The video on the Odebrecht corruption scandal—"Nos gobiernan puros mafiosos" (We are governed by the mafia)—is also a good example of *La Pulla*'s attempt to expose the dishonesty of the ruling class beyond partisan politics (La Pulla, 2018c).

In its coverage of the history and current situation of political violence in Colombia, *La Pulla* has continued to address the peace process between the government and the guerrillas and its role in the ongoing tensions and polarization of the country. The video "El plebiscito sacó la peor porquería de Colombia" (The referendum got the worst out of Colombia) explains the ideological and moral issues involved in the controversial peace accords' national referendum (La Pulla, 2016a). The show deconstructs the political manipulations undertaken by both the Santos government and the opposition when promoting their campaigns for or against the peace accords. While *La Pulla* criticizes all of the fallacies associated with the anti-accords campaign, it also explains the problematic issues of accepting the conditions of the FARC, as in the video "Why Are They Gonna Give FARC a Huge Ammount [*sic*] of Money?" (La Pulla, 2016g). In a similar vein, the show criticizes the possibility of the FARC leader known as "Timochenko" (Rodrigo Londoño Echeverri) becoming president of the country (this episode was one of the top performing videos, gathering more than five million views on Facebook) (El Espectador, 2017).

Recognizing the role that drug trafficking has played in Colombia's history, *La Pulla* also attempts to educate viewers about the current significance of this illegal activity. In "Classic Lies about Drugs in Latin America," the show dispels misinformation about the relationship between drugs and violence, capos, national economies, and rural workers, relating the phenomenon to deeper sociopolitical realities of the region (La Pulla, 2017b). Similarly, another video deconstructs myths about Pablo Escobar, questions the glorification of the drug trafficker in popular culture, and reminds the audience of his criminal activities (La Pulla, 2019b). In terms of foreign policy, *La Pulla* has extensively covered the implications of the humanitarian crisis in Venezuela, explaining the problematic histories and roles of both the Right and the Left (La Pulla, 2017g). The show has decisively criticized the Chavist authoritarian government and Nicolás Maduro's policies (La Pulla, 2019a), while also ridiculing the right-wing discourse that encourages an invasion of Venezuela (2018i) and promotes xenophobia against Venezuelan immigrants (2018f).

As can be seen in the varied examples of *La Pulla*'s coverage, the show produces content that is critical of diverse ideological and political views. This nonpartisan, independent, and inquisitorial spirit counters the prevalent sociopolitical polarization in public debate (usually built on misinformation, ignorance, or an appeal to established emotional beliefs) with arguments based on research and evidence. The producers want their arguments and perspectives to affect the central spheres of public conversation: "We did not want to be an alternative media outlet, because the alternative stays in the margins. We wanted to be at the center and make the powerful shake. We wanted our episodes to be seen by congresspeople, by presidents. And I think that is what journalism should aspire to" (Baena, personal interview, 2022). From this engaged and critical perspective, *La Pulla* has also covered other important and sensitive issues in Colombia, such as environmental pollution (La Pulla, 2018e), abortion (2016e), the role of religion in sociopolitical debates (2017d), the challenges of educators in the country (2017e), and sexual workers' rights (2017c).

During the pandemic, like other online satiric shows of the region, *La Pulla* focused on informing the audience about the evolution of the health emergency and countering the abundant misinformation (La Pulla, 2020b, 2020c). For example, the show solidly dispelled fake news and conspiracy theories about secondary effects of the vaccines (La Pulla, 2021b) and corruption and irregularities around them (2021c). The pandemic, nevertheless, did not take all the attention away from other important national and global issues, such as the controversial 2022 Colombian elections (La Pulla, 2022a, 2022b, 2022c) or a discriminatory TikTok algorithm that was censoring critical information about China (2020a). Many of *La Pulla*'s pieces have also stretched the original short-duration episodes into longer videos and experimented with new formats.[13] Baena stated: "Throughout the evolution of the project, we have understood that journalism's capacity for transformation is infinite. We can push the borders and limits of our profession. We have even done theater plays with our reports. It never ends. We have always seen *La Pulla* as an unfinished product" (personal interview, 2022).[14]

The show's innovative journalistic content has been recognized in relation to struggles for gender equality. In 2016, the show's coverage about same-sex couples' right to adopt children obtained the prestigious Simón Bolívar National Journalism Award (La Pulla, 2016d). For *La Pulla*, the struggle for LGBTQ rights has paralleled its feminist perspective against a patriarchal society. In the video "¿Por qué el feminismo no es un asco?" (Why is feminism not disgusting?), Baena deconstructs prevalent prejudices about feminist views while explaining challenges that women face in Colombia's traditionally sexist society (La Pulla, 2016f). Unsurprisingly,

Figure 5. *Las Igualadas*, a video column on gender issues hosted by Mariángela Urbina, offers a new generational feminist view against patriarchal structures of power and sexist media representations in Colombia. Film still.

her perspectives on these topics have generated sexist aggression from anonymous trolls. "The debate often has to do with the fact that I am a woman," she said to *Semana* ("Nos emberracamos," 2016). Considering her pioneering role as a female political satirist in Colombia's media, this observation is indicative of a deeper underlying issue. Within the history of generalized violence in the country, women and marginalized groups have been more vulnerable than others. *Las Igualadas*, a sister show of *La Pulla*, has also dealt with this problem.

Las Igualadas: Journalism with a Gender Perspective in a Conservative and Violent Society

Created in March 2017 and following a similar format to *La Pulla*, *Las Igualadas* is a YouTube video series on gender issues from a feminist perspective. Also born out of *El Espectador*, it had a three-person team at its outset: host Mariángela Urbina, a twenty-five-year-old journalist who soon became a national public feminist; Viviana Bohórquez, a lawyer and activist; and Juan Carlos Rincón, opinion editor of the newspaper. With almost three hundred thousand subscribers to the *Las Igualadas* YouTube channel and videos reaching two million views as of 2022, it has become popular among young people not only in Colombia but also in Mexico and Spain, with 60 percent of the audience being women under twenty-five (Agudo, 2019) (see figure 5).

Using ironic, direct, and fast-paced language, *Las Igualadas* established an ongoing critique of the sociopolitical reality of the country from a gendered perspective. It approached, for example, the debate about the peace accords, focusing on the ways they affected women and vulnerable groups; young people's understanding of notions of a peaceful society in relation to equality for all (Las Igualadas, 2019d); the deep connections between sexism and politics in Colombia, as evidenced in the discourse of politicians on both sides of the aisle (2018c, 2019e, 2019j, 2019o); and the particular challenges that immigrant Venezuelan women face in the country (2018g). This gendered approach to the national reality is particularly relevant because of the history of violence that women have suffered in Colombian society.

Colombian women, particularly Afro-descendant and Indigenous women, were victims of violence and displacement throughout the national conflict (Brown, 2019; Fiscó, 2005; Goldscheid, 2020). Twenty thousand cases of sexual violence against women were reported during the half century of fighting before the 2016 accords were signed (Moloney, 2018). Different forms of sexual, psychological, and physical violence against women were used as a war strategy to spread terror among communities, according to a report by the Inter-American Commission on Human Rights (2006). Meanwhile, women's roles as primary caretakers continued during the conflict, putting them "in charge of keeping the family together, figuring out how to survive after being displaced, leading searches for disappeared relatives, all at the expense of their own mental health" (Brown, 2019).

Women's rights organizations pushed to include a subcommission on gender in the peace agreements to respond to the specific needs of women and LGBTQ victims. However, these sections of the peace deal have been the least implemented, according to a 2018 report by the Kroc Institute for International Peace Studies at the University of Notre Dame. Thus, violence has continued, with the most vulnerable groups—Afro-descendant, Indigenous, rural, lesbian, bisexual, and transgender women, as well as women with disabilities—disproportionately affected without state protection or access to justice (Goldscheid, 2020). Rights defenders, politicians, and leaders who are women have also faced gender-specific violence, including rape and threats against their children (Forst, 2018; Zulver, 2019).

Outside the context of war, the situation is also worrying. One woman is killed on average every three days, with fifty-five cases of sexual violence reported daily, according to the National Institute of Legal Medicine and Forensic Sciences (Moloney, 2018). Most offenders are partners, former partners, stepfathers, fathers, neighbors, or uncles of the victims. More than 74 percent of survivors are girls under the age of fourteen (Brown, 2019). According to a 2018 United Nations report, one in three Colombian women has been physically abused by her partner, with a higher incidence among older and less educated women (ONU Mujeres, 2018). Adding to these statistics are the hundreds of thousands of Venezuelan women who immigrated to Colombia to escape the crisis in their own country. Most of these crimes go unpunished, since most women do not denounce their abusers. Often, women are believed to "provoke" violence with their behavior, such as wearing short skirts or being out at night, perpetuating Colombia's macho culture, which condones violence, blames women for the abuse inflicted on them, and perpetuates traditional repressive roles (Moloney, 2018).

Responding to these problematic issues, *Las Igualadas* has denounced discrimination (Las Igualadas, 2017h, 2019p), sexual violence (2017i, 2018l, 2018m, 2019a, 2019g, 2019n), and sexual harassment (2017a, 2017d, 2017f, 2017g, 2019f) in different environments while trying to fill a gap in sexual education in the media, social institutions, and public discourse. At the same time, the show seeks to destigmatize negative ideas about feminism in Colombian society (Las Igualadas, 2019h, 2019m) while educating viewers on contemporary debates on gender (2018d, 2018f) and the LGBTQ movement (2019b). As part of this critical and educational perspective, it covers issues such as abortion (Las Igualadas, 2018a, 2019r), contraceptives (2018n), teen pregnancy (2018k), toxic relationships (2017b), online pornography (2017c, 2017j, 2019i), online dating (2019l), mental health (2019c), plastic surgery (2018h), female masturbation (2017e), virginity (2018j), HIV relationships (2018p), and sexuality and disabilities (2019q). In this sense, the show fosters conversation about sensitive gender issues in a still prejudiced and conservative society. Similar to *La Pulla*, it combines irony, information, and analysis with an angry tone that stems from frustration and social trauma, connecting with feminist voices that use humor as "a survival kit" (Ahmed, 2017) to provide models for affective orientations to sustain their sociopolitical work during periods of crisis (McAuliffe, 2023) and popular misogyny (Banet-Weiser, 2018).

At the same time, *Las Igualadas*' producers highlight the role of the press in empowering women and marginalized groups. They point out the need for journalists to include a gender perspective when covering the most urgent sociopolitical issues of the country. For Urbina, traditional journalism's authority is based on being the voice of the unheard, and in this light, "the press has a historical debt to women" (Esteban, 2018). Urbina also acknowledges the importance of new digital technologies and platforms for expanding the reach of what she calls *periodismo de género* (gender journalism) and refocusing the news agenda on women's rights (Esteban, 2018). With its postmodern ironic twist, *Las Igualadas* reflects on the traditional role of the media in reproducing gender prejudices and stereotypes. The show not only analyzes the prevalence of male views and sexism in audiovisual culture (Las Igualadas, 2019k, 2019s), but also exposes celebrities, personalities, YouTubers, and journalists who engage in sexist or homophobic behavior (2018e, 2018g, 2018o). Many of these reports have ended in legal suits against the newspaper and the producers. In 2020, a court ordered *Las Igualadas*, *El Espectador*, and the publisher Fidel Cano Correa to rectify content accusing a religious leader of gender violence. The resolution was appealed, but the Foundation for Press Freedom denounced this legal attempt as an effort to intimidate journalists and promote self-censorship on gender issues ("Decisión contra Las Igualadas," 2020).

Las Igualadas' social critiques have produced a backlash of sexist aggression against its journalists. Comments on social networks are full of rage, with threats of rape and murder (Forero-Aponte, 2018). For Urbina, the internet has become one more place where gender violence is performed and reproduced: "Social media reflect[s] the violence that we experience every day. . . . One time I received the following threat, 'Insolent feminazi, a bullet in your forehead'" (quoted in Esteban, 2018).[15] This insult—feminazi—has become a recurrent label meant to disqualify feminist struggles for empowerment. Likening women fighting for their rights to repressive fascists has been a strategy of (usually) threatened and threatening men, who perceive these critiques as an attack on their privileges supported by patriarchal structures (a similar discursive fallacy to what the US alt-right has referred to as "white genocide").[16] In a satiric video, *Las Igualadas* deconstructed the notion of feminazi (Las Igualadas, 2018b). With daily life examples in which the word might be used, Urbina shows how the term seeks to disregard women who denounce gender inequality and harassment at home, at work, and in other social environments. The video also summarizes the strategies that *Las Igualadas* embodies: humor, irony, solid information, and critical thinking as resources to expose sexism and resist violence.

Conclusion

In alliance with a traditional media outlet and other funding organizations, *La Pulla* and *Las Igualadas* became influential in public debate by filling a nonpartisan informational gap in Colombian media while also developing sociopolitical critique in a country with a history of violence that has concretely affected journalists, satirists, activists, women, LGBTQ people, and other minorities. In the so-called postconflict era, these satiric digital shows tackled the prevalent national tensions after the longest civil war conflict in the Western hemisphere. With a combination of humor, irony, investigation, analysis, and, notably, frustration and anger at a violent and unequal society, these satiric shows seek to educate and develop a deeper conversation about Colombia's historical processes, political corruption, and social prejudices. In this effort, *La Pulla* counters the prevalent political polarization (specifically surrounding the peace accords between the government and the guerrillas) with a critical and nonpartisan perspective on political actors and ideological views. Similarly, *Las Igualadas* counters gender violence and prejudice with uncensored educational information and examples of how sexism and homophobia are ingrained and performed in Colombian society. While the show clearly denounces different patriarchal structures, it also seeks to educate and empower women, with a focus on the new generations. In this sense, it, like *La Pulla*—both shows hosted by young women—takes a pedagogical and activist role (advocating for gender journalism, for example) and exemplifies the need for more female voices in contemporary Latin American satire and political infotainment.

These online satiric shows also implemented a successful hybrid business model. In many ways, each project functions as a small start-up within a parent company. The *La Pulla* and *Las Igualadas* teams are employees of the newspaper and use its platform for distribution and recognition, but they keep their editorial and economic independence and have developed their own styles and audiences while rejuvenating the *El Espectador* brand. While the newspaper announced in 2018 that its website would be behind a metered paywall, the digital shows have remained free on all platforms. The recognition and popularity of these shows, however, does not translate into traditional commercial revenue or monetization. Their irreverent tone alienates advertisers, and the producers prefer not to insert ads or plug products in the shows. Grants from foundations and nonprofit organizations have been an important source of funding, as well as public talks and workshops at universities, organizations, and schools. Nevertheless, their alliance with *El Espectador* has remained an essential component for legal protection, mentoring advice, and intergenerational collaboration.

In addition to their hybrid business models, these shows became especially appealing to young urban audiences by producing heavily glocalized content focused on national and regional sociopolitical news agendas. While strongly influenced by recent US political television satire (such as *The Daily Show* and *Last Week Tonight*), these Colombian cases successfully combined their foreign influences with local tradition (particularly Jaime Garzón's irreverent humor). In this sense, they created a uniquely scathing, glocal voice that tapped into national tensions following global formats and styles. In a context where the pandemic, social inequalities, and the controversial peace accords intensified the political polarization in the country, these shows have tried to explain the multilayered reality behind the simplistic arguments of the Left and the Right, offering cathartic interpretations based on solid arguments. This nonpartisan approach— from a progressive, inclusive, and democratic system of values—seems to be a constant in other online satiric shows of the region, as evidenced in the following chapters.

Notes

1 *La Pulla* covered the controversial tax reform and the mass protests, for example (La Pulla, 2021a, 2021d).

2 "Básicamente las Pullas que hicimos hace seis años se pueden poner hoy (con una cifra un poquito peor) y se mantienen. [Y esto también se muestra con otras realidades latinoamericanas] porque a los latinoamericanos nos une una corrupción enquistada y una violencia muy marcada."

3 Because of financial problems following the assassination of *El Espectador*'s editor, Guillermo Cano Isaza, and a bomb attack on its newsroom, the newspaper was sold in 1997 by the Cano family to the Santo Domingo Group, which remains committed to the independent editorial stance of the publication. Despite being part of a bigger media conglomerate, *El Espectador* has been internationally praised for its professionalism and defense of freedom of expression (Gutiérrez Roa, 2021; Mioli, 2016; "UNESCO/Guillermo Cano," n.d.).

4 "Empezamos siendo una columna absolutamente rabiosa en la que nos quejábamos del mundo en que vivíamos y del país que habitábamos. Después, encontramos un

tono un poco más sarcástico, un poco más cínico, más explicativo, pero sin dejar atrás la identidad de queja. Pero de queja con argumentos. Nos vamos a quejar por lo que nos dejaron, pero esto tiene unos datos, unas cifras y una reportería detrás."

5 Scholars have increasingly paid attention to the use of traditional stereotypes of women to justify their exclusion from public life (Cook & Cusack, 2010), and the way that contemporary female comedians and other performers challenge those norms, reinventing the tradition of the unruly woman (Petersen, 2017) and going beyond the trope of the "angry feminist" (Barbara, 2010).

6 "El periódico nunca nos ha censurado ningún episodio. Pero como hacemos parte de un grupo más grande de medios que puede complicar los intereses, nos protege tener nuestra propia financiación. De alguna forma, nos blinda ante el grupo grande."

7 "Cada quince días hacemos un consejo de redacción. Ahí definimos los temas que pueden ser 'pullables' y que podemos investigar en un tiempo definido. Luego entre todos hacemos el guion, y al final Fidel Cano lo revisa y le da la estocada final."

8 "No creo que hubiéramos podido hacer *La Pulla* en ningún otro medio colombiano. En los otros medios hay muchos filtros para hacer contenidos periodísticos. *El Espectador* siempre se ha caracterizado por ser muy libre en su estructura. El trabajo del periodista es muy libre e independiente, pero también riguroso con la información. *El Espectador* ha sido uno de los pocos medios de Colombia no se ha arrodillado al poder. A pesar de que es parte de un grupo grande, es un medio que sigue dando batallas y valora la libertad de expresión por sobre cualquier cosa."

9 "Es que 'La Pulla' no es periodismo equilibrado, sino opinión. Opinión basada en argumentos. . . . Que nosotros tomamos posición. Que le apuntamos a todo el mundo, sin defender a unos y atacar a otros. Y que no estamos de acuerdo con aquello de que, en plena etapa de posconflicto y reconciliación, con nuestro tono supuestamente estamos polarizando. . . . Desde el principio hemos dicho que 'La Pulla' es apenas el inicio de una discusión más profunda."

10 "Un mensaje para el doctor Uribe y todos los que nos ven. Odiamos a la guerrilla. Odiamos a los paramilitares. Y nuestras únicas armas son la palabra y esta cámara. Saben por qué tenemos que hacer esta advertencia? Para que no nos maten."

11 Another example of a journalist's reaction to this violence is a phrase that was uttered on live television by César Londoño, sports journalist and colleague of Jaime Garzón, the night that the comedian was murdered: "Here ends the sport reports. . . . Shitty country" (Hasta aquí los deportes. . . . País de mierda). Instead of just seeing this moment as an accidental outburst on live television, many who shared his frustration and anger with the dangerous environment went on to resignify the phrase ("A 20 años," 2019).

12 "Todos los problemas sociales se enmarcan en uno macro: seguimos siendo un país violento. Solo este año ya llevamos 87 masacres y más de 1400 líderes asesinados después de la firma del acuerdo de paz. Y yo ya me cansé en la Pulla de hacer este conteo de líderes asesinados. Podemos visibilizar el tema pero no sabemos cómo pararlo."

13 Baena explained about the longer pieces, "At the beginning, we did three- or four-minute videos because we thought that people were not going to watch our content and we needed to get their attention quickly. Now we do pieces that go up to forty minutes. And we can do it because we have things to say, and we know that that time is necessary to develop the information that we have" (personal interview, 2022).

14 "A través de este proyecto hemos entendido que la capacidad de transformación del periodismo es infinita. Incluso podemos empujar nuestras propias fronteras y límites de nuestra profesión. Nosotros hemos hecho hasta obras de teatro con esto. No se agota. Siempre hemos concebido a La Pulla como un producto inacabado."

15 "Las redes sociales son un reflejo de la violencia que vivimos todos los días. . . . Una vez me escribieron 'Feminazi insolente, tiro en la frente.'"

16 As Green (2019, p. 51) notes, the term *white genocide* has "become a meme that amplifies and inflates the discourse of reverse racism and engenders fear among whites that immigration, interracial relationships and children, and diversity initiatives and practices (among other public and private forms of racial integration) are leading to the elimination of whites."

References

21 años sin Jaime Garzón. (2020, August 12). *Fundación para la Libertad de Prensa.* https://flip.org.co/pronunciamientos/21-anos-sin-jaime-garzon

A 20 años del asesinato de Jaime Garzón: "¡País de mierda!" (2019, July 13). *Colombia Informa.* https://www.colombiainforma.info/a-20-anos-del-asesinato-de-jaime-garzon-pais-de-mierda/

Agudo, A. (2019, January 29). "La prueba de que el feminismo es un movimiento plural es que discutimos entre nosotras." *El País.* https://elpais.com/elpais/2019/01/28/planeta_futuro/1548701511_859026.html

Ahmed, S. (2017). *Living a feminist life.* Duke University Press.

Alsema, A. (2016, October 18). How Colombia's newspapers consistently misinformed the public on the armed conflict. *Colombia Reports.* https://colombiareports.com/colombias-newspapers

Alsema, A. (2019, September 9). The crucial role of independent media in Colombia's peace process. *Colombia Reports.* https://colombiareports.com/the-role-of-independent-media

Arroyave Cabrera, J. A. (n.d.). Colombia. *Media Landscapes.* https://medialandscapes.org/country/colombia

Ávila, A. (2019, April 30). Medios de comunicación y libertad de prensa. *El País.* https://elpais.com/internacional/2019/04/30/colombia/1556581971_362007.html

Baddour, D. (2018, February 28). Satirical video column brings new life and audience to traditional Colombian newspaper's opinion section. *LatAm Journalism Review.* https://latamjournalismreview.org/articles/satirical-video

Banet-Weiser, S. (2018). *Empowered: Popular feminism and popular misogyny.* Duke University Press.

Barbara, T. (2010). *Feminism and affect at the scene of argument: Beyond the trope of the angry feminist.* Temple University Press.

Barrios, M., & Miller, T. (2021). Voices of resilience: Colombian journalists and self-censorship in the post-conflict period. *Journalism Practice, 15*(10), 1423–1440.

Barrios, M., Vega, L., & Gil, L. (2019). When online commentary turns into violence: The role of Twitter in slander against journalists in Colombia. *Conflict & Communication Online, 18*(1). http://www.cco.regener-online.de/

Becerra, L. (2019, September 27). En Colombia se desinforma por WhatsApp y Facebook revela estudio de Universidad de Oxford. *La República.* https://www.larepublica .co/economia/en-colombia-se-desinforma-por-whatsapp-y-facebook-revela -estudio-de-oxford-2914148

Brown, K. (2019, May 9). For many women in Colombia, peace never arrived. *Aljazeera.*

Caballero, M. C. (2000). The Colombian press under siege. *Harvard International Journal of Press/Politics, 5*(3), 90–95.

Cancino-Borbón, A., Barrios, M., & Salas-Vega, L. (2022). When reporters make the news: Narrated role performance during Colombia's post-conflict with the FARC guerrilla group. *Journalism Studies, 23*(1), 88–107.

Colombian forces committed "serious" abuses during protests: UN. (2021, December 15). *Al Jazeera.*

Cook, R., & Cusack, S. (2010). *Gender stereotypes: Transnational legal perspectives.* University of Pennsylvania Press.

Daniels, J. P. (2018, December 11). Colombia journalism project aims to bring untold stories of war to light. *Guardian.*

Day, A. (2022). Mothers and whores: Female performers and comedic controversies. *Studies in American Humor, 8*(1), 32–50.

Day, A. (2023). Gender and Genre in Hannah Gadsby's *Nanette. Television & New Media.* Advance online publication. https://doi.org/10.1177/15274764231201966

Day, A., & Green, V. (2020). Asking for it: Rape myths, satire, and feminist lacunae. *Journal of Women in Culture and Society, 45*(2), 449–472.

Decisión contra Las Igualadas incrementa la autocensura frente denuncias de violencia de género. (2020, November 25). *Fundación para la Libertad de Prensa.* https:// flip.org.co/pronunciamientos/decision-contra-las-igualadas-incrementa-la -autocensura-frente-denuncias-de-violencia-de-genero

El Espectador. (2017, November 9). *#LaPulla: Timochenko merece llegar a la presidencia* [Video]. Facebook. https://www.facebook.com/elespectadorcom/videos/ 10155984169344066

El Gran Electrón. (2016, March 30). *La pulla: Ahora resulta que si hay apagón va a ser culpa nuestra* [Video]. YouTube. https://www.youtube.com/watch?v=zcfgmfaPIig

Esteban, P. (2018, March 7). Conozca a las santandereanas creadoras de "Las Igualadas." *Vanguardia.* https://www.vanguardia.com/entretenimiento/galeria/conozca-a -las-santandereanas-creadoras-de-las-igualadas-PDvl426669

Estos son los valores que defiende "El Tiempo," según su propietario Luis Carlos Sarmiento Angulo. (2021, December 4). *Revista Semana.* https://www.semana

.com/nacion/articulo/estos-son-los-valores-que-defiende-el-tiempo-segun-su
-propietario-luis-carlos-sarmiento-angulo/202139/

Fattal, A. (2019, August 30). Ex-FARC's leader call to arms is bad news for Colombians. *New York Times.*

Finley, J. (2016). Black women's satire as (Black) postmodern performance. *Studies in American Humor, 2*(2), 236–265.

Fiscó, S. (2005). Atroces realidades: La violencia sexual contra la mujer en el conflicto armado colombiano. *Papel Político, 17*, 119–159.

Foggin, S. (2021, June 22). "The risk you run": Colombia's women protesters on sexual violence. *BBC.* https://www.bbc.com/news/world-latin-america-57553316

Forero-Aponte, Á. (2018, April 23). Female empowerment; male rage. *Bogotá Post.* https://thebogotapost.com/female-empowerment-male-rage-feminism/29254/

Forst, M. (2018, December 3). United Nations special rapporteur on the situation of human rights defenders. https://www.ohchr.org/Documents/Issues/Defenders/StatementVisitColombia3Dec2018_EN.pdf

Garcés-Prettel, M., Jaramillo, L., Arroyave Cabrera, J., & Avila-Majul, A. (2019). Libertad de prensa y conflicto armado en Colombia: Un análisis desde la autonomía profesional percibida por los periodistas colombianos. *Saber, Ciencia y Libertad, 14*(1), 21–34.

García, A. (2016, October 10). De por qué odiamos a las Farc (y no tanto a los paras). *La Perorata.* https://laperorata.wordpress.com/2016/10/10/de-por-que

García-Marrugo, A. (2013). What's in a name? The representation of illegal actors in the internal conflict in the Colombian press. *Discourse & Society, 24*(4), 421–445.

Goldscheid, J. (2020, May 27). Gender violence against Afro-Colombian women: Making the promise of international human rights law real. *Columbia Human Rights Law Review.* http://hrlr.law.columbia.edu/hrlr-online/gender-violence

Gómez, I. (2001). Colombia: The war against journalists. *Nieman Reports, 55*(1), 9–12.

Gómez-Giraldo, J. C., & Hernández-Rodriguez, J. C. (2009). Libertad de prensa en Colombia: Entre la amenaza y la manipulación. *Palabra clave, 12*(1), 13–35.

Gómez-Giraldo, J. C., Hernández-Rodriguez, J. C., & Gutiérrez-Coba, L. M. (2010). Los noticieros de la televisión colombiana "en observación." *Palabra clave, 13*(2), 217–250.

Green, V. (2019). "Deplorable" satire: Alt-right memes, white genocide tweets, and red-pilling normies. *Studies in American Humor, 5*(1), 31–99.

Gutiérrez Roa, É. (2021, June 11). 134 years of defending freedom of expression. *DW.* https://corporate.dw.com/a-57847120

Hide, S. (2019, August 13). Jaime Garzón: The day the laughter stopped. *Bogotá Post.* https://thebogotapost.com/jamie-garzon-the-day-the-laughter-stopped/40134/

Higuera, S. (2020, August 13). 21 years after the assassination of the Colombian journalist Jaime Garzón, not all culprits have been convicted. *LatAm Journalism Review.* https://latamjournalismreview.org/articles/21-years-after

Human Rights Watch. (2020). Colombia. In *World report 2020: Events of 2019* (pp. 142–150). Seven Stories Press.

Inter-American Commission on Human Rights. (2006). *Violence and discrimination against women in the armed conflict in colombia.* Organization of American States.

Klobucista, C., & Renwick, D. (2017, January 11). Colombia's civil conflict. *Council on Foreign Relations.* https://www.cfr.org/backgrounder/colombias-civil-conflict

KROC Institute for International Peace Studies. (2018). *Informe Especial del Instituto Kroc y el acompañamiento internacional, ONU Mujeres, FDIM y Suecia, al seguimiento del enfoque de género en la implementación del Acuerdo Final.* KROC Institute.

La gran encuesta de la parapolítica. (2007, May 4). *Revista Semana.* https://www.semana .com/nacion/articulo/la-gran-encuesta-parapolitica/85319-3/

La Pulla. (2016a, October 13). *El plebiscito sacó la peor porquería de Colombia* [Video]. YouTube. https://www.youtube.com/watch?v=A4VcX4FAIaY

La Pulla. (2016b, June 23). *La Pulla answers your questions (Part I)* [Video]. YouTube. https://www.youtube.com/watch?v=bN—fLG7ZPo

La Pulla. (2016c, April 28). *La Pulla: It's really hard to trust the Police* [Video]. YouTube. https://www.youtube.com/watch?v=J_QAl1jrEuE

La Pulla. (2016d, April 14). *La Pulla: Let gay people adopt* [Video]. YouTube. https://www .youtube.com/watch?v=lQltHKv2DtY

La Pulla. (2016e, May 4). *La Pulla: No more lies about abortion* [Video]. YouTube. https:// www.youtube.com/watch?v=85macWLHZ3w

La Pulla. (2016f, November 24). *¿Por qué el feminismo no es un asco?* [Video]. YouTube. https://www.youtube.com/watch?v=upSi1siOsig

La Pulla. (2016g, September 20). *Why are they gonna give FARC a huge ammount* [sic] *of money?* [Video]. YouTube. https://www.youtube.com/watch?v=UbI-SbsC5Ns

La Pulla. (2017a, March 2). *10 steps to be assassinated in Colombia* [Video]. YouTube. https://www.youtube.com/watch?v=v6b1emMACrw

La Pulla. (2017b, October 26). *Classic lies about drugs in Latin America* [Video]. YouTube. https://www.youtube.com/watch?v=kI6pNzP3zIM

La Pulla. (2017c, August 17). *Dejen de tratar a las prostitutas como imbéciles* [Video]. YouTube. https://www.youtube.com/watch?v=i2y56aRDShE

La Pulla. (2017d, September 6). *The Game of Thrones of Pope Francis in the Vatican* [Video]. YouTube. https://www.youtube.com/watch?v=lajgPnzqbqY

La Pulla. (2017e, June 1). *¿Por qué los profesores se la pasan de paro en paro?* [Video]. YouTube. https://www.youtube.com/watch?v=yoQR2vvL3xU

La Pulla. (2017f, November 23). *This is how Uribe silences his critics* [Video]. YouTube. https://www.youtube.com/watch?v=HO0GiTmevgM

La Pulla. (2017g, July 13). *Venezuela is fucked up everywhere* [Video]. YouTube. https:// www.youtube.com/watch?v=deaC-dIDQQY

La Pulla. (2018a, May 17). *Gustavo Petro NO merece ser presidente* [Video]. YouTube. https://www.youtube.com/watch?v=szbjBDWeALQ

La Pulla. (2018b, April 26). *Ivan Duque is the worst candidate to the presidence* [sic] *(or that's what we think)* [Video]. YouTube. https://www.youtube.com/watch?v= KEAitu_-F50

La Pulla. (2018c, November 22). *Nos gobiernan puros mafiosos* [Video]. YouTube. https://www.youtube.com/watch?v=iq9AbL3-D6A

La Pulla. (2018d, March 1). *¿Por qué nadie se mete con Álvaro Uribe?* [Video]. YouTube. https://www.youtube.com/watch?v=B_D0q1joElI

La Pulla. (2018e, March 28). *¿Por qué todos tan callados con el derrame de petróleo en Santander?* [Video]. YouTube. https://www.youtube.com/watch?v=uSYZ7hIZsTc

La Pulla. (2018f, September 6). *Venezuelans: Do not come here!* [Video]. YouTube. https://www.youtube.com/watch?v=RuQx6DxUp9c

La Pulla. (2018g, October 18). *Ya es hora de invadir Venezuela* [Video]. YouTube. https://www.youtube.com/watch?v=DhtWp2cQM_8

La Pulla. (2019a, January 17). *Nicolás Maduro, el mejor "presidente" del mundo* [Video]. YouTube. https://www.youtube.com/watch?v=YIvAK425zjc

La Pulla. (2019b, March 7). *Pablo Escobar is a hero* [Video]. YouTube. https://www.youtube.com/watch?v=_Ele0_I1h_w

La Pulla. (2020a, July 16). *El video que TikTok no quiere que veas* [Video]. YouTube. https://www.youtube.com/watch?v=dKFiRabL1-c

La Pulla. (2020b, July 24). *Nos llegó el PEOR momento del coronavirus* [Video]. YouTube. https://www.youtube.com/watch?v=39sGup0z460

La Pulla. (2020c, September 3). *¿Se fue el coronavirus? Cómo no ser un estúpido en el fin de la cuarentena* [Video]. YouTube. https://www.youtube.com/watch?v=ol2rqQMzx2Y

La Pulla. (2021a, April 29). *A esto se debe la rabia contra la reforma tributaria* [Video]. YouTube. https://www.youtube.com/watch?v=_UOxOjqc-Ek

La Pulla. (2021b, April 22). *Así juegan con las vacunas en América Latina* [Video]. YouTube. https://www.youtube.com/watch?v=kvl8JwHW9E8

La Pulla. (2021c, December 2). *Así lo manipulan con las vacunas* [Video]. YouTube. https://www.youtube.com/watch?v=nv6SGw3j-gs

La Pulla. (2021d, May 21). *Paro en Colombia: ¿Por qué la gente sigue protestando?* [Video]. YouTube. https://www.youtube.com/watch?v=JHu1qdZjb98

La Pulla. (2022a, February 17). *Así quieren engañarlo en elecciones* [Video]. YouTube. https://www.youtube.com/watch?v=e8rvEhqbmP4

La Pulla. (2022b, February 3). *Estas son las familias sucias e intocables del Congreso* [Video]. YouTube. https://www.youtube.com/watch?v=IDXPwB3-19s

La Pulla. (2022c, March 9). *No vote por estos candidatos al Congreso* [Video]. YouTube. https://www.youtube.com/watch?v=_iqxSBUvmGc

Las Igualadas. (2017a, October 24). *11 trucos para no ser un acosador sexual en el trabajo* [Video]. YouTube. https://www.youtube.com/watch?v=KLKYqtfeyB8

Las Igualadas. (2017b, June 27). *19 síntomas de que tu novio es un maldito loco* [Video]. YouTube. https://www.youtube.com/watch?v=3MjHE1qx9oY

Las Igualadas. (2017c, October 10). *A las mujeres también nos gusta el porno y otras cositas* [Video]. YouTube. https://www.youtube.com/watch?v=3kggcVvQwx8

Las Igualadas. (2017d, November 7). *A los hombres como Nacho Vidal y Maluma también los acosan sexualmente* [Video]. YouTube. https://www.youtube.com/watch?v=5FoHU-B5V6o

Las Igualadas. (2017e, July 25). *La Masturbación es una delicia así te hayan dicho lo contrario* [Video]. YouTube. https://www.youtube.com/watch?v=WKEzh5Jdj_k

Las Igualadas. (2017f, September 26). *Las universidades de Colombia son un infierno para las mujeres* [Video]. YouTube. https://www.youtube.com/watch?v=_s7qR3YOzKs

Las Igualadas. (2017g, November 21). *Las viejas son unas exageradas, ahora a todo le llaman acoso* [Video]. YouTube. https://www.youtube.com/watch?v=RqkKeQQ3ns0

Las Igualadas. (2017h, March 7). *Lo que toda mujer debe saber antes de su primer trabajo* [Video]. YouTube. https://www.youtube.com/watch?v=lDHP98BJeYw

Las Igualadas. (2017i, August 8). *Nos están matando porque nos obligan a dormir con el enemigo* [Video]. YouTube. https://www.youtube.com/watch?v=LbgKAmqSUrU

Las Igualadas. (2017j, April 18). *¿Por qué no puedo mandar fotos desnuda tranquila?* [Video]. YouTube. https://www.youtube.com/watch?v=GBNu-k8htyc

Las Igualadas. (2018a, December 11). *Abortar es un alivio* [Video]. YouTube. https://www.youtube.com/watch?v=1cQEKAo6Opw

Las Igualadas. (2018b, March 6). *Así es un día de oficina en la vida de una feminazi* [Video]. YouTube. https://www.youtube.com/watch?v=iF3H3hQlc5w

Las Igualadas. (2018c, June 12). *Duque vs Petro: ¿Quién es mejor para las mujeres?* [Video]. YouTube. https://www.youtube.com/watch?v=A-nCzEolHOU

Las Igualadas. (2018d, June 5). *El daño de la ideología de género* [Video]. YouTube. https://www.youtube.com/watch?v=kf2zsIWVb44

Las Igualadas. (2018e, October 30). *¿Es Cristiano Ronaldo un violador?* [Video]. YouTube. https://www.youtube.com/watch?v=fLON6a4373k

Las Igualadas. (2018f, April 17). *¿La ideología de género va a homosexualizar a los niños?* [Video]. YouTube. https://www.youtube.com/watch?v=qQsv7mS2p8A

Las Igualadas. (2018g, February 13). *Las denuncias de 5 mujeres contra Nicolás Arrieta* [Video]. YouTube. https://www.youtube.com/watch?v=E1WVCp6QC0A

Las Igualadas. (2018h, April 10). *Las peores mentiras sobre cirugías estéticas* [Video]. YouTube. https://www.youtube.com/watch?v=Qy0lLJjSmus

Las Igualadas. (2018i, February 20). *Lo peor de ser venezolana en Colombia* [Video]. YouTube. https://www.youtube.com/watch?v=DXInV7uSTvg

Las Igualadas. (2018j, October 9). *Mentiras que le dañan la primera vez a cualquiera* [Video]. YouTube. https://www.youtube.com/watch?v=CsOJYtL_eyI

Las Igualadas. (2018k, September 4). *Mentiras sobre el embarazo adolescente* [Video]. YouTube. https://www.youtube.com/watch?v=wdRFz1MY8iU

Las Igualadas. (2018l, May 1). *Mi abuelo me acorraló y manoseó* [Video]. YouTube. https://www.youtube.com/watch?v=4W-6cCknYfc

Las Igualadas. (2018m, May 8). *¿Por que no todas las mujeres gritamos cuando nos violan?* [Video]. YouTube. https://www.youtube.com/watch?v=aA0Kq_DMm6I

Las Igualadas. (2018n, July 11). *Sacarlo antes de venirse y otras mentiras* [Video]. YouTube. https://www.youtube.com/watch?v=vTOZoGUkxv8

Las Igualadas. (2018o, September 18). *¿Se merecía el golpe Eileen Moreno?* [Video]. YouTube. https://www.youtube.com/watch?v=DK9tcQ5EFzs

Las Igualadas. (2018p, December 4). *¿Tendrías sexo con una persona con VIH?* [Video]. YouTube. https://www.youtube.com/watch?v=iuwwMIygjr4

Las Igualadas. (2019a, March 19). *#AMíTambién El violador dormía en mi propia casa* [Video]. YouTube. https://www.youtube.com/watch?v=-10-TL3Lhv4

Las Igualadas. (2019b, June 25). *Así ha sido la revolución LGBT en 50 años con Las Cardachians, Endry Cardeño y Christian C.* [Video]. YouTube. https://www.youtube.com/watch?v=RsuDL-rWAKA

Las Igualadas. (2019c, April 23). *Consejos para cuidar tu salud mental* [Video]. YouTube. https://www.youtube.com/watch?v=fpMSzOyH7rk

Las Igualadas. (2019d, September 17). *Diez cosas que debes saber sobre paz para no pasar por ignorante* [Video]. YouTube. https://www.youtube.com/watch?v=yqxxxrpgKN8

Las Igualadas. (2019e, July 2). *Donald Trump: ¿Un presidente violador?* [Video]. YouTube. https://www.youtube.com/watch?v=RBLpLyL0uJ8

Las Igualadas. (2019f, August 13). *El extranjero que promueve el acoso contra mujeres en Medellín* [Video]. YouTube. https://www.youtube.com/watch?v=BGgk7Y77A-I

Las Igualadas. (2019g, May 21). *El falso chamán que abusaba mujeres durante el yagé* [Video]. YouTube. https://www.youtube.com/watch?v=pC0uPjAUjMg

Las Igualadas. (2019h, April 2). *El feminismo y el machismo son la misma cosa* [Video]. YouTube. https://www.youtube.com/watch?v=0lVal6FBSHk

Las Igualadas. (2019i, June 18). *El hombre que publicó 17 videos íntimos sin permiso* [Video]. YouTube. https://www.youtube.com/watch?v=FoWXBNbv1-E

Las Igualadas. (2019j, February 26). *Hollman Morris nos cree idiotas* [Video]. YouTube. https://www.youtube.com/watch?v=W7t8kKp9Jtc

Las Igualadas. (2019k, August 20). *¿La casa de Papel es una serie machista?* [Video]. YouTube. https://www.youtube.com/watch?v=MhP99LgV7V8

Las Igualadas. (2019l, February 5). *Los peores tipos que te puedes encontrar en Tinder* [Video]. YouTube. https://www.youtube.com/watch?v=4XlıHE0vhyOI

Las Igualadas. (2019m, August 27). *MÉXICO: ¿Por qué están tildando a las feministas de violentas y vandálicas?* [Video]. YouTube. https://www.youtube.com/watch?v=cB7Aopy3SLY

Las Igualadas. (2019n, September 22). *Periodista denuncia violencia sexual por editor del diario El Colombiano de Medellín* [Video]. YouTube. https://www.youtube.com/watch?v=RIX0pp3xmTE

Las Igualadas. (2019o, August 2). *Petro es machista, así diga lo contrario* [Video]. YouTube. https://www.youtube.com/watch?v=p20NyY_qsu0

Las Igualadas. (2019p, May 28). *Por estas razones ser mujer trans y lideresa es muy difícil* [Video]. YouTube. https://www.youtube.com/watch?v=zon-4zKrE0w

Las Igualadas. (2019q, March 26). *¿Por qué las mujeres con discapacidad no deberían tener hijos?* [Video]. YouTube. https://www.youtube.com/watch?v=wjdS5XWAv44

Las Igualadas. (2019r, September 24). *¿Por qué mueren las mujeres por abortos en Ecuador y El Salvador?* [Video]. YouTube. https://www.youtube.com/watch?v=T4B3DssKNcQ

Las Igualadas. (2019s, July 9). *Tres películas con mujeres protagonistas que todas deberíamos ver* [Video]. YouTube. https://www.youtube.com/watch?v=g-CgS4doylk

Lauria, C. (2004). Reporters under fire in Colombia. *NACLA Report on the Americas, 37*(4), 36–37.

Martinez, M. (2018, June 7). La Pulla's wildly popular YouTube videos (born at a 130-year-old newspaper) are bringing hard news to young Colombians. *Nieman Lab.* https://www.niemanlab.org/2018/06/la-pullas

McAuliffe, J. (2023). How to feminist affect: Feminist comedy and post-truth politics. *Philosophy and Social Criticism, 49*(2), 230–242.

Mioli, T. (2016, March 15). Colombian newspaper *El Espectador* marks 129 years with campaign for forgiveness. *LatAm Journalism Review.* https://latamjournalismreview.org/articles/colombian-newspaper-el-espectador

Miranda, B. (2016, October 3). Las razones por las que el "No" se impuso en el plebiscito en Colombia. *BBC Mundo.* https://www.bbc.com/mundo/noticias-america-latina-37537629

Moloney, A. (2018, February 1). To end violence against Colombian women, "look inside homes": government. *Reuters.* https://www.reuters.com/article/idUSKBN1FL6PZ/

Mora, R. A. (2016). Jaime Garzón's trickster discourse: His messages, social commentary, and legacy in Colombian comedy. *International Journal of Cultural Studies, 19*(5), 519–534.

Moreno Quevedo, A. (2023, February 10). Luis Carlos Sarmiento Angulo: 90 años del hombre que definió una era del mundo empresarial colombiano. *Forbes.* https://forbes.co/2023/02/10/editors-picks/luis-carlos-sarmiento-angulo-90-anos-del-hombre-que-definio-una-era-del-mundo-empresarial-colombiano

"Nos emberracamos, pero con argumentos": La Pulla. (2016, June 10). *Revista Semana.* https://www.semana.com/enfoque/articulo/la-pulla-maria-paulina-baena-cuenta-como-nacio-y-polarizacion-que-genera/477235/

ONU Mujeres. (2018). *El progreso de las mujeres en Colombia 2018: Transformar la economía para realizar los derechos.*

Otis, J. (2018, May 1). Amenazas de muerte hacen que el caricaturista colombiano Matador deje de publicar en las redes sociales. *Committee to Protect Journalists.* https://cpj.org/es/2018/05/amenazas

Páramo, A. (2016). Una tarde con los cerebros detrás de La Pulla de *El Espectador. VICE.* https://www.vice.com/es/article/nnp8mx/una-tarde

Petersen, A. H. (2017). *Too fat, too slutty, too loud: The rise and reign of the unruly woman.* Plume.

Prager, A., & Hameleers, M. (2021). Disseminating information or advocating peace? Journalists' role perceptions in the face of conflict. *Journalism, 22*(2), 395–413.

Rodriguez, C. (2011). *Citizens' media against armed conflict: Disrupting violence in Colombia.* University of Minnesota Press.

Sánchez, G. (Coord.). (2013). *¡Basta ya! Colombia: Memorias de guerra y dignidad.* Grupo de Memoria Histórica.

Turkewitz, J. (2021, May 18). Why are Colombians protesting? *New York Times.*

UNESCO/Guillermo Cano World Press Freedom Prize. (n.d.). *UNESCO.* https://www.unesco.org/en/prizes/cano

Uprimny, R. (2017, July 22). Sátira, calumnia y democracia. *El Espectador.* https://www.elespectador.com/opinion/satira-calumnia-y-democracia-columna-704386/

YouTube. (n.d.a). *El Espectador* [Channel]. https://www.youtube.com/user/Elespectadorcom

YouTube. (n.d.b). *La Pulla* [Channel]. https://www.youtube.com/channel/UCu2cUfy1hmjlcfZHzvVuEgg

Zulver, J. (2019, October 1). "Based in hatred": Violence against women standing in Colombia's elections. *Guardian.*

4

Apocalyptic Satire in Argentina's Macri/Kirchner Polarized Society

Guille Aquino's *El Sketch*

In December 2020, amid the pandemic, a soccer match between Argentinean "progressives" and "fascists" is about to be played on a neighborhood field in Buenos Aires. The opposing players appoint Guille Aquino, an alleged neutral observer, to be the referee. It's a very important game: they have been playing intensely against each other for the past ten years, and they need to determine the ultimate winner. The captain of the progressives' team describes some of his players: a feminist woman (politically militant, pro-abortion, bisexual, always with a defensive attitude, someone who sees in the referee whistle a phallocentric symbol), a neo-hipster (who allegedly lives in the trendy Palermo Soho, likes IPA beers, plays Jenga, and is an LGBTQ ally and bicycle rider), and an activist for the legalization of marijuana (who is smoking from a pipe), among others. They use inclusive language, want to eliminate the patriarchal state, and seek to "cancel" their adversaries. The fascists' team includes a racist taxi driver who complains about social protests, a police officer who is ready to shoot any suspicious person, an Opus Dei priest who is always trying to "recruit" underage kids for the team, and a doorman who enjoys hitting immigrants, homeless people, and his wife. Using a variety of sexist, homophobic, and racist expressions, the fascists call for bribing the referee, repressing their adversaries with violence, paying tribute to the military dictatorship, and drinking chlorine dioxide to treat COVID-19. Guille, the improvised referee, just wants to get on with the game. He insists that both teams stop insulting each other and start playing. When the game is finally about to begin, all members of both teams put on the Argentinean national team's shirt and get their smartphones from their pockets. "What are you doing? What happened to the game?" Guille asks. "This is it. We are tweeting against each other," one of the captains replies. "This game was never meant to be played on the field, just in social media," the other captain clarifies. "Then, who wins in real life?" Guille asks. "Nobody," the captains reply. "In real life, we are both useless."

"Progres vs. fachos" (December 23, 2020) is a video from *El Sketch*, a satiric online series created in 2016 by comedian Guille Aquino in Buenos Aires (Aquino, 2020c). Combining foreign comedy referents with local humor and rock traditions, *El Sketch*'s short videos (of around five minutes) tackle the prevalent national tensions and ideological contradictions of contemporary Argentina, a country that has been intensely polarized between the Left and the Right during the past few decades. From the 2001 economic crisis to the pandemic, a new wave of sociopolitical satire has captured the tensions and implications of this polarization, also known as *la grieta* (the crack or ideological gap). With millions of views on YouTube, Instagram, and Facebook, *El Sketch* has gone viral in Argentina but has also been noticed in other urban centers of the region. While it tackles sociopolitical polarization within the country, it also exposes other global problems, such as discrimination, gentrification, bigotry, and global warming. Reflecting the complex scenario of Macrism/Kirchnerism in Argentina, *El Sketch* illuminates the role of satire in contemporary polarized democracies, challenges to prevalent progressive and conservative views, and the way that multilayered satire navigates transgression and political correctness. It also presents an apocalyptic view of the country's current sociopolitical environment, which intensified during the pandemic.

Crisis and Ideological Polarization in Argentina

In 2015, millionaire Mauricio Macri, the mayor of Buenos Aires and former president of Boca Juniors (one of the country's most popular soccer teams), was elected president of Argentina. For the very first time since the country's democratic transition in the 1980s, a right-wing political party (Cambiemos), in alliance with other parties, gained national power via democratic elections. Macri's election was perceived as evidence of a broader right turn in the region—along with the election of Jair Bolsonaro in Brazil and Sebastián Piñera in Chile—and it intensified the polarization that has existed in Argentina since 1946, when the presidential victory of General Juan Perón divided the population into antagonistic camps of Peronism (rooted in the working class, state-based social protection, and nationalism) and anti-Peronism (rooted in the conservative middle and upper classes, favoring deregulation of the private sector and, later, the free market) (Azzolini, 2016). Since the country's transition to democracy, not a single non-Peronist president had been able to finish a regular term in office. Macri did, but his government was unable to realize its promised free market reforms or to dismantle the statist economic model left in place by twelve years of Kirchnerism (the Peronist faction led by Néstor Kirchner and later his wife, Cristina Fernández de Kirchner [CFK]).

During the Kirchnerist period (2003–15), the country recovered from the 2001 economic crisis, the economy grew based on the exportation of products (such as soybeans), and unemployment and poverty decreased significantly. Kirchnerism implemented a variety of progressive social measures (such as rights for women, LGBTQ citizens, and retirees). It appealed to Argentina's working classes by expanding social welfare programs, spending heavily on energy and transport subsidies, and defending workers' rights (Smink, 2015). However, CFK was also accused of being a corrupt populist and becoming increasingly authoritarian and polarizing. In this last regard, the *campo-gobierno* (field-government) conflict in 2008 was a breaking point. It was an agricultural strike, consisting of a lockout and roadblocks, in which the agricultural production sector protested against the government's decision to increase taxes on soybean and sunflower exports (Fair, 2008). The conflict, which lasted for more than three months, worsened when the protests were coupled with a transportation industry strike and the food supply to the cities was threatened. The confrontation evidenced the increasing polarization in the country. While Néstor Kirchner reappropriated the terminology and rhetorical strategies of Peronism during his term (2003–7) (Muñoz & Retamozo, 2008), the *campo-gobierno* conflict led the government of CFK and the opposition to frame the issue using old social dichotomies. Her government referred to the conflict in terms of "the people versus the oligarchy" and compared the agricultural leaders with the repressive *golpistas* (coupists) of the past, who aimed to "besmirch the memory of Perón and Evita" (Fernández de Kirchner, 2008). While the government used terms like oligarchy, guerillas, and *golpistas*, the opposition responded with terms like lefties, Montoneros, and terrorists (Colacrai, 2012). The polarization also reflected a growing tension between the government and the media. As a response to the negative coverage, CFK promoted a communications law (the Audiovisual Communication Service Law, Ley de Servicio de Comunicación

Audiovisual) that sought to limit the power of the Clarín Group, which was the largest media conglomerate in the country and was critical of the government. The constant tension between these camps only grew after this point.

Kirchnerism left power in 2015 with a high degree of discredit because of accusations of corruption and judicial convictions against some of its leaders. Nevertheless, it remained a powerful actor as Macri's political opposition. It maintained strong connections with its societal core not only through the memory of the good old days of redistributive policies associated with the commodity boom, but also because of the retained power of CFK. Her slogan, *La patria es el otro* (The motherland is your fellow citizen), a phrase encouraging solidarity and national belonging, maintained its antagonism to Macri's ideas of "inclusion through consumption" (ideas based on the increasing availability of consumer credit, the growing precarity of employment, and the spread of individualist ideologies). The Macrist ideology was based on the myth of meritocracy and individual entrepreneurship, framed as an antidote to what many interpreted as the limitations of CFK's populism (Anria & Vommaro, 2019; Mason-Deese, 2019).

Nevertheless, by the end of Macri's government in 2019, the national scenario was different. Argentina was facing steep economic decline, unaffordable foreign debt (the country was once again in a virtual default situation), a budget deficit, currency depreciation, and inflation rates of 53.8 percent (Instituto Nacional de Estadísticas y Censos, 2020), a record high across three decades. In line with these indicators, poverty increased to 40.8 percent and indigence to 8.9 percent (Observatorio de la Deuda Social Argentina, 2020); national unemployment rose to 10 percent of the economically active population for the first time in years; and health indicators were rapidly deteriorating. For Anria and Vommaro (2019), the difficulties Macri's government faced in implementing its reformist program were explained by his lack of political resources and the inconsistency of his right-wing coalition in programmatic terms (with business owners, for example, maintaining short-term thinking and particularistic, poorly coordinated behavior). But more importantly, the policy legacies of the previous Kirchnerist governments became severe obstacles to Macri's reformist project. They constrained his attempts to make drastic cuts on public spending, given the visibility and popularity of these social programs. Macri was forced to apply a gradualist approach by slowly reducing subsidies to the middle classes and public transportation, pursuing public-private partnerships rather than complete privatization, and even leaving some of CFK's social programs in place (such as the universal child allowance). At the same time, representatives of Kirchnerism in Congress were among the most visible opponents of the bills proposed by the Macri government, and a diverse set of social movements, popular organizations, and political parties—from the feminist movement and popular economy workers to more traditional trade unions—came together to build a broad anti-neoliberal front that retained a high capacity to mobilize and blocked attempts to remove state protections (Mason-Deese, 2019). They critiqued not only Macri's economic program, but also his racist and xenophobic policies.

In this highly polarized context, CFK felt that Macri's government was trying to repudiate her by putting her party's main leaders in jail, while Macri government officials believed that the opposition was trying to radicalize social protests to overthrow the president. Even years later, conservative sectors consider CFK to be a corrupt populist who sought impunity for her crimes and corruption and accuse her of being close to Nicolás Maduro of Venezuela and other leftist autocrats. Meanwhile, a large part of the Left considers Macri and his allies to be neoliberal criminals that ran up a huge foreign debt only to steal these dollars for their own benefit through a mechanism of capital flight and a servile attitude toward imperialist interests (Abal Medina, 2020). This tension evidences again one of Argentina's structural problems: a political landscape dominated by two social coalitions that lack the capacity to impose their own project but are strong enough to block the other's (Malamud, 2019).

The confrontation highlights the prevalence of what Argentines call *la grieta*, referring to the strong sociopolitical and cultural polarization between the main two political groups. It reflects the transnational Left/Right and liberal/conservative dichotomies, but is shaped by the complex variable of Peronism (Villanueva & Aguerre, 2020). While some differences relate to, for example, benefits and rights for the poor, immigrants, the LGBTQ community, and other minority groups, the broader political division is based on age, social class, and ideology (Ipar & Catanzaro, 2017). The divisions have affected friendships, families, social groups, and relationships, and are manifested in social media (Kessler & Feuerstein, 2020) and even in dating apps, with Argentina's Tinder embracing the gap to filter romantic connections (Gonzalez, 2019). It is within this complex social texture of antagonistic cultural logic that Guille Aquino's humor operates.

A Bitter Satire of Polarization for an Ideologically Confused Generation

Guille Aquino is an Argentinean comedian who became popular because of his viral satiric video series *El Sketch*, published online weekly on his social media platforms and aired concurrently on a national television station. Aquino, a millennial scriptwriter of television entertainment shows and a theater director, also performed the popular character Paco Cambiasso on the television show *Duro de Domar* (Hard to tame) and wrote and starred in the acclaimed humorous play *Antisocial*. Through all this, *El Sketch*—with more than 120 videos between 2016 and 2020—remains his more holistic satiric take on contemporary Argentinean national debates, which can also be applied to other Latin American realities. "There is something in the urban world of ideologically confused, mean, middle-class people that works in many places," he said (personal interview, 2019).[1]

The national relevance of Aquino's humor is strongly connected to the sociopolitical tensions during Macri's government:

> The political context increasingly influenced our content. When we began doing *El Sketch* at the end of 2016, the themes were generic. The television station where the show was broadcast did not want us to get into politics. We did not have much interest either. But in 2017, we were on a news channel and the context was different. In 2018 and 2019, it was unavoidable. It became clear that the crisis was going to be central to most episodes of the show. (personal interview, 2019)[2]

In fact, Aquino began working independently on *El Sketch* because, at the beginning of Macri's tenure, he lost his job as a scriptwriter for a production company with a progovernment editorial stance. The ideological polarization of the moment is present in many *El Sketch* videos, in which Aquino unveils the inconsistencies of political dichotomies (Kirchnerism versus Macrism, progressive versus fascist, Left versus Right) and the stereotypes associated with them. In "La nueva Argentina" (The new Argentina), for example, the sketch shows Guille running into a friend on the street who is carrying a suitcase (Aquino, 2019h). The friend says he is moving out of the country because people like Guille voted "wrongly," and he cannot stand to live anymore in a country of populism, welfare, high taxes, drugs, and homosexuality. Despite their differences, they say goodbye and declare that they will miss each other. However, Guille's friend walks only a few more steps in the other direction, sets his suitcase on the floor, and places a piece of tape painted with the colors of the Argentine flag on the ground. He declares that his side of the tape is a new country—the separatist Republic of Argentina—for those who voted "well." Guille is not allowed in this new republic, which is populated with conservative media figures, strong anti-immigrant policies, transnational investments, and an increasing but manageable foreign debt, and which has no poverty. Guille accuses him of inhabiting an imaginary country and suggests that they should build something together. The friend agrees, then, to build a wall to separate the two nations further. In "Abuela vs república" (Grandmother versus the republic), Guille goes to the hospital to visit his dying grandmother (Aquino, 2019b). The doctor warns him that she might be gone at any moment and that she has not been reading newspapers, watching television, or following the news in any form. It's election week 2019, and the dying grandmother is a fervent Macrist. Guille must lie to her to make her last moments alive pleasant. The first lie is that Macri was re-elected, and his government has accomplished all its socioeconomic promises. When she finally dies, leaving him a package of huge debts, Guille and the doctor acknowledge that the "worst has already passed." These two videos are representative of Aquino's attempt to satirize *la grieta* and the profound divide in Argentina's society, affecting friendships and family relations. In an environment of irreconcilable ideological perspectives, death and artificial geopolitical demarcations are presented as extreme outcomes of historical confrontations.

Despite these differences, Aquino also highlights the existence of an increasing cynicism toward politics. In "Apolítico" (Apolitical), Guille interrupts his friends watching the presidential debate and turns off the television to plug in his iPhone (Aquino, 2019e). He then explains that he does not care about debates and elections; he comes from a long line of apolitical families. A friend confronts him over his views, and Guille forces a debate in support of his own idea to create the first apolitical party in Argentina. He explains that he has no platform of ideas because some of the main national issues—such as poverty, retirement pensions, education, human rights, gender inclusion, and foreign relations—are too politicized. The sketch ends with Guille convincing his friends to adopt an apolitical view of the country. In "Amiga diputada" (Congresswoman friend), Guille visits a friend who has just been elected to Congress on a conservative ticket (Aquino, 2019d). He is surprised that she obtained more than a hundred thousand votes. She explains: "Look at me. Cute woman, young, blue eyes, and supporting anti-abortion campaigns. How many people like this can you find? Just one. Me." Recalling all the trouble that she got into dur-

Figure 6. *El Sketch*, created in 2016 by comedian Guille Aquino in Buenos Aires, tackles some of the prevalent national tensions and ideological contradictions of contemporary polarized Argentina. Film still.

ing her youth, which was filled with parties and excessive behavior, both realize that the one thing she did not do was have a clandestine abortion. She knows nothing about politics; having a strong anti-abortion stance is her only political capital. The video exposes the opportunistic, cynical, and hypocritical behavior of politicians who combine extreme conservative views to appeal to a fanatical base, despite having an immoral personal life and social decisions (see figure 6).

These political tensions are framed within a context of permanent economic crisis and hyperinflation, with concrete social consequences. Aquino exposes the manifestations of the crisis without adopting a partisan tone and goes beyond the surface of the problem. In "Guillerma," for example, he points out the abuses that domestic workers suffer while satirizing the moral miseries of an exploitative upper class that seeks to seem benevolent and justify its privilege (Aquino, 2019g). In "Palermo Indie," he targets an urgent problem of metropolitan cities: access to affordable housing and gentrification (Aquino, 2019m). In "Américas Anónimas" (Americas Anonymous), Aquino explicitly expands his humorous critique to the common problems of Latin American countries (Aquino, 2019c). In an imitation of the environment of a rehabilitation meeting for addicts, different countries—Chile, Mexico, Bolivia, Peru, Colombia, Uruguay, and Argentina—sit in a circle and relate their main problems (foreign debt, corruption, political violence, drug trafficking, violations against human rights, and inequality, among others). After diverse confrontations, they realize that they share a common characteristic: their acritical surrender to neoliberal hegemony incarnated in the influence and role of the United States in the region.

At the core of Aquino's critiques is an effort to unveil the moral double standards in a contradictory and hypocritical society. The comedian aims to make viewers reflect on and question their own ideological beliefs and the narratives in which they are sustained. In the video "Homofobia positiva" (Positive homophobia), for example, he critically analyzes prejudices against LGBTQ people that in today's world might be disguised as tolerance (Aquino, 2017b). In "Novia Nazi" (Nazi girlfriend) and "Novia anti dr@ga" (Anti-drugs girlfriend), he shows the moral misery of an unexpectedly fascist woman hidden in plain sight amid today's youth culture (Aquino, 2017c, 2019k). In "Planeta tierra" (Planet earth), he portrays the contradictions and moral entitlement of certain environmentalists while conveying a desperate commentary on our responsibility and impotence in the imminent climate catastrophe (Aquino, 2019n). In "Amigo cura" (Priest friend) he targets religion and the Catholic Church through the caricature of a corrupt priest who, after finding God in his rehabilitation from drugs, is obsessed with business opportunities and moneymaking (Aquino, 2018). In all these examples, there is a progressive and moral perspective that, nevertheless, is constantly questioned and renegotiated within the video. Aquino explains these internal ideological battles:

> Our public opinions and perspectives tend to be so solemn and dignified that the actions of a person could never live up to them. We all want a better world, but we lack the personal resources to achieve it and we become hypocritical. We cannot fully embody our values, which are usually very contradictory, whether you are a conservative or a progressive. (personal interview, 2019)[3]

In today's digital world, social media outlets offer endless platforms to display these frequently contradictory, hypocritical, and dignified opinions. "We are all victims of today's freedom to express our opinions on multiple platforms. Like the world needs to know what we are thinking. Each of us is like his own marketing division. And now we not only express our opinions, we need to create an impact, be controversial, extremist, on point, ironic. I find that funny" (personal interview, 2019).[4] This critical perspective, which finds humor in its own flaws, connects with a self-reflective comedic tradition and debates about the challenges of counter-cultural movements to remain transgressive and resist commodification. It links back to the Argentinean cultural relationship between humor and rock music.

Rock and Humor in Argentina

Wearing a ratty old white Velvet Underground T-shirt, black pants, and shades, Guille Aquino has a rocker aesthetic: messy hair on top with the sides shaved, a scrawny beard, and sometimes a few fingernails painted black. He smokes cigarettes and drinks beers on- and off-camera. Aquino has adopted not only the rocker aesthetic, but also the attitude and a cul-tural debt to the tradition of Argentina's *rock nacional* (national rock), an eclectic cultural movement with a particular sociopolitical history in-grained in the country's urban identity since the 1960s. Argentina's *rock na-cional* is a label used for a variety of musical genres that are practiced and produced in the country and that developed as part of a large antiestablish-ment culture. During its foundational and golden era, underground and counterculture musicians combined diverse styles of Anglo rock 'n' roll with local music traditions (principally, tango and folklore), infusing the movement with its own hybrid identity. In addition, these artists were pio-neers in utilizing the Spanish language in their rock lyrics and in including local themes and references. The movement narrated turbulent historical moments: military dictatorships, political violence, repression, and socio-economic crisis. Its relevance and mysticism were based in an antiauthori-tarian sentiment, which offered space for generations of youth to question the hegemonic and patriarchal values of conservative Argentinean society (Manzano, 2014). Aquino considers this tradition to be a central part of his identity, and he pays tribute to it in his videos, with soundtracks of iconic artists like Charly García, Babasónicos, and Andrés Calamaro. At the same time, he jokes about some of the stereotypes and other cultural associa-tions related to the rock music industry.

The complex relationship between Argentinean humor and rock was developed most prevalently by *Peter Capusotto y sus videos* (Peter Capus-otto and his videos), a satiric television show during the Kirchner era that parodied *rock nacional* culture and its relationship with Argentinean idio-syncrasies. Hosted by Diego Capusotto and produced by Pedro Saborido, comedians of the so-called underground generation of the 1980s, the show was the most watched on Argentinean public television and became regionally popular due to its successful early presence on the web. Mimicking a documentary style and various television genres, *Peter Capusotto y sus videos* ridiculed stereotypes, celebrities, and popular culture's myths while exposing their inconsistencies and absurdities (and their influence and power). One of the most controversial characters was Bombita Rodríguez, a 1970s new wave singer committed to the armed struggle of the left-wing Peronist guerrilla organization Montoneros. Combining cheesy love songs with radical left-wing guerrilla messages, this character captured the increasing tension between the Right and the Left after the 2001 crisis and during the Kirchnerism period while revisiting Argentina's political history since Perón and the role of the media and the entertainment industry in the process. Similarly, Capusotto's characters, such as Micky Vainilla (a Nazi pop singer) and Violencia Rivas ("the precursor of punk rock in Argentina"), became part of a satiric discourse that not only questioned *rock nacional*'s contradictions (its distancing from the countercultural and antiauthoritarian ideals that supposedly marked its origins and defined its cultural mythology, and its embrace of commercial strategies, prejudiced attitudes, and superficial spectacle), but also carried out a structural critique of the entertainment industry and media culture in Argentina.

"It was very smart," said Aquino, referring to Capusotto's humor. "It was like saying in 2002: what if we just make fun of how ridiculous the rockers have become? Rock was the last untouchable bastion of counterculture. To make it the object of a joke was very precise and surprising. It will remain forever" (personal interview, 2019).[5] Since then, there have been many debates about "the death of rock." The Capusotto character that most directly ridiculed the commoditization of the movement was Pomelo, a parody of a national rock star (closely resembling real musicians such as Juanse from the Argentine R & B rock band Los Ratones Paranoicos) (see, e.g., Peter Capusotto y sus, 2010). Pomelo absurdly embodied many vices of the drug-driven, self-obsessed, and wicked celebrity artist, suggesting the death of rock's rebelliousness as part of today's society of spectacle. Through this character, Capusotto criticized the commoditization of countercultural expression, revealing not only the discursive emptiness of celebrity culture but also the responsibility of audiences (converted into acritical consumers) in the death of the rock utopia. Speaking about this death, Aquino said:

> I think rock was doomed to die and that was the beginning of its
> death. In the past years, all the accusations of rape and sexual harass-

ment against rock stars evidenced the decline of the movement, and how shitty many of those people were. At least in the way we understood it: four dudes playing guitar, doing drugs, hooking up with hot girls, and creating cool songs. I think that idea has died. (personal interview, 2019)[6]

Humor in Argentina has frequently been referred to as the "new rock," in terms of its capacity to challenge the status quo and to question power. An early example of this occurred in 2007, when the fictional Pomelo appeared on the cover of the Argentine *Rolling Stone* magazine as Artist of the Year. This metatextual gesture not only exemplified the adoption of postmodern and self-referential irony within local rock culture and the Argentine media, but also highlighted the idea that the most rocker attitude at this point was to satirize the rock movement itself. Nevertheless, Aquino acknowledges his cultural debt to a tradition that has also defined his art:

It's very difficult to separate oneself from something that one loved so much [referring to the rock movement]. In my case, I can ridicule it but also appreciate it. And I think it's okay to approach issues like that. We can have different opinions about an issue. Rock was foundational for me and shaped my identity, but I can also make fun of it, of what I am. I can also practice this type of self-reflective sense of humor because I'm a cisgender white man. (personal interview, 2019)[7]

Acknowledging his positionality within his artistic options also seems to be a way for Aquino to rethink the limitations of a traditionally male-dominated, homophobic, racist, sexist, and classist cultural and media environment. Furthermore, Aquino's humor usually targets and problematizes his own positionality as part of his fictional universe, connecting with prevalent anxieties and social debates of the millennial generation about prejudices and political correctness.

Television Humor, Prejudices, and Political Correctness

Since Perón introduced television to Argentina in 1951, television humor has evolved significantly. Landi (1992) identified three generations of television humor in Argentina. The first, between 1960 and 1970, is made up of amateur actors who came from street fairs, circuses, comedy theaters, and the radio. Their humor is *costumbrist* and based on the exploitation of social stereotypes.[8] The second generation, which took to television screens in the mid-1970s, based its humor on sexual misunderstandings. This generation's era ended with the death of comedian Alberto Olmedo in 1988. The third generation, which extended through the 1990s, included actors of the café-concert.[9] Their humor was acidic and grotesque; the most prominent performer was Antonio Gasalla. Moglia (2013) has suggested a fourth generation, with its origin in the new Argentinean theater of the 1980s underground generation. This generation includes actors like Diego Capusotto, Alfredo Casero, Fabio Alberti, and Mex Urtizberea, who entered television on the absurdist and surrealist comedy program *De la cabeza* (From the Head, 1992–93). This generation also consolidated what has been called intratelevision parody (Colacrai, 2012; Moglia, 2009) or post-television humor (Fraticelli, 2013), in which social stereotypes are progressively replaced by media stereotypes.[10] As one of the most outstanding comedians of this intratelevision parody generation, Capusotto was a protagonist in some of the most salient programs of this period: *Cha cha cha* (1993–97), *Todo por dos pesos* (Everything for two pesos, 1999–2002), and, starting in 2006, *Peter Capusotto y sus videos*.

While Aquino's humor has important connections to Capusotto's generation (such as the countercultural spirit influenced by the rock movement), he is part of what can be considered a fifth generation, which is digital, ultrasensitive to debates about social discrimination and prejudice, and raised mostly with foreign comedy references:

> Our generation mainly watched foreign television. My main influences were *The Simpsons*, *Seinfeld*, American and British humor in general. Very little Latin American or Hispanic humor. . . . Actually, five years ago I stopped watching any local television. Not even humor. For me, a great comedy show today is *Better Call Saul*, which is not really a humorous one. (personal interview, 2019)[11]

In a similar vein, Aquino has paid tribute to one of the most transgressive and complex contemporary global comedians. He interviewed Sacha Baron Cohen's Borat when the British satirist was promoting his latest movie before the 2020 US election (Aquino, 2020a). A connection between the humor of Baron Cohen and Aquino is the attempt to satirize divergent perspectives (liberal and conservative, for example) through multilayered characters that unveil diverse forms of prejudice. In this sense, and in line with a new generational sensitivity toward humor, Aquino distances himself from traditional Latin American television comedy that reproduces stereotypes, particularly in terms of gender, class, and race. He finds it not only outdated, but also superficial and bereft of creative effort. Aquino's humor navigates satiric transgression and political correctness through in-depth scriptwriting, unexpected angles on social issues, morally complex characters, and acknowledgment of the comedian's own positionality. From the perspective of an urban, heterosexual, middle-class, white male, Aquino's self-reflective humor recurrently seeks to, for example, question gender norms and deconstruct masculinity. In "Padre Argentino" (Argentinean father) (Aquino, 2019l), "Día de los enamorados" (Valentine's Day) (2019f), and "Chica promiscua" (Promiscuous girl) (2017a), he challenges social expectations of women's roles and behaviors under the male gaze within family and romantic relationships. In his comedic universe, sexuality is presented as a constant negotiation between rejecting gender prejudices and, at the same time, not being completely ridiculous. Issues such as abortion, pregnancy, promiscuity, and parental responsibility are used to reflect on our own (progressive or conservative) views on such matters.

While Aquino's humor is positioned at a progressive ideological stance, he also acknowledges that humor is a complex issue, particularly in today's environment of political correctness: "If you begin to analyze humor or any piece of comedy with today's parameters, you will never end. It's one paradox after another. You think: ironic consumption is normalizing a social problem, but at the same time it is attacking and criticizing it" (personal interview, 2019).[12] This statement highlights a constant issue that contemporary humor faces when approaching sensitive topics, at a time when there are new and more visible sensitivities toward a variety of matters, and social media has become a tool for canceling unacceptable or misunderstood discourses and behaviors. There is a moral concern between the intention of the jokes, the effects they might produce, and what can be considered truly transgressive in today's culture. The role of comedy and popular culture in normalizing social prejudices is a recurrent topic in contemporary Argentine alternative humor. A new wave of feminist comedians, for example, has tackled issues of sexism and violence against women. One of the most prominent voices is Malena Pichot, a comedian who began as a YouTube star and then created different online shows about gender issues, as described in chapter 2. Pichot's rise to fame happened at a time when sexism and violence against women were being highly discussed in Argentina, a time that also gave rise to the #NiUnaMenos (Not One Less) antifemicide protest movement. The demonstration that launched #NiUnaMenos—held at the Congressional Plaza in Buenos Aires, on June 3, 2015—was supported by media campaigns, attended by nearly three hundred thousand people, and backed by women's rights groups, unions, political organizations, and the Catholic Church. Responding to this movement in her work, Pichot has frequently participated in public debates about feminism in Argentina and has strongly reacted to sexist remarks by public figures. Aquino's comedy establishes connections with this context, but at the same time, he highlights the importance of craftsmanship and constant reinvention:

> If before, comedians made fun of women or gay people and we laughed at jokes about butts, now the target seems to be the white millionaire man who is against minorities. And that is becoming the easy joke. For me, humor is defined by the effort you put into the work. I see a lot of comedy that is ideologically aligned with what I think, but I don't like it, because I don't see significant creative effort in it. . . . At the end, it is about the heart and how you feel it. Humor is popular, physical, and not intellectual. You feel something and you cannot explain why. It is a mystery. (personal interview, 2019)[13]

This statement is essential to an understanding of the core intentions of comedy that is sociopolitical but recognizes itself primarily as a form of art. While Aquino's satire does present a set of moral and ideological values, its main concern has to do with the creative process and the indecipherable effect of art that goes beyond laughter. It stands by the romantic and Wildean idea that aesthetic pleasure is ranked over its possible meanings. These meanings, nevertheless, are also important and usually mediated by contemporary entertainment formats and media platforms.

Self-Reflective Humor, Independence, and Apocalyptic Scenarios

Postmodern humor tends to be metareferential and self-reflective (Alonso, 2018). Comedians mock television, radio, and popular culture formats; humor magazines satirize news and journalism languages. Comedians have increasingly perceived the media as central to upholding the status quo, and its malpractices as dangerous in promoting misinformation and ignorance. In "Palermo News," Aquino targets the rotten logic of news editors that make distorted or fake news into a professional norm (Aquino, 2019a). Playing a newly hired news writer attending his first editorial meeting, Aquino faces a professional culture that has developed the skill to transform urgent social problems into feel-good stories that support the establishment and the prevalent neoliberal mentality. In contrast to the satiric news parody format (like the one used in the magazine the *Onion*), Aquino uses real headlines and news stories from the local media to satirize the ridiculous framing and editorial mentalities that lead to the distortion of relevant information. He is attacking not just the content or the format, but the ideological and moral implications of the decision-making process that leads to what we call news.

In the internet era, Aquino also targets his own platform and today's digital culture, acknowledging his own responsibility in public discourse. In "Nacional meme" (National meme), for example, he mocks those who think that creating a political meme is today's most significant act of civic participation (Aquino, 2019j). In "Los influencers" (The influencers), he unveils the cynicism of a generation defined by social media identities (Aquino, 2019i). He says: "It's probably a defense mechanism, a critique of what we do. Maybe we are also part of the problem. It's like a disclaimer, our way to say that we do not do humor to anesthetize or numb people. Because revenge against the world is not here [in the humor]; it's somewhere else" (personal interview, 2019).[14] The "somewhere else" is the real world, and it is a difficult market. In 2019, Aquino began making money from YouTube, but his project's sustainability comes mainly from selling videos to television. "But that money is not enough," he says. "I also have a theater play and people come to see the show. I make more money from my play than from doing the videos" (personal interview, 2019).[15] For Aquino, working with limited resources is a personal decision and a declaration of principles. In contrast to many other YouTubers or social media influencers, he does not have direct advertising or sponsors. "Maybe it is because of our type of humor," he says. "I could do the videos and make more money; I could sell them to other places. But I know that the more money they [television producers] give you, the more influence they want to have in the content. If you want freedom, you need to do it for free" (personal interview, 2019).[16]

In this sense, Aquino is part of an independent wave of digital satirists who have created alternative and hybrid business models not controlled by the pressures of advertising or mainstream television networks. For example, the digital satiric news show *Pais de boludos* (Country of Jerks), launched in 2017 and hosted by Federico Simonetti and Ivana Szerman, combined YouTube revenue with audience donations and funding (YouTube, n.d.b). Ezequiel Campa, a comedian popular on social media for his character Dicky del Solar (a parody of a bigoted right-wing rugby player), also combined the creation of independent digital content with the promotion of his stand-up and commercial shows (YouTube, n.d.a). These are some Argentine examples of a regional trend among independent media producers of exploring new alternatives to fund risqué content. During the pandemic, social media platforms offered increasing visibility to independent producers trying to reach "captive" audiences (in lockdown), in the context of scarce entertainment television production and the increasing dissemination of fake news, opening more alternatives for funding opportunities to digital comedians (Provéndola, 2020).

In fact, it was at this time that Aquino took the opportunity to make his first movie, which he released online through an on-demand platform in 2021, available to rent for US$10. The one-hour movie is titled *Guille Aquino Presidente* (President Guille Aquino) (Aquino, 2022). The storyline describes how, amid a world crisis, Guille wakes up one day as the president of Argentina and must deal with the responsibility, the corruption, and, mainly, the opposition. The movie is an extended version of *El Sketch* that condenses many of its recurrent sociopolitical topics, but instead of Guille being a powerless average citizen who is constantly judging and criticizing society, he now embodies a newly elected president whose main task is to "close the gap" (*cerrar la grieta*). "A typical *El Sketch* character usually just points out what he thinks is right or wrong, but now he is in a place where he has all the power and chokes on his own words. All that he thinks could work, fails loudly," Aquino explained to *Diario con Vos* (Guille Aquino en Radio Con Vos, 2022).[17] Through absurdist inversions, the movie also offers new controversial national interpretations. It shows, for example, a tour de force dialogue in which President Guille converses with the leader of the opposition, a conservative and cynical woman politician with whom he also has sexual tension. While describing many of the most urgent national problems, the two characters argue about responsibility for the political crisis and the divisions and failures of the country. They finally agree that the main culprit is "the people" (*el pueblo*), a "caste" with unrealistic expectations too far away from the needs of politics. "But what if for the first time we the politicians listen to the people?" President Guille asks. "Sure," the opposition leader answers. "Who do you want to listen to? The lower class, which does not want to die? The middle class, which is trying to survive? Or the rich, which is trying to live fucking the other two classes?" In this scenario of corruption and unequal connivance among people of all classes and the opposing political tenets, the only possible outcome seems to be the imminent extermination of national democratic societies as we know them. In the context of the COVID-19 pandemic, this conclusion aligns with Aquino's satiric construction of apocalyptic scenarios in his sketches during the global emergency. In "El último porteño" (The last *porteño*) and "Sobre el fin del mundo" (About the end of the world, a parody of the Netflix movie *Don't Look Up*), Aquino recapitulates the main sociopolitical critiques developed throughout the years of his show, leading to the annihilation of *porteños* (citizens of Buenos Aires) first, and then the rest of the world (Aquino, 2020b, 2021). Apocalyptic scenarios intensified by the pandemic became, then, in Aquino's satiric world, the result of decades of polarization, prejudice, violence, selfishness, indifference, and corruption, and might be the only solution to "close the gap," as a character states in "Sobre el fin del mundo."

Conclusion

In the context of the sociopolitical polarization surrounding the election of President Macri and the subsequent socioeconomic crisis, Guille Aquino's humor became a lucid exploration of the national tensions intensified by the political right turn after twelve years of Kirchnerism in Argentina. Targeting *la grieta*—the contemporary version of the old antagonism between liberals and conservatives, shaped by the complex variable of Peronism—his satiric videos offer a lens to understand the divisions between generations, social groups, and even families and friends while also questioning our own ideological beliefs and the narratives in which they are sustained.

While Aquino's critiques are developed from a progressive perspective, he aims to unveil the moral double standards of what he sees as a contradictory and hypocritical society (both in its liberal and its conservative versions). Therefore, the comedian tends to challenge and renegotiate his own ideological beliefs within the videos. This critical perspective, which finds humor in its own flaws, connects with a self-reflective comedy tradition that has during the past few decades caricatured the decay of countercultural movements—such as *rock nacional*—and their challenges to remain transgressive and resist commoditization. While humor in Argentina has frequently been referred to as the "new rock," in terms of its capacity to challenge the status quo and to question power, Aquino's work also questions satire's capacity to promote real social change while highlighting its artistic nature.

In the context of the #MeToo movement and the increasing visibility and public debates about social prejudices (such as racism, sexism, homophobia, and xenophobia), Aquino's humor usually targets and problematizes his own positionality—white, male, heterosexual, urban, middle-class—as part of his comedic universe, connecting with prevalent anxieties and social debates of the millennial generation. Distancing himself from the comedy tradition that noncritically reproduces prejudices and stereotypes, Aquino uses his humor to negotiate satiric transgression and political correctness through morally complex characters, scriptwriting that seeks unexpected angles, and the continuous deconstruction of his own privilege and positionality. Similarly, Aquino also targets his internet platforms and today's digital culture, including memes, influencers, YouTubers, and news. He exposes the contemporary moral and professional mentalities behind media content creation, acknowledging his own (often failed) responsibility in public discourse.

Aquino's *El Sketch* is exemplary of a new generational sensitivity toward humor in Latin America that deals critically with national and regional sociocultural and political issues, while appealing to young urban audiences exposed to transnational media formats. While heavily influenced by the Anglo satire tradition, it also establishes a dialogue with local trends and popular culture, creating a unique glocal voice that taps into national and regional tensions, particularly the ideological polarization of Argentina and Latin America. At the same time, Aquino is part of an independent wave of digital satirists who have created alternative and hybrid business models to avoid the pressures of advertising or the control of mainstream television networks. His online platform offers the comedian the visibility to promote his offline shows while also allowing him to share his content with television stations without renouncing editorial control. The challenging context of the pandemic encouraged Aquino to expand and experiment with new formats such as an online, on-demand movie. It also influenced his content thematically, resulting in his embrace of an apocalyptic perspective that functions as a resolution to his sociopolitical critiques. This pessimistic attitude also relates to other cases in the region, like the Peruvian ones analyzed in the next chapter.

Notes

1 "Hay algo ahí en el mundo urbano de gente mala de clase media ideológicamente confusa, que funciona en varios lados."

2 "El contexto político fue cada vez influyendo más. Cuando comenzamos a hacer el Sketch a finales de 2016 era muy genérico. En el canal donde estábamos no querían hacer política. Nosotros tampoco teníamos mayor interés. Pero en 2017 salíamos en

un canal de noticias y la coyuntura era distinta. En 2018 y 2019 fue ineludible. Era claro que la crisis iba a ocupar la mayoría de los capítulos."

3 "Son tan solemnes las opiniones y las posturas que el accionar de un ser humano jamás puede estar a la altura de lo que cree. Todos queremos un mundo mejor, pero en el camino quedás siempre corto de recursos, hipócrita. No estás a la altura de tus pensamientos, que por lo general son muy contradictorios, ya seas facho o progre."

4 "Todos somos víctimas de la libertad actual de opinar en múltiples plataformas. Como si el mundo necesitara saber lo que pensamos. Y cada uno es como su propia división de marketing. No puedo solo opinar, tengo que causar un impacto, tengo que ser polémico, extremista, ir al hueso, irónico. Me parece que hay chiste en eso."

5 "Le pusieron una gran inteligencia. Fue como decir en 2002: 'che, ¿y si hacemos puros chistes de lo pelotudos que son los del rock?,' que era como el último bastión intocable de la contracultura. Convertir eso en el objeto de la burla fue muy preciso y sorpresivo. Y quedó para siempre."

6 "Creo que el rock estaba condenado a morir y ese fue el principio de la muerte. En los últimos años la cantidad de denuncias que salieron de músicos de bandas grosas o indies por violación, abusos y por ser gente muy mierda terminó de matarlo. Al menos como lo entendemos: cuatro hombres tocando la guitarra, que se comen minitas, hacen unos temas cancheros y son medio drogadictos y faloperos. Creo que eso murió."

7 "Es muy difícil desarraigarse de algo que uno quiso tanto. En mi caso, es una especie de burla, y de un abrazo también. Me parece que está bien tratar así todos los temas. No tenés que opinar una sola cosa. Algo puede ser fundacional, que marcó mi identidad y me forjó, pero también me puedo burlar de eso, de lo que soy. Además siendo hombre, cisgénero, blanco, tenés permitido el sentido de humor sobre vos mismo. Porque podés."

8 The best-known examples of this period are Pepe Biondi, José Marrone, Juan Verdaguer, and Juan Carlos Calabró. Additionally, Tato Bores, the acclaimed host, actor, political humorist, and "comic actor of the nation," had a successful artistic career of about fifty years. He worked in television from 1957 until 1993, three years before his death.

9 The notion of the café-concert or café-chantant, a type of musical establishment where drinks and food are served, comes from the French Belle Époque. While not as political or controversial as the cabaret tradition, its performances were sometimes risqué.

10 In a mediatized society, television genres become the target of jokes: telenovelas, music video clips, journalistic programs, talk shows, and other hybrid and infotainment genres are stripped and deconstructed in order to expose their artificiality. "If before television humor picked up social elements and situations to transform them into comedy, today the tendency of television humor confirms that the television universe offers enough material to make humor. The social stereotypes were progressively replaced by media stereotypes" (Moglia, 2009, p. 5).

11 "Para mí nuestra generación viene más de ver cosas de afuera. Mis principales influencias son de ver los Simpson, Seinfeld, humor yanqui, inglés. Muy poco humor

latino o en castellano. . . . Y desde hace cinco años que corté todas las cadenas. No veo nada. Para empezar ya no veo humor o lo consumo en otros formatos. Para mí una gran serie de humor de ahora es Better Call Saul, que no tiene nada de humor."

12 "Si te ponés a desmenuzar el humor o cualquier pedacito de comedia con los parámetros de hoy, no terminas nunca. Es una paradoja sobre otra paradoja. Pensás: el consumo irónico está tapando o facilitando que un problema social persista, pero a la vez lo está exhibiendo y denunciando, pero también lo está normalizando."

13 "Si antes nos burlábamos de una mina y de un puto y nos reíamos con chistes de un culo, ahora es sólo del hombre blanco, millonario, que va contra cualquier minoría. El facho es el nuevo target. De vuelta se está convirtiendo en un facilismo. Para mí el humor se define en el esfuerzo que le ponés. Yo veo un montón de comedia que está cerca de lo que yo pienso ideológicamente, pero no me gusta, porque no se esforzaron. . . . Para mí, lo que juega es el corazón y cómo lo sentís. El humor es popular, físico y no es intelectual. Te deja sintiendo algo y no se puede explicar porqué. Es un misterio."

14 "Debe ser como un medio de defensa. Es una crítica a lo que hacemos nosotros. El Sketch mismo se pone al centro. Quizá también somos parte del problema. Es como un disclaimer: nuestra manera de decir que nosotros no hacemos humor para anestesiar. Porque la revancha no está acá; está en otro lado."

15 "Este año empecé a monetizar en YouTube y es poca plata. Lo puedo sustentar porque vendo el producto a la tele. Igualmente, eso se queda atrás. También tengo una obra de teatro y la gente viene a ver el show. Yo gano más plata con el teatro que haciendo los videos."

16 "Yo no tengo marcas detrás [que me auspicien]. Y de hecho tengo muy pocas ofertas. Quizá por nuestro tipo de humor. Veo otros en Internet que su contenido es 90% publicidad. No entiendo cómo eso puede tener éxito. . . . Yo podría hacer los videos y ganar más plata. Podría venderlos en otros lugares. Pero para mí es clave que cuanta más plata te dan para hacerlo, más te rompen las bolas y más incidencia van a tener en el contenido. . . . ¿Querés libertad? Hacelo gratis."

17 "Teníamos mi personaje de los sketches que siempre señala lo que está bien, lo que está mal, y pensamos ponerlo en un lugar donde tenga todo el poder y que se atragante con sus propias palabras, que todo lo que el creía que podía funcionar fracase estrepitosamente."

References

Abal Medina, J. (2020). Peronism back in power in Argentina: Economic crisis and political stability. *Latin American Policy, 11*(1), 148–153.

Alonso, P. (2018). *Satiric TV in the Americas: Critical metatainment as negotiated dissent.* Oxford University Press.

Anria, S., & Vommaro, G. (2019, October 29). In Argentina, a "right turn" that wasn't and left-Peronism's unlikely comeback. *NACLA Report on the Americas.* https://nacla.org/news/2019/10/28/argentina-elections-pink-tide-kirchner

Aquino, G. (2017a, April 18). *Guille Aquino // El Sketch – Chica Promiscua* [Video]. You-Tube. https://www.youtube.com/watch?v=DTaEF6Tg7x8

Aquino, G. (2017b, May 31). *Guille Aquino // El Sketch – Homofobia positiva* [Video]. YouTube. https://www.youtube.com/watch?v=Ne1PnKNdvqU

Aquino, G. (2017c, March 28). *Guille Aquino // El Sketch – Novia Nazi (ex skinhead)* [Video]. YouTube. https://www.youtube.com/watch?v=fpuMLM1rT94

Aquino, G. (2018, October 2). *El Sketch – Amigo cura* [Video]. YouTube. https://www.youtube.com/watch?v=vliyd3Xk_-A

Aquino, G. (2019a, February 15). *Guille Aquino – El Sketch – Palermo news (malas noticias)* [Video]. YouTube. https://www.youtube.com/watch?v=zvg1CxZ4N5k

Aquino, G. (2019b, August 17). *Guille Aquino - Sketch – Abuela vs republica* [Video]. YouTube. https://www.youtube.com/watch?v=6fOdnb0y4wo

Aquino, G. (2019c, November 23). *Guille Aquino – Sketch – Americas Anonimas* [Video]. YouTube. https://www.youtube.com/watch?v=RoI25zLFROI

Aquino, G. (2019d, June 22). *Guille Aquino - Sketch – Amiga diputada* [Video]. YouTube. https://www.youtube.com/watch?v=Ie-TtXFjgG8

Aquino, G. (2019e, October 20). *Guille Aquino - Sketch – Apolitico* [Video]. YouTube. https://www.youtube.com/watch?v=WLQE-2Iduh4

Aquino, G. (2019f, August 10). *Guille Aquino - Sketch – El dia de los enamorados* [Video]. YouTube. https://www.youtube.com/watch?v=2r-AY-Qwasw

Aquino, G. (2019g, September 9). *Guille Aquino - Sketch – Guillerma* [Video]. YouTube. https://www.youtube.com/watch?v=bIicYLeD1yQ

Aquino, G. (2019h, November 2). *Guille Aquino - Sketch – La nueva Argentina* [Video]. YouTube. https://www.youtube.com/watch?v=O-aKP-AGg-Y

Aquino, G. (2019i, March 30). *Guille Aquino - Sketch – Los influencers* [Video]. YouTube. https://www.youtube.com/watch?v=TprjToPif7U

Aquino, G. (2019j, March 30). *Guille Aquino - Sketch – Nacional meme* [Video]. You-Tube. https://www.youtube.com/watch?v=VjV8eAUE1bM

Aquino, G. (2019k, August 31). *Guille Aquino - Sketch – Novia anti dr@ga* [Video]. You-Tube. https://www.youtube.com/watch?v=nejteO-hcSQ

Aquino, G. (2019l, June 15). *Guille Aquino - Sketch – Padre Argentino* [Video]. YouTube. https://www.youtube.com/watch?v=OPbxGGbmbgw

Aquino, G. (2019m, July 6). *Guille Aquino - Sketch – Palermo indie* [Video]. YouTube. https://www.youtube.com/watch?v=fOwrSinTfXs

Aquino, G. (2019n, September 28). *Guille Aquino - Sketch – Planeta tierra* [Video]. You-Tube. https://www.youtube.com/watch?v=11NhrPW557E

Aquino, G. (2020a, October 23). *Guille Aquino – Entrevista a Borat ft. Sacha Baron Cohen* [Video]. YouTube. https://www.youtube.com/watch?v=LkTWrRVfokQ

Aquino, G. (2020b, July 25). *Guille Aquino - Sketch - El Último Porteño ft. Guzman & Belloso* [Video]. YouTube. https://www.youtube.com/watch?v=a1lbAl6Ur50

Aquino, G. (2020c, December 23). *Guille Aquino - Sketch - Progres vs Fachos* [Video]. YouTube. https://www.youtube.com/watch?v=Liy3BzGdqi4

Aquino, G. (2021, December 28). *Guille Aquino & Netflix – No miren arriba, Argentina* [Video]. YouTube. https://www.youtube.com/watch?v=vxek6KS9aXo

Aquino, G. (2022, July 22). *Guille Aquino Presidente* [Video]. YouTube. https://www
.youtube.com/watch?v=Tj9iImrUlXs

Azzolini, N. (2016). Enemigos íntimos: Peronismo, antiperonismo y polarización
política en Argentina (1945–1955). *Identidades, 6*(2), 142–159.

Colacrai, P. (2012). Bombita Rodríguez, el cepillo a contrapelo de la memoria. *Trama de
la Comunicación, 16,* 57–67.

Fair, H. (2008). El conflicto entre el gobierno y el campo en la Argentina: Lineamientos
políticos, estrategias discursivas y discusiones teóricas a partir de un abordaje
multidisciplinar. *Iberoforum, 3*(6), 82–106.

Fernández de Kirchner, C. (2008, July 15). Conflicto del campo, Néstor Kirchner en la
Plaza de los Dos Congresos. http://www.cfkargentina.com/conflicto-del-campo

Fraticelli, D. (2013). Una periodización de los programas cómicos: Paleo, Neo y Humor
Post-televisivo. *Imagofagia, 8.* https://www.asaeca.org/imagofagia/index.php/
imagofagia/article/view/581

Gonzalez, C. (2019, October 1). "Si votas Macri (o Kirchner), ni me mires": La polarización política argentina invade Tinder. *RT.* https://actualidad.rt.com/
actualidad/328902-polarizacion-politica-argentina-invadir-tinder

Guille Aquino en Radio Con Vos: "Los argentinos somos medio infelices y quejo-
sos, pero con sentido del humor." (2022, January 21). *Diario con vos.* https://
diarioconvos.com/2022/01/21/guille

Instituto Nacional de Estadísticas y Censos. (2020). *Índice de precios al consumidor
(IPC): Diciembre de 2019.* https://www.indec.gob.ar/uploads/informesdeprensa/
ipc_01_20578B3E8357.pdf

Ipar, E., & Catanzaro, G. (2017, November 16). Nueva derecha y autoritarismo social.
Revista Anfibia. http://revistaanfibia.com/ensayo/nueva-derecha

Kessler, G., & Feuerstein, E. (2020, September 30). Twitter, el laboratorio político. *Revista Anfibia.* http://revistaanfibia.com/ensayo/twitter

Landi, O. (1992). *Devórame otra vez: Qué hizo la televisión con la gente, qué hace la gente
con la televisión.* Planeta.

Malamud, A. (2019, June 25). Argentina is polarized: Or is it? *Americas Quarterly.*
https://www.americasquarterly.org/article/argentina-is-polarized-or-is-it/

Manzano, V. (2014). "Rock nacional" and revolutionary politics: The making of a youth
culture of contestation in Argentina, 1966–1976. *Americas, 70*(3), 393–427.

Mason-Deese, L. (2019). A changing tide in Argentina? *NACLA Report on the Americas,
51*(4), 316–322.

Moglia, M. (2009, November 4–6). *Fútbol y rock: Innovación temática del humor televi-
sivo* [Paper presentation]. V jornadas de jóvenes investigadores, Buenos Aires.

Moglia, M. (2013). Violencia Rivas. Análisis de un personaje humorístico: una mujer
furiosa. *Revista Punto Género, 3,* 47–64.

Muñoz, M. A., & Retamozo, M. (2008). Hegemonía y discurso en la Argentina con-
temporánea: Efectos políticos de los usos de "pueblo" en la retórica de Néstor
Kirchner. *Perfiles Latinoamericanos, 31,* 121–149.

Observatorio de la Deuda Social Argentina. (2020, February 11). *La pobreza en agenda:
10 años de medición de las deudas sociales en la Argentina.* https://uca.edu.ar/es/

noticias/la-pobreza-en-agenda-10-anos-de-medicion-de-las-deudas-sociales-en
-la-argentina

Peter Capusotto y sus. (2010, October 14). *Peter Capusotto y sus Videos - Pomelo - 3°
Temporada - Programa 10* [Video]. YouTube. https://www.youtube.com/watch?v
=zhnbh2blcMI

Provéndola, J. I. (2020, March 17). Instagram y una solución humorística al coronavirus. *Página 12.* https://www.pagina12.com.ar/253543-instagram-y-una-solucion
-humoristica-al-coronavirus

Smink, V. (2015, October 27). Qué ganó y qué perdió Argentina durante el kirchnerismo.
BBC Mundo. https://www.bbc.com/mundo/noticias/2015/10/151022_elecciones
_argentina_kirchnerismo_vs

Villanueva, D., & Aguerre, T. (2020, February 3). La polarización después de la grieta.
Revista Anfibia. http://revistaanfibia.com/ensayo/la-polarizacion-despues-la
-grieta/

YouTube. (n.d.a). *Ezequiel Campa* [Channel]. https://www.youtube.com/channel/
UCfknJn7W2MRC25I0b5nHdDw

YouTube. (n.d.b). *Pais de Boludos* [Channel]. https://www.youtube.com/channel/
UCMdE59YbYbSqkiZT_DPM4Dg

5

Satiric Literacy and Marginal Sociopolitical Critique in Post-Fujimori Peru

Gente Como Uno and El Cacash

The daughter of a Peruvian president explains that she does not like abortion and that she is not a complete feminist because she shaves, an art curator clarifies that men will not turn gay by going to art shows, a fashion designer suggests how to achieve a "poverty" look, a reporter discusses how many jars of jelly a journalist could charge for biased coverage, a rock guitar player denies that all musicians are drug addicts and enemies of progress, and a dating blogger elucidates why women still date men despite gender violence. These were some of the local Peruvian personalities interviewed by a fictional hyperconservative and bigoted interviewer—someone who defended "national progress" at all costs—as part of *Gente Como Uno* (People like us, *GCU*), a digital satiric show that parodied social prejudices and sensationalistic biases in Peruvian media, rooted in the country's recent political history.

The authoritarian regime of Alberto Fujimori (1990–2000) heavily controlled and co-opted mass media, particularly national television and the tabloid press (Conaghan, 2002, 2005; Degregori, 2000; Fowks, 2000; Macassi, 2001; Wood, 2000). Not only did this control lead to flagrant cases of corruption, but the regime also used the sensationalist press and entertainment media as part of its propaganda machine. After the fall of Fujimori, Peru restored a precarious democracy in a deeply divided society with fragile social institutions and a general crisis of political representation (Barrenechea & Sosa-Villagarcia, 2014; Cotler, 2013; Crabtree, 2010; Dargent, 2009; Levitsky & Cameron, 2003; Tanaka & Vera, 2007; Vergara, 2013). Nevertheless, the democratic transition coincided with national macroeconomic growth and a celebratory discourse on Peruvian identity exhibited in media and marketing campaigns as part of the transnational branding of the country. Between 2001 and 2016, Peru successfully reduced poverty but failed to expand social and educational programs to reach much of the population, evidencing the huge inequalities across social groups and geographic areas. The fissures of the so-called Peruvian miracle became more evident in 2020–21 amid political instability (with four presidents within a year), social turmoil, a devastating public health crisis (the COVID-19 pandemic), and a highly controversial presidential election in the *bicentenario* (the two hundredth anniversary of the independence of the country). These were the consequences of a severe institutional crisis and polarization (Camacho & Sosa-Villagarcia, 2021; Medina Rivas Plata, 2021; Zarate & Casey, 2019), with the mainstream media taking an increasingly conservative and biased role in supporting right-wing candidates and reactionary discourses (Alonso, 2022b). Peruvian digital satire has reflected these sociopolitical tensions.

This chapter analyzes the cases of *Gente Como Uno*, a niche and politically incorrect satiric show distributed by the portal Útero.pe that caricaturized national television's right-wing prejudices between 2014 and 2017,[1] and El Cacash (The Poopie), a popular YouTuber who has since 2012 impersonated a gang member hosting a satiric news show called *El Desinformado* (The uninformed), and who describes his work of criticizing the political class as "scratching the tiger's balls" (personal interview, 2019). The analysis of the first case, focusing on the online comments of the show, introduces the notion of satiric literacy in a society experiencing an educational crisis and a mediascape polluted with discriminatory content and fake news, while the second case illuminates the tensions of the country's recent political instability, giving voice to the younger generation's saturation with traditional media. Through exaggerated or marginal personas, *GCU* and El Cacash are also interpreted as new DIY venues of transgressive satire that question a long tradition of prejudiced national comedy and a history of sensationalism in the media.

From Fujimori's Media Dictatorship to Democracy's Satiric Infotainment

On April 5, 1992, President Fujimori headed a self-coup (*autogolpe*), which implied closing Congress and the courts. This event marked the first major authoritarian move of a government democratically elected in 1990 that became popular for stabilizing the economy through neoliberal policies (by the late 1980s, high inflationary rates had reached over 7,500 percent, while the GDP had decreased by 30 percent) and defeating the radical left-wing terrorist group Sendero Luminoso (Shining Path). The self-coup ended twelve years of a precarious democratic system and marked a new constricted period for journalism and the media in Peru. On the day of the coup, the country's newspapers, magazines, and television and radio stations were "visited" by troops, which remained in place for forty hours. The military detained journalists and opposition politicians but then released them in response to international pressure.

After the coup, Fujimori falsely proclaimed the continuing freedom of the Peruvian press. This blatant lie was sustained because most of the media collaborated, at least indirectly, with the coup (Gorriti, 1993). The military intervention ensured that the press encouraged a positive public perception of the coup through uniform noncritical coverage (Wood, 2000). From that day forward, the government of Fujimori—through the National Intelligence Service, led by the president's adviser Vladimiro Montesinos—maintained tremendous control of the media via a wide network of corruption and mafia operations (Conaghan, 2002, 2005; Degregori, 2000; Fowks, 2000; Macassi, 2001; Wood, 2000) in which media owners and journalists were bribed to express a progovernment editorial stance. Fujimori used the media as a mouthpiece for the authoritarian regime to disqualify any oppositional figures through defamation and sexist, racist, and homophobic insults. The overwhelming government propaganda machine also led to the disproportionate growth of sensationalist media and the trivialization of national television content. The tabloid media became extremely popular, garnered high ratings and circulation, and mainly (but not exclusively) targeted the Peruvian lower classes. This strategy also shifted attention away from relevant social issues and developed a society with an appetite for spectacle and infotainment, to the detriment of freedom of expression. This period of Peruvian history has been called "Latin America's first media dictatorship," and Fujimori's presidency has been described as one of the best examples of the relations among neopopulism, neoliberalism, and mass media (especially television) in Latin America (Boas, 2005; Roberts, 1995; Weyland, 2001, 2003).

During Fujimori's administration, the media in general became increasingly frivolous, acritical, and entertainment driven. Media spectacles grew, distracting public attention from national politics and violations against human rights. *Chicha*, or sensationalist publications, became the most outrageous and "trashy" products.[2] Designed to appeal to the less-educated segment of the Peruvian population, these tabloids, displayed in all *kioskos* (street newsstands), used slang in headlines and news articles, portrayed partially nude women on the front page, and focused coverage on murders, rapes, and local celebrities (Gargurevich, 1991, 2000). At the same time, the government and the undermined media encouraged the success and popularity of new entertainment television programs and infotainment formats, such as the talk show *Laura en América* and the paparazzi show *Magaly TeVe*. Fully embracing sensationalism, conservative rhetoric, and a paternalistic attitude toward the low-income classes, these were two of the most popular shows in Peru during the 1990s. Like most of the media, they served the government's authoritarian discourse in direct and indirect ways (both spouting propaganda and shifting attention away from relevant social issues).

During the Fujimori years, television political humor was also co-opted by the regime. For example, Carlos Álvarez, one of the most famous comedians of the last few decades in Peru, was hired to satirize oppositional leaders on the state television channel and took part in Fujimori's electoral campaigns (Alonso, 2020; Hildebrandt, 2008; Vivas Sabroso, 1999). Some comedians tried to resist the political pressures, like the team behind *Los Chistosos* (The funny ones), a satiric infotainment radio show hosted by veteran comedian Guillermo Rossini and other talented impersonators. Broadcast on Radio Programas del Perú (RPP), a radio station also co-opted by the regime, the show tried to be neutral within a censored environment and so mildly satirized diverse political groups ("Los chistosos," 2015; Pajares, 2012).[3] During the last year of the Fujimori government, one of the few spaces critical of the government on national television was the satiric infotainment show *Beto a saber*, which demonstrated the power of the combination of political satire and journalism to critique the authoritarian regime (Alonso, 2010). This show was, nevertheless, an exception at the time.

In addition to its political role, humor in Peruvian television and mainstream media has, for the most part, reproduced discrimination and prejudice (Sue & Golash-Boza, 2013). Two of the most controversial cases have been the characters La Paisana Jacinta (Peasant Jacinta) and El Negro Mama. Created by comedian Jorge Benavides, these characters offensively parodied Indigenous and Black Peruvians, respectively. Peruvian media humor has also developed a similar framing for other marginalized groups, such as LGBTQ people, and, from a male *criollo* (Creole) perspective, it has been based on aggression toward the Other (Huerta, 2019). Homophobic, sexist, classist, and racist jokes have always been part of popular entertainment shows on national television. Examples are the long-running television shows *Trampolín a la fama* (Springboard to fame, 1966–96) and *Risas y salsa* (Laughter and salsa, 1980–99), and the *cómicos ambulantes* (street comedians) who became popular on national television during the 1990s.

The colonization of reality during Fujimori's government that was enacted by saturating the media with startling images, vulgar entertainment, and floods of misinformation led to what Degregori (2000) has called "the decade of the antipolitics." For Degregori, the 1990s were marked by a lack of critical discourse in the political sphere and media, where images, sensationalism, and spectacle ruled over debate, analysis, and argumentation. The fall of the Fujimori regime also happened in spectacular terms, similar to the ones that supported the regime. Fujimori's fraudulent reelection in 2000 evidenced how the regime's corruption had taken over most national institutions. Leaked images of Vladimiro Montesinos at the National Intelligence Service bribing a congressperson became the first of a series of videos exposing corruption at the highest levels. These *vladivideos*, as they were dubbed, broadcast by an alliance of oppositional groups on a recently created cable channel, led to the president's resignation via fax in November 2000 while he was in Japan. Upon his extradition to Peru, Fujimori was sentenced in 2009 to twenty-five years in prison for violating human rights.

In a society deeply divided by inequality, exclusion, and ethnic and social discrimination (Cadena, 2011; Comisión de la Verdad y Reconciliación, 2004; Flores Galindo, 1994; Matos Mar, 2004; Nugent, 1992; Portocarrero, 1993; Thorp et al., 2006; Thorp & Paredes, 2010; Vargas Llosa, 1996) and governed by weak institutions and a discredited political class (Barrenechea & Sosa-Villagarcia, 2014; Cotler, 2013; Dargent, 2009; Tanaka & Vera, 2007; Vergara, 2013), the democratic transition exhibited the endemic crisis of political representation in the country. In the "democracy without parties" that was Peru (Crabtree, 2010; Levitsky & Cameron, 2003), the gap between the state and society was not closed after Fujimori, with the weaknesses of the institutions evidenced in the low approval of political leaders. The media also tapped into this discontent. President Alejandro Toledo's government (2001–6) faced an oppositional mainstream press, which sought to recover its watchdog role after Fujimori yet frequently used sensationalism to deliver accusations—a possible legacy of spectacle but renamed "freedom of expression" in the new democracy. New shows that combined journalism with entertainment became the most outspoken critics of the government. Examples were *La Ventana indiscreta* (Rear window), an innovative show within the investigative journalism genre often criticized for sensationalism, and *El Francotirador* (The sniper), a satiric infotainment television show hosted by celebrity journalist Jaime Bayly, who years later would launch an atypical presidential campaign to become the first "bisexual, impotent, and agnostic" president of Peru, evidencing the triumph of political spectacle in Peruvian democracy (Alonso, 2015a).

In 2004, President Toledo, who dipped to an 8 percent citizens' approval rating, accused the press of a plot to remove him from power through a series of corruption allegations involving his closest collaborators (Felch, 2004; Mahshie, 2005). The crisis led to public debates on the role of journalism in democracy and the limits and ethical parameters of the press when taking an openly oppositional role. Consequently, the new democratic political establishment and its economic elites sought to reinforce their links with traditional media. A common cause became the construction and consolidation of the Marca Perú (Peru Brand), an intense marketing and branding campaign to promote Peruvian culture, products, and industries, such as gastronomy and tourism (Cánepa & Lossio, 2019; Cuevas-Calderón, 2016; Hirsch, 2020). Rebranding Peruvian cultural identities, it was established as part of an official discourse that celebrated the country's macroeconomic growth, fueled by high commodity prices overseas, a growing mining sector, and an expanding middle class of consumers (Zarate & Casey, 2019). Between 2001 and 2016, Peru successfully reduced poverty but failed to expand social programs to reach much of the population, evidencing the huge inequalities across social groups and geographic areas. Moreover, despite the so-called Peruvian miracle, the country experienced an educational crisis. According to a 2017–18 report by the World Economic Forum, Peru's education system ranked 127th of the 137 countries analyzed. It was the South American country that least invested in education (3.7 percent of the GDP, in comparison to at least 6 percent in countries like Brazil, Venezuela, and Bolivia) ("Cinco retos," 2018). Not surprisingly, the low quality of education has translated into a persistence of social prejudices. In 2013, a national study found that 83 percent of students in elementary school thought that girls needed to be quiet for the boys to respect them, and 68.7 percent believed that boys who play with dolls resemble "little girls" ("En Perú," 2019). To address ingrained discrimination in schools, the Peruvian Ministry of Education has tried to include components related to gender equality in the curriculum.

However, conservative groups—evangelical and Catholic associations in alliance with Fujimorism—have fought back against these measures, accusing the Ministry of Education of trying to "homosexualize" their children (Fowks, 2017). The prevalence of sensational and prejudiced content in the media has paralleled this educational crisis, with the decade of the 1990s materializing as a crucial moment in the merger of conservatism, ignorance, and entertainment in the mass media.

During the democratic transition, the national mainstream media was not particularly active in questioning social inequalities and contradictions. On the contrary, it grew progressively intolerant of watchdog journalists as polarization increased. During Alan García's government (2006–11), investigative teams exposed high-profile corruption in the government until several of those critical journalists were fired from mainstream media outlets. The 2011 presidential race between right-wing Keiko Fujimori (the daughter of the incarcerated ex-dictator) and leftist Ollanta Humala (a former military leader with a nationalist platform) showed the media outlets of El Comercio Group, the biggest media conglomerate in the country, taking the side of Fujimori (Alonso, 2011). Their coverage was so clearly partial that even novelist and Nobel laureate Mario Vargas Llosa, perceived by many as conservative, canceled his collaborations with the newspaper *El Comercio*, while many other journalists pointed out the recurrent editorial biases. Since then, the evident support of right-wing politicians by traditional media has intensified during national elections, in many cases suspending professional and ethical guidelines of journalism. This partisanship has become particularly problematic because of the concentration of the media in conglomerates. Since 2013, El Comercio Group has controlled 70 percent of annual advertising in print, television, and digital media; 80 percent of newspaper circulation; and 78 percent of the readership of dailies in the national market, according to a study by *Ojo Público* and *Reporteros Sin Fronteras* (Castilla, 2016). In 2016, three media companies—El Comercio Group, ATV Group, and Latina Group—dominated 84 percent of the Peruvian television market. Lack of diversity in the media coincided with the boom of competition reality shows (such as the popular *Esto es guerra* [This is war] and *Combate* [Combat]), while critical journalists (such as the iconic César Hildebrandt, a Peruvian Walter Cronkite) disappeared from national television, increasingly replaced by right-wing pundits (such as Phillip Butters, a local version of Bill O'Reilly). Peruvian political television infotainment and hybrid genres thus evolved from (1) entertainment formats including political (mis)information during the Fujimori regime (*Laura en América, Magaly Te Ve*), to (2) traditional journalistic formats that included entertainment elements to criticize corruption during the fall of the Fujimori regime and the democratic transition (*Beto a saber, La Ventana indiscreta*), to (3) the strengthening of television infotainment as simulacra of politics and a potential political platform (*El Francotirador*), while most of the media adhered to a neoliberal status quo and tended to favor right-wing discourses and reactionary politics (Alonso, 2016).

While popular humor in the mainstream media has rarely questioned power or the status quo, there is an important transgressive satiric tradition in the alternative Peruvian press, from the emblematic magazine *Monos y monadas* (Monkeys and funny faces, founded in 1905) to publications of the twenty-first century such as *Dedomedio* (Middle finger) and *El Panfleto* (The pamphlet, a digital satiric news publication that connects with a transnational history of news parody magazines like the *Onion* [United States], *Charlie Hebdo* [France], the *Clinic* [Chile], and *Barcelona* [Argentina]) (Alonso, 2019). In the time of the internet, new critical voices emerged, offering alternative satiric interpretations of reality in a society used to lowbrow, prejudiced, and discriminatory humor. A pioneer of Peruvian digital infotainment is the portal Útero.pe, which began in 2005 as a blog created by journalist Marco Sifuentes, who has been recognized as the most influential digital journalist in the country by several polls and publications. With more than fifteen years of publishing under the slogan of *Webeo disfrazado de periodismo (y al revés)* (Playfulness on the web disguised as journalism [and the other way around]), Útero.pe became an established brand and a popular digital news and entertainment portal in the Peruvian mediascape. In terms of video blogs, examples include *La Habitación de Henry Spencer* (The room of Henry Spencer), a popular YouTube interview channel created in 2007 by Luis Carlos Burneo and an early example of a DIY and digital-native audiovisual production, and *El Diario de Curwen* (2014–present), which became a representative of political infotainment on YouTube by explaining complex national issues with accessible and simple language (YouTube, n.d.b, n.d.c). Since then, digital infotainment and political humor on the internet have expanded into a variety of styles and formats, influenced by international satiric references, the turbulent national political context, and local sociocultural tensions. *Gente Como Uno* and El Cacash are two examples of these satiric approaches.

Experimental Parody of Prejudice and Ignorance in a Literal Society: The Case of *Gente Como Uno*

On October 26, 2014, *La República*, one of the biggest newspapers in Peru, published a story with the following title: "Brad Pitt Spits on Interviewer for a Question about Jennifer Aniston."[4] The story referred to Pitt's appearance on the US satiric online show *Between Two Ferns with Zach Galifianakis*. In this parody of television talk shows, host Galifianakis mockingly interviews American celebrities who are aware of the satiric, politically incorrect edge of the show and respond accordingly. The ironic dimension of the show is evident in the absurdist humor of the apparently improvised and amateur host and his awkward interactions with and provocations of the interviewees. It is also highlighted in the precarious set and the constant parody of media and advertising practices. Nevertheless, *La República*'s story unironically described what had happened during the interview, completely missing the metatextual humor and references. The Peruvian coverage of this story exemplified a disconnect between ironic texts and their literal interpretation in societies where audiovisual comedy has for the most part been univocal and domesticated as slapstick, impersonation, and prejudiced jokes.

A few months before the aforementioned story was published, *Gente Como Uno* (People like us, *GCU*), a satiric online television show, was launched in Peru. On ten consecutive Wednesdays, a five- to eight-minute video, previously uploaded to YouTube, was released on Útero.pe, a popular news and entertainment portal based in Lima. Each episode featured an interview with a local personality such as the daughter of a former president of the country, a political analyst, a feminist artist, a fashion designer, a provocateur/writer, a rock musician, or a leftist sociologist (see figure 7). During these interviews, *GCU*'s fictional host—a hyperconservative, sexist, racist, homophobic, and ignorant interviewer, dressed in a serious dark suit and glasses, with generous amounts of gel in his hair and visible electric pink socks—confronted his guests, reproducing and magnifying some prevalent social prejudices in Peru (as seen daily on national television and in the press) to ridicule them and expose their absurdity. References to nonexistent or misleading polls, opinions disguised as facts, and biased questions were some of the parodied television journalism practices, and themes discussed in the interviews sought to question notions of national "progress," social prejudices, cultural discrimination, and local stereotypes in general.

Figure 7. *Gente Como Uno*, a niche satiric interview show and an experimental intervention by the author of this book, caricatured Peruvian national television's right-wing prejudices in post-Fujimori Peru. Film still.

A disclaimer at this point is essential: I, Paul Alonso, the author of this book, was one of the creators of *GCU*. I also played the role of the fictional host. Media producer Luis Delgado and I designed the show to "approach a variety of social and political tensions from a satiric perspective that considered political correctness a way to hide prevalent prejudices," as publicized in Útero.pe's initial announcement of the launch of the show ("Lanzamiento," 2014). Delgado and I had already worked together on a digital television show called *Otra pregunta* (Another type of question) for Terra TV, a transnational news and entertainment media outlet. On *Otra pregunta*, we interviewed dozens of the most prominent celebrities, politicians, and artists in the country. Professionally, I had also conducted journalistic interviews for more than a decade with cultural and political personalities for national and international media. This journalistic background, we felt, gave us credibility and access to Lima's media world. For us, *GCU* was an attempt to experiment with new types of critical audiovisual humor that we considered nonexistent in Peruvian media. We engaged in parody—understood as a voice speaking in someone else's discourse but with "a semantic intention that is directly opposed to the original one" (Bakhtin, 1984, p. 193)—of traditional Peruvian news and entertainment television, with the intention of inciting reflection and reevaluation of mainstream media practices, logic, and prejudices.[5]

While designing *GCU*, we borrowed from different satiric referents (such as *Da Ali G Show, The Colbert Report,* and *Between Two Ferns*) to configure the dynamics of the show and the host's character. We took the parodic dimension of Stephen Colbert as a hyperconservative pundit, gave it a local twist modeled after some Peruvian equivalents to Fox News' Bill O'Reilly, and infused it with the politically incorrect tone and aberrant questions of Sacha Baron Cohen's Ali G. Conscious of our low-budget, independent enterprise and influenced by *Between Two Ferns*, we decided to highlight and even intensify the precariousness of the production. In parallel with the forced acting and improvisational host, we emphasized the unstable lighting, sound, and editing techniques to create an amateur, "homemade" feel. From Galifianakis, we also took the awkward silence after an inappropriate question and the intention of violating as many television rules as possible. The episodes were shot in the living room of an apartment in Miraflores (an upper-middle-class neighborhood in Lima) with a green screen, and the help of a small crew of friends. All the interviewees were informed that *GCU* was a satiric show and that the host was a fictional character. Nevertheless, they did not know the questions in advance; nor had they seen any previous episodes before. We intended to shock them and give them the space and freedom to either confront or agree with the host's extravagant, erroneous, and prejudiced opinions, as a reflection of how people react to these prevalent attitudes in daily Peruvian life and media.

Each episode was released through Útero.pe and promoted on the portal's popular social media accounts (Facebook and Twitter, at the time), with a sensational headline that parodied clickbait styles. The first episode was an interview with Carla García, the daughter of former president Alan García, one of the most controversial political personalities in the country. It was published with the headline "I Have Never Masturbated a Dog" (Gente Como Uno, 2014a). The quote was part of her response to a humorous question recalling an infamous video of Kenji Fujimori, son of the former dictator, in which he appears to be playing erotically with his dog. The satiric frame of the joke implies that all offspring of Peruvian presidents might have zoophile tendencies. Carla García was also at the time a columnist and media personality known for her pieces on women's and LGBTQ rights, and her progressive stances toward abortion and gay marriage. The blurb for the story cited some of the topics discussed in the interview: "How to recognize someone gay in Lima? Is abortion a trend among the youth? Will Congress approve marriage between feminists?" During the interview, García ambivalently adapted to the codes of the satiric conversation, stating that she was not a complete feminist because she shaved; that she thought that gay people, feminists, and priests should be allowed to get married (to adults); and that she did not *like* abortion. She also corrected the interviewer about her father's second name, denying that he was the Antichrist, before addressing the camera to tell the audience not to masturbate dogs. In addition to one video episode that was a midseason summary, the other video episodes of *GCU* included the following titles and blurbs:

Episode 2: "Would Nadine [the Peruvian First Lady at the time] Be a Good Housewife?" Interview with political analyst José Alejandro Godoy. "Why do the enemies of progress protest for access to clean water? How to keep confronting our Chilean enemies." (Gente Como Uno, 2014g)

Episode 3: "Are Artists More Special Than You?" Interview with art curator Luisa Fernanda Lindo. "Is art a monopoly of women and homosexuals? What is the maximum amount of art shows that a man can go to before turning gay? Is premature ejaculation a problem for sensitive artists? Are we being scammed by art galleries that do not follow the Catholic Church anymore?" (Gente Como Uno, 2014h)

Episode 4: "We Asked a Sociologist How to Eliminate *Chicha* Culture and His Answer Will Make You Dance Cumbia." Interview with sociologist Santiago Alfaro, whose work deals with marginal cultures and music traditions. "How do La Tigresa del Oriente and Wendy Sulca [both kitsch popular culture icons] affect Marca Perú? Has *chicha* culture betrayed its main promoter, Alberto Fujimori? After evicting the workers of La Parada [an informal market], what other places do we need to evict people from to get rid of *chicha* culture?" (Gente Como Uno, 2014f)

Episode 5: "Are Spaniards Still Better Than Peruvians?" Interview with Spanish pornographic writer Hernán Migoya. "Who better represents Peruvian women: Tula Rodríguez [a former showgirl and television host] or Martha Meier [a conservative journalist and media owner]? What are the differences between homosexuals and rapists? Is the wrong type of Spaniard arriving in Peru?" (Gente Como Uno, 2014i)

Episode 6: "Do Women Incite Street Harassment with Their Cleavage and Desires to Find a Boyfriend?" Interview with blogger María José

Osorio, known for her writing on dating from a feminist perspective. "How to recognize a virgin in Lima. What are the best strategies to seduce a woman online? If the main risk of violence and death to women is men, why do they keep dating us?" (Gente Como Uno, 2014c)

Episode 7: "Was the Fujimori Government the Golden Years of the Peruvian Press?" Interview with influential digital journalist Marco Sifuentes, founder of Útero.pe. "Will it ever be possible to combine journalism with the internet? What is a fair fee for a journalist to charge for biased coverage?" (Gente Como Uno, 2014b)

Episode 8: "We Asked a Rock Musician about K-Pop and His Answer Will Make You Smoke Cocaine." Interview with Walter Cobos, guitarist of the band Ni Voz Ni Voto. "Do Peruvian bands deserve to be played on the national radio? Are all musicians the enemies of progress? Is K-pop the future of rock?" (Gente Como Uno, 2014e)

Episode 9: "We Asked a Fashion Designer about White Peruvian Models and His Answer Will Make You Feel Cholo." Interview with fashion designer Edward Venero. "Why is the fashion world filled with homosexuals and drug addicts? How to obtain an 'extreme poverty' look. In addition to vomiting, cocaine, and liposuction, what are other tips to stay in good shape? Should we move the capital of fashion from Bangladesh to Puno [one of the poorest regions of the country]?" (Gente Como Uno, 2014d)

The episodes of GCU were uploaded to YouTube privately and only made public when the story was ready to be published on Útero.pe. Then, the story was promoted on Útero.pe's popular social media accounts with the embedded video. Most online comments and reactions to the episodes came from these platforms, but some also came from GCU's YouTube and Facebook accounts. The reactions were immediate, visceral, and polarized, with a majority taking the show literally and criticizing its production and content, while a minority praised the show for its innovation and risk-taking attitude. An analysis of 393 online comments, divided into three categories, showed the main interpretations of and reactions to GCU: 67 percent of comments were negative, 19 percent were positive, and 14 percent were neutral. Most of the negative comments were insults directed toward the interviewer, the producers, and the portal Útero.pe. Concerning the negative comments that elaborated on their perspective, we found that most of them clearly did not understand *GCU* as a parody of a television show and took the content literally. Examples include the following:

This guy with the pink socks doesn't know what he's talking about. You better learn how to do an interview and not come off as an asshole![6]

How silly and ignorant is this interviewer? He doesn't know anything, a young man full of prejudices just repeating his social segment's views of popular culture.[7]

In the name of God, what a shameful show. It does not have good sound, and the color is all wrong. Publish the complete interviews without cuts [edits]. . . . I didn't know about this show, but I won't watch it again. Starting with the headline, everything is offensive.[8]

Can someone explain to me what kind of reporter this is? . . . Who asks these types of questions? It's shameful to watch the interview. . . . SO UNPLEASANT![9]

I was going to tell [the interviewer] to fuck himself until I read it was "humor and parody," but I think this time, the humor and irony went too far.[10]

Does this dude interview like that on purpose? Or is he just from Lima?[11]

A few negative comments did understand the show as parody and elaborated on their critique, arguing that it was not their type of humor or that it did not work for them. In contrast to the visceral negative reactions, the positive comments frequently mentioned the exceptionality of *GCU* within Peru's audiovisual humor landscape. These comments also responded to the negative commentators, pointing out their flawed readings, highlighting the satiric nature of the show, and making connections with other international comedy references. Examples of these interventions follow:

This type of humor is very good, but Peru is not ready for it. [The media] has imposed such simple and stupid humor on us that people cannot recognize parody and sarcasm. What can you expect if you eat shit every day.[12]

There are people in the audience that do not distinguish between parody and what is real. I don't exactly know why that is. Would it be that our media system is so putrid that people cannot make those distinctions? Or would it be that the average Peruvian has scarce intelligence? Would it be both? In any case, we are fucked. What a shame![13]

We should have this type of show on national television. Damn conformism![14]

People in this country need to develop reading comprehension skills. What part of SATIRE did you not understand? It's like Borat.[15]

I love this *Colbert Report* cholo.[16]

I see from the comments that people are not familiar with dry and sarcastic humor. Watch *Between Two Ferns*. It's different than what Stephen Colbert does.[17]

I love to see how people tear their hair out with the *GCU* videos. They definitely don't know how to read the show and that's why they don't understand it.[18]

GCU was discontinued after the first season ended. Nevertheless, it was relaunched a year later with a format of satiric reports based on the news agenda, more similar to well-known international examples of the genre, such as *Last Week Tonight with John Oliver*. While viewership remained within its niche, the number of comments was drastically reduced and most were positive. Online commentators welcomed the resurgence of the show, and some compared it to other national and international digital shows that they watched. In any case, the reception was not as uncomfortable as it was in the first season, which evidenced the challenges of interpreting complex and multilayered satiric texts in a mediascape dominated by sensational and prejudiced content, and a national context of educational crisis. These challenges should be considered when one is evaluating audiences' *satiric literacy*—the ability to access, analyze, and interpret polysemous, ironic, and metareferential satiric texts—which can be considered part of a wider conceptualization of media literacy, an important issue to ponder in a context marked by ideological polarization and the rise of fake news. A subsequent period of political crisis and the pandemic further evidenced this problem.

The Pandemic, the Media, and the Political Crisis in the Year of the *Bicentenario*

Beginning with the government of President Pedro Pablo Kuczynski (2016–18), Peru has experienced an increasingly severe institutional crisis and political instability (Camacho & Sosa-Villagarcia, 2021; Medina Rivas Plata, 2021; Zarate & Casey, 2019), with four presidents in power within a year and continuous social turmoil. The chaotic circumstances can be traced to 2018, when President Kuczynski and an obstructionist Congress controlled by Keiko Fujimori were in a struggle for power. The Fujimorist majority in Congress boycotted the executive's initiatives and aimed to censor its ministers. It ultimately promoted Kuczynski's resignation based on his alleged links to the Lava Jato corruption scandal, a Brazilian investigation that revealed bribery and money laundering across the region and that incriminated former presidents and leading national politicians (Keiko Fujimori herself was detained for several months in connection with the scandal, and ex-president Alan García killed himself to avoid being detained) (Zarate & Casey, 2019). Kuczynski resigned in 2018 after videos of vote-buying negotiations to avoid his first impeachment were made public. Martín Vizcarra, then vice president, replaced Kuczynski.

Vizcarra was initially popular because of an anticorruption and reformist agenda that led him to close Congress in 2019 and call for early legislative elections. Despite the measure's early popularity, it resulted in extended tensions after the new Congress was installed. A few months later, on March 6, 2020, the first Peruvian case of COVID-19 was reported. Decades of underinvestment in the health-care system and the unsustainability of pandemic lockdowns in a country where most people are employed in the informal economy led Peru to be among the countries with the highest rate of COVID-19 deaths in the world, and to report the worst economic contraction in the region, pushing nearly 10 percent of the national population back into poverty (Angelo & Mauvais, 2021; Pighi, 2020).

Amid the public health and economic crisis, political groups were focused on attacking one another. Congress's decision to vacate Vizcarra at the end of 2020 (just eight months before the 2021 election), accusing him of corruption in charges that many considered politically motivated, unleashed a scenario of popular revolt. Vizcarra's removal, promoted by congresspeople also accused of corruption, was executed under the weak and constitutionally controversial legal concept of "permanent moral incapacity," a term originally indicating a lack of mental or psychological ability to exercise power, not an ethical deficit (Medina Rivas Plata, 2021). Manuel Merino, president of Congress, took power after Vizcarra, but lasted less than five days in office. Popular revolts against the political usurper, consisting mostly of young Peruvians organized on social media, became the largest demonstrations of the past two decades in the country. Police repression led to the killing of two young men, with hundreds injured and others reported missing. Merino was forced to resign, and Francisco Sagasti—one of only nine congresspeople without open criminal proceedings at the time—was elected interim president until the elections of 2021, the *bicentenario* (the two hundredth anniversary of the Peruvian Republic).

The 2021 elections reflected citizens' disaffection with and distrust of the country's institutions and officials (Angelo & Mauvais, 2021; Cameron & Sosa-Villagarcia, 2021; Pighi, 2021). A significant percentage of voters chose populist, antisystem candidates from all sides of the ideological spectrum, and blank votes ranked second in number of ballots. The two candidates who made it to the presidential runoff received barely 33 percent of the vote combined during the first round. Pedro Castillo—a leftist schoolteacher from a rural area, with no governing experience—faced right-wing Keiko Fujimori. Although both candidates ran with populist and socially conservative discourses, they presented different views on the economy and the role of the state. For many analysts, the election was perceived as driven by contention over the neoliberal economic model that had dominated the country for the past three decades, whose failures had been evidenced by the pandemic (Cameron & Sosa-Villagarcia, 2021; Taj & Turkewitz, 2021). Castillo, campaigning as an outsider with some worrisome antidemocratic ideas and collaborators, channeled voters' anger over corruption, the economic crash, and the marginalization of rural Peruvians amid the crisis of the pandemic. He focused his political program on a call for a new constitution to replace the one established by Alberto Fujimori in 1993. Keiko Fujimori, inundated with corruption accusations and facing prison time, defended her father's constitution and the economic model it protected (Cameron & Sosa-Villagarcia, 2021). After a highly polarized electoral campaign, Castillo won by less than 1 percent of the vote, and Fujimori claimed electoral fraud without proof. While the Trump-inspired political move sought to delay and damage the credibility of the process, the US Department of State, the Organization of American States, and the European Union all deemed the election free and fair (Tegel, 2021).

The media took an essential and biased role in covering the polarizing campaign (Higuera, 2021; Salazar, 2021; Vergara, 2021). Most national television sided with Fujimori without exhibiting any tendency for balance or following electoral coverage regulations; its coverage was permeated with veiled or open propaganda. The partisanship of the media was reminiscent of how Alberto Fujimori had co-opted national television and the popular press during his authoritarian regime in the 1990s. For example, influential news shows chose their sources and analysts largely to support Keiko Fujimori's campaign (Salazar, 2021). One of the most embarrassing cases was when the national news show *Cuarto poder* (Fourth state) interviewed a former marine who said that he had proof, based on mathematical theory and cryptology experience, that there was fraud against Fujimori in the runoff election. His absurd conspiracy theory, discredited later by many experts, was broadcast on national television without questioning from any of the experienced journalists interviewing him. This type of biased and partisan coverage had already led to the dismissal and resignation of many critical journalists and producers from América TV and Canal N (channels owned by the editorial groups El Comercio and La República) who refused to take a pro-Fujimori and anti-Castillo stance (Higuera, 2021; Mella & Prado, 2021).

Furthermore, the media had already become an amplifier and source of "fake news" about the pandemic (Livise, 2021; Ñaupas, 2021). The clearest example was the coverage of the right-wing television station Willax TV, owned by businessman Erasmo Wong (also the owner of a supermarket chain). Some of the most dangerous fake news spread by Willax TV on its political news shows aimed at discrediting the effectiveness of COVID-19 vaccines (some of these shows said that the vaccines could make people sicker or convert them into cell phones, or claimed that getting the Chinese vaccine was like "injecting water" into the veins), promoting medicines (such as ivermectin) without scientific evidence, and presenting fake polls and documents promoting conservatives and attacking progressives. During the mass protests against Merino in 2020, a Willax TV show presented fake evidence about alleged weapons used by protesters to justify police repression.

Critically, however, during such protests, young people increasingly turned to social media to organize politically and to share legal and medical information. In a country with still relatively low internet penetration (68 percent), social media networks became the most popular source of news (70 percent), and reputable digital-native outlets such as *IDL-Reporteros* and *Ojo Público* reaffirmed their relevance as independent journalism sources, according to the Reuters Institute (Cueva Chacón, 2021). Furthermore, the context of the pandemic and the political crisis encouraged the creation of a variety of new alternative digital-native journalism projects, such as *La Encerrona* (The confinement) and *Sálvese quien pueda* (Every man for himself) (Alonso, 2022a). From the satiric infotainment perspective, the YouTuber El Cacash confirmed himself as a prevalent humorous voice to narrate the chaotic scenarios of a country eroded by corruption.

Criticizing Corruption through a Marginal and Criminal Voice: The Case of El Cacash

At twenty-three years old, before becoming the popular Peruvian YouTuber known as El Cacash, Gerardo García wanted to do stand-up comedy. "Since I was a kid, I watched Eddie Murphy, George Carlin, and Richard Pryor," he explained, referring to his early comedic influences (personal interview, 2019). It was 2012, and he did not know how to get into the Peruvian stand-up circuit or if there even was one. His girlfriend suggested that he broadcast his jokes and humorous monologues on the internet, at a time when the first wave of Peruvian YouTubers was becoming popular. García's first character was El Juan Ber Uan, a parody of emerging influencers and enthusiastic young producers of internet videos. "All of them seemed so happy, so positive. I wondered where the gloominess of life was. So, I decided to parody them. Because it is impossible to be so exultant, unless you are on cocaine all the time" (personal interview, 2019).

His decision to parody the language and mannerisms of the emerging stars of the platform that he was using connected with a recurrent, metareferential feature of contemporary satire: the critique of one's medium as a way of acknowledging its flaws and manufactured, mediated reality. His critique of some prevalent features of the first wave of Peruvian YouTubers was then expanded in 2016 to other domains with his most popular character, El Cacash, the parody of a boisterous local gangster who, shirtless and with a piece of cloth tied on his head, comments on sociopolitical national news and criticizes corruption and the media.

> I studied in a school in Zárate [a working-class neighborhood in Lima]. And when we got out of school, the gangsters would rob us of everything, even our pencils and notebooks. El Cacash is a parody of those *pirañas* [lit. piranhas; refers to young urban thieves, gangsters,

and criminals]. El Cacash is a parody of them. The character was born out of my frustration. I even stopped taking pencils to school. (personal interview, 2019)[19]

In the tradition of marginal comedy, in which the subject parodies his oppressor and resists through humor, El Cacash is also a character that condenses a variety of social vices: he is misogynistic, coarse, criminal, drug-driven, and violent.[20] However, he is also a victim of a system that marginalizes a significant portion of Peruvian youth by denying them access to education and employment. This might be why El Cacash is always angry with the political system, the government, and the establishment in general. From his criminal perspective, he attacks the structural corruption of the national institutions. One might think that a felonious character like El Cacash would be on the side of corruption and ignorance; however, through a humorous ideological juxtaposition, he defends a progressive agenda. He is a liberal gangster. While his comedy initially dealt with social stereotypes, national idiosyncrasies, and popular culture, it eventually evolved into its most recognizable impersonation: the news commentator.

I have always read the news, and I like to grumble. I turn on the television and I get mad. The lies in the media are shameless. That's why I always wanted to do a news show, but I felt lazy. But one day, I was walking on the street, and I see a poster of Mónica Delta [a television news host] promoting her comedy show. That's when I thought: if this jerk can do stand-up, I'm going to do a news show. (personal interview, 2019)[21]

García named his news show, hosted by El Cacash, *El Desinformado* (The Uninformed), a comprehensive satiric commentary on the daily news agenda. He adapted the format of internationally popular satiric infotainment news shows (à la *The Daily Show* or *Last Week Tonight*) for a Peruvian audience, using local slang (a lot of it, which makes it difficult to understand for any non-Peruvian person and even for Peruvians without knowledge of urban marginal jargon) and constant references to local popular culture. In this way, with more than 1,200 videos uploaded on his YouTube channel as of 2022 (YouTube, n.d.a), El Cacash has approached the most controversial issues of national politics: presidential impeachments and resignations, the Lava Jato corruption scandal, the humanitarian pardon of Alberto Fujimori, tensions between the president and Congress, and allegations of corruption on the part of leaders of diverse political parties (see

Figure 8. El Cacash (Gerardo García), a popular Peruvian YouTuber and fictional gang member turned host of the satirical news show *El Desinformado*, connected with the younger generation's saturation with traditional media and the political establishment. Film still.

figure 8). During the pandemic, he also provided thorough coverage of the government's measures in response to the health emergency while dismantling fake news and addressing the sociopolitical tensions of the 2021 presidential elections. In these videos, he acerbically criticizes politicians of different ideological factions, offering context, pointing out inconsistencies, and always coming up with new, offensive nicknames for political leaders and news protagonists. While El Cacash criticizes left-wing and right-wing politicians alike, he maintains special indignation for the corruption and political responsibility of Fujimorism (he calls it "the orange poop," the color of the party's logo) and the biases of the national media, which he accuses of spreading fear and disinformation during the pandemic and the political crisis (personal communication, 2022).

As part of his daily professional routine, García reads diverse sources of information, rigorously fact-checks his content, and seeks to further interpret the more relevant or insufficiently discussed issues of the news agenda. However, he distinguishes his work from that of journalism, and highlights his role as a comedian:

I respect investigative work very much, and I do not consider myself a journalist. I'm a *rebotador de información* [information spreader]; I will never say anything important that has not yet been published. I offer a condensed version of the news, so people can draw their conclusions. . . . Sometimes, however, people have accused my show of having double moral standards. And I say to them: El Cacash is a shirtless dude wearing a piece of cloth on his head and speaking like a gangster. If you completely believe what he is saying, the problem is yours. (personal interview, 2019)[22]

The comedian, in this sense, relies on his audience for a significant portion of the interpretational work and encourages them to seek diverse sources of information and to develop media and satiric literacy skills. At the same time, while the character El Cacash speaks without filters and from a marginal perspective—creating a sense of honesty and probably articulating some unspoken truths—he does not pretend to be objective, unbiased, or even realistic. His exaggerated and boisterous performance parodies those gangsters that overperform their marginality. "I've had gangster friends, and they speak normally among themselves," García explained. "But if an unknown person shows up, they begin to speak with more slang and more aggressively, to show the new guy that this is not his neighborhood, that he needs to be careful because this is not his home" (personal interview, 2019). In this sense, gangsters are also playing characters. If traditional television newscasters wear suits and ties to create the impression of seriousness and professionalism to disguise their editorial biases, El Cacash overstresses his marginality to not be taken too seriously. This is highlighted by the warning/disclaimer included at the beginning of each *El Desinformado* video: "This newscast includes content that might be perceived as very, very tawdry and offensive, motherfucker. So, if you have virgin ears or a serious political position, you better not watch it."[23] Digital audiences, nevertheless, have continued watching his work for many years. His YouTube channel had more than 275,000 subscribers as of 2022, and he has significant followings on Facebook and Instagram.

Despite the offensive tone of El Cacash, and in contrast to most national television humor and tabloid culture, García does not make fun of historically marginalized groups.

I don't like the humor that objectifies women. And I also do not paint my face brown to make fun of gangsters. I find that offensive. Usually, that type of [sexist and racist] humor does not have a wider goal. All comedy has a target or victim. With that type of [sexist and racist]

humor, the represented character is the victim. There is no target beyond that. With El Cacash, I found my target: politics and the news.
(personal interview, 2019)[24]

Economic sustainability has always been a fundamental challenge for
independent digital producers like García. While he is part of the YouTube
Partner Program (which, according to him, "only covers the water and
electricity bills"), the rest of his funding comes from brand sponsorships.
"One knows which offers to take, and which ones not to," explains García,
referring to any possible conflict of interest or limitations to his editorial
content (personal communication, 2019). At the same time, the sustainability of his work also depends on a constant negotiation of boundaries
and limitations established by the platform. He has experienced censorship
from YouTube. Due to a variety of complaints about his content, his You-
Tube account was suspended for a month, and he could not upload new
videos. He appealed the decision of the social media giant and was finally
able to continue using his account.

García worked briefly on television when El Cacash served as a cor-
respondent for *Hashtag*, a comedy news show broadcast on the television
station Frecuencia Latina, but the show was canceled after two months.
He remains acutely aware of the difficulties of his humor trespassing the
editorial filters of traditional television stations, even when they embark
on a progressive adventure:

> The show was too politically correct until El Cacash appeared. . . . I'm
> not too interested in working for television. [Owners, editors, and
> producers] tell you too much about what it is that you can say or not.
> I come from the internet medium, which until now has been mostly
> open [to uncensored speech]. But if there is an opportunity on televi-
> sion, I'd probably take it. Work is work, and I need it. (personal inter-
> view, 2019)[25]

Rather than migrating to television, though, García has taken his character on the road with a variety of stand-up comedy shows and has established his work as part of an interconnected wave of digital-native media
start-ups that combine political information, social analysis, and popular
culture/entertainment. Instead of competing among themselves as most
traditional and commercial media outlets do, these new entrepreneurial
sites coexist and collaborate. An emblematic example is *La Liga electoral*
(The electoral league), which García appeared on in 2021 (Ferraro, 2021).

Through this project, several prevalent alternative, digital-native news and entertainment sites such as *Sálvese quien pueda*, *La Encerrona*, Útero.pe, and *El Diario de Curwen*, along with El Cacash and various digital journalists and influencers, provided collaborative coverage of election days. More recently, additional satiric voices on social media—such as political scientist Carlos León Moya and comedian Jaime Ferraro—have further amplified the network of alternative sources of information and sociopolitical critique in Peru's digital mediascape.[26]

Conclusion

Through excessive and exaggerated characters, *Gente Como Uno* and El Cacash are rare examples of Peruvian audiovisual satire that targeted, with different approaches, the country's political Left and Right, the national ideological polarization, and the biased role of the media in supporting a conservative status quo. Referring frequently to the impact of the Fujimori regime on Peruvian society, both cases criticized the corrupt relationship of the media with the political establishment as well as the sensationalist practices inherited from Fujimori's media dictatorship, which led to a prevalence of partisanship, propaganda, and fake news in public discourse.

GCU's fictional, hyperconservative, bigoted host, who defended "national progress" at all costs, parodied the right-wing biases and tabloid practices of television news and entertainment, and questioned media discourse on the Peruvian miracle (which lauded the country's macroeconomic growth despite persisting social inequality and discrimination). The host's politically incorrect and offensive remarks sought to evidence the levels of prejudice that prevail in public discourse and other aspects of social life, in contrast to the celebratory narratives of "progress" and "development."

A few years later, in the face of the latest political crisis and the COVID-19 pandemic, El Cacash targeted the corruption of leaders from different political and ideological factions that led to a national sociopolitical and economic collapse, and the role of the media in developing disinformation campaigns and reproducing political propaganda and fake news. From his criminal perspective as a marginal (but liberal) gangster, El Cacash has sought to be the voice of reason in a corrupt reality, suggesting that it takes a low-life criminal to expose a white-collar one (alluding to dishonest politicians, journalists, and media owners).

These cases contrast with a tradition of humor in Peruvian media generally reduced to slapstick, impersonation, and prejudiced jokes that reinforce discrimination against historically marginalized groups. Both cases engage in politically incorrect satire as part of a transgressive satiric act that seeks to expose and question social vices such as racism, homophobia, sexism, and classism. In the case of *GCU*, an analysis of online comments shows that a significant number of viewers interpreted the show literally and did not understand the critical nuances of the multilayered satire. This raises the issue of satiric literacy in a country experiencing an educational crisis, where television humor has been dominated by the reproduction of prejudices and journalism has normalized tabloid and reactionary discourses. Nevertheless, the fact that some commenters understood the satiric dimension of the show and desperately tried to communicate it to the ones that were not getting it might be a sign of a desire for a more complex humor landscape in Peru. In the case of El Cacash, he addresses the interpretational aspect of his newscast with explicit warnings and disclaimers at the beginning of each episode to remind viewers of his comedic intention and to encourage them to also check other sources of information. At the same time, his over-the-top, marginal, coarse, and criminal performance seems to position his character more overtly and unambiguously.

Both *GCU* and El Cacash were inspired by foreign satiric references adapted to Peruvian urban reality. *GCU* borrowed from international productions such as *Da Ali G Show*, *The Colbert Report*, and *Between Two Ferns* in the dynamics of the show and the host's character. The sociopolitical and cultural critiques, nevertheless, targeted local elites' prejudices, hegemonic national media discourses, and Peruvian television personalities. In the case of El Cacash, his creator was inspired by the transgressive US stand-up comedy tradition of George Carlin, Richard Pryor, and Eddie Murphy, while his newscast, *El Desinformado*, follows the satiric infotainment format of shows such as *The Daily Show* and is based on analysis and deconstruction of the news agenda. Connecting with the tradition of marginal comedy that resists through humor (like Mexico's Brozo, *el payaso tenebroso* [the creepy clown]), El Cacash's coarse and felonious persona deploys Peruvian underworld slang and local popular culture references, making the understanding of his language a hyperlocal endeavor.

While *GCU* was a niche, transient, and early experiment of transgressive digital satire, García's El Cacash has become established as a popular, constant, and influential satiric character, with a significant number of loyal followers on social media. Through sponsorships, supporters' donations, and commercial stand-up comedy shows, García has been able to fund his continuous production of digital content. He also became part of a new wave of progressive satire and alternative digital media ventures in Peru, which—in contexts such as the 2021 presidential election—create alliances to cover and analyze the news as a way to counterbalance the poor performance of the national mainstream media.

Notes

1 While it was not as prominent as the other cases of this book in terms of viewership and impact, *GCU* is included here as a hyperalternative experiment and firsthand intervention by the author to gain wider insight about the production, circulation, and interpretation of digital satire and to introduce the concept of satiric literacy.

2 The term *chicha*, which comes from a traditional Peruvian beverage, is also used to refer to the diverse popular culture of Lima, which reflects the intrinsic *mestizaje* of contemporary Peruvian society. In music and other cultural manifestations, it has developed an original aesthetic and narrative of popular life. But the media world appropriated the term for vulgar sensationalism.

3 After the fall of the Fujimori regime, the news parody radio show also made its way onto television as *24 minutos* and *24 minutazos*. According to Rossini, the TV show was canceled because President Alejandro Toledo took offense at its parodies (Pajares, 2012).

4 Other mainstream media outlets, such as *RPP*, also published the story (e.g., "Brad Pitt," 2014).

5 Connecting with Bakhtin's ideas of carnival and its dialogic nature, parody seeks the "creation of a decrowning double" (Bakhtin, 1984, p. 127), a "superimposition of texts" (Hutcheon, 1985) that offers new ways to make sense of conventional genres. In relation to parodic, satiric exaggeration of traditional media texts, many authors have pointed out the work of media critics to advance "media literacy" and contribute to the evolution of genres (Achter, 2008; Anderson & Kincaid, 2013; Baym, 2009; Baym & Jones, 2013; Druick, 2009; Gray, 2005; Gray et al., 2009; Kumar, 2012; Low & Smith, 2007; Saunders, 2008).

6 "Este pata de las medias rosadas, no sabe de lo que habla mejor infórmate para poder sostener una entrevista y no quedar como un webon!"

7 "Pero que tipo más tonto e inculto el entrevistador. No sabe nada, un hombre joven lleno de prejuicios y repitiendo lugares comunes de su sector social respecto a la cultura popular."

8 "Por dios santo, qué vergüenza de programa, ni buen sonido y mal croma y pon la entrevista entera sin cortes. . . . No conocía este programa y desde luego no pienso verlo nunca mas. . . . Solo el titulo de esto ofende."

9 "Alguien me puede explicar qué clase de reportero es este? Quién fórmula estas preguntas? Vergüenza ajena me da ver la entrevista. . . . TAN DESAGRADABLE!"

10 "Yo iba a mandarlo a la mierda hasta que leí 'humor crítico y parodia.' Pero creo que del humor y la ironía se pasaron."

11 "Este weon entrevista asi al proposito? o solo es limeño?"

12 "Este tipo de humor es muy bueno pero Perú no está preparado para él. Nos han acostumbrado a un humor tan simple y baboso que no reconocen la acidez de la parodia y el sarcasmo. Tambien, si comes caca todos los días."

13 "Hay gente en la audiencia que no distingue entre la parodia y lo real. No sé exactamente a qué se deba esto. ¿Será que nuestro sistema de medios está tan putrefacto como para que se detecte dicha distinción, o será que los peruanos son, en promedio, escasos en inteligencia? ¿Será ambos? Sea cual fuese la opción: estamos cagados, ¡qué lástima!"

14 "Este tipo de programa deberían pasar en los canales abiertos. Maldito conformismo."

15 "Falta más comprensión de lectura en este país que parte de es una SÁTIRA no entendieron a lo Borat."

16 "Me encanta este Colbert Report, pero cholo."

17 "Por los comentarios veo que la gente no está familiarizado con el humor seco y sarcástico, vean Between Two Ferns para entender a lo que apuntan que no es lo mismo de lo que hace Colbert."

18 "Me gusta ver como gente se rasga las vestiduras por ver los vídeos de GCU, definitivamente no saben leer, y por ello no entienden de que va este programa."

19 "Yo estudié en un colegio de Zárate. Y cuando salíamos del colegio, [los pandilleros] nos robaban todo, los lapiceros, los cuadernos, los libros. El Cacash es una parodia de estos pirañas. Nace de la impotencia en sí. Porque nos robaban todos los días. Yo hasta dejé de llevar lapiceros al colegio."

20 Another Latin American example of this type of character is Mexico's Brozo, *el payaso tenebroso* (the creepy clown). Brozo is a bawdy, misogynistic, politically incorrect clown with a raspy voice. With his green hair and decadence, Brozo is a bitter and incensed character who speaks with resentment and cynicism. He uses sour humor and vulgar expressions to criticize the social and political realities of Mexico, with a special focus on the country's elites (Alonso, 2015b).

21 "Yo siempre he leído noticias y me encanta renegar. Prendo la televisión y me indigno. La mentira es descarada. Por eso, siempre quise hacer un noticiero, pero me daba flojera. Hasta que un día caminando vi un afiche que anunciaba que Mónica iba a hacer un show de comedia. Ahí dije: si esta huevona hace stand up, yo voy a hacer un noticiero."

22 "Respeto mucho el trabajo de investigación y no me considero un periodista. Soy un rebotador de información; nunca voy a decir algo que no está ya publicado. Yo doy un condensado de las principales noticias para que la gente saque sus conclusiones. . . . A veces me han acusado de doble moral. Y yo digo: el Cacash es un huevón con un polo en la cabeza hablando como piraña. Si tú confías completamente en eso, el problema es tuyo."

23 "El siguiente noticiero contiene material que puede resultar bastante pero bastante berraco pe conchesumare. Así que si tienes oidos vírgenes o una posición política seria, mejor no lo veas."

24 "El humor de calatas no me gusta. Y con el Cacash, yo no me pinto la cara para hacer de piraña y decir que son marrones. Eso me parece ofensivo. Además, ese tipo de humor no tiene un objetivo. Toda comedia tiene una víctima. Con ellos [el humor sexista y racista], el personaje es la víctima. No hay objetivo más allá de eso. Con el Cacash, yo encontré mi víctima: la política y las noticias."

25 "Era muy políticamente correcto, hasta que salía yo. . . . No me interesa tanto la tele, porque te dicen mucho lo que puedes o no decir. Yo vengo de este medio [Internet], que hasta ahora había sido muy abierto. Pero si se da la oportunidad, chamba es chamba. Y yo la chapo."

26 Jaime Ferraro's satiric work has become particularly relevant in deconstructing how privilege operates in Peru. By portraying a white man from an exclusive Lima neighborhood who is seemingly unaware of his entitlement, Ferraro explores the stark social differences that define Peru's deepest sociopolitical conflicts, with a focus on class, race, and socioeconomic status (Polivision Atlanta, 2023).

References

Achter, P. (2008). Comedy in unfunny times: News parody and carnival after 9/11. *Critical Studies in Media Communication, 25*(3), 274–303.

Alonso, P. (2010, May 24). Beto Ortiz: "Estoy harto del personaje que tengo que interpretar." https://paulalonso.wordpress.com/2010/05/24/beto-ortiz (Reprinted from *Dedo Medio, 31,* 32–36).

Alonso, P. (2011, May 30). Bloque de medios peruanos toma partido por Keiko Fujimori en segunda vuelta de elecciones presidenciales, dice estudio. *LatAm Journalism Review.* https://latamjournalismreview.org/es/articles/bloque-de-medios

Alonso, P. (2015a). The impact of media spectacle on Peruvian politics: The case of Jaime Bayly's *El francotirador. Journal of Iberian and Latin American Studies, 21*(3), 165–186.

Alonso, P. (2015b). Infoentretenimiento satírico en México: El caso de Brozo, el Payaso Tenebroso. *Cuadernos.Info, 37,* 77–90.

Alonso, P. (2016). Peruvian infotainment: From Fujimori's media dictatorship to democracy's satire. *Bulletin of Latin American Research, 35*(2), 210–224.

Alonso, P. (2019). Satiric magazines as hybrid alternative media in Latin America. *Latin American Research Review, 54*(4), 944–957.

Alonso, P. (2020). *Otra pregunta / Carlos Alvarez (2)* [Video, filmed 2012]. YouTube. https://www.youtube.com/watch?v=OwWxXa0Fi5c

Alonso, P. (2022a). Hybrid alternative digital-native media in Latin America during the pandemic: Two Peruvian cases of entrepreneurial journalism hosted from Spain. *Journal of Latin American Communication Research, 9*(1–2), 3–28.

Alonso, P. (2022b). *Treinta años de entretenimiento y política en el Perú: De la dictadura mediática al espectáculo de la democracia (1992–2022)*. Editorial Planeta.

Anderson, J., & Kincaid, A. (2013). Media subservience and satirical subversiveness: *The Daily Show, The Colbert Report*, the propaganda model and the paradox of parody. *Critical Studies in Media Communication, 30*(3), 171–188.

Angelo, P. J., & Mauvais, C. (2021, June 1). Will Peru's polarized election bring more instability? *Council on Foreign Relations*. https://www.cfr.org/in-brief/will-perus -polarized-election-bring-more-instability

Bakhtin, M. (1984). *Problems of Dostoevsky's poetics*. University of Minnesota Press.

Barrenechea, R., & Sosa-Villagarcia, P. (2014). Perú 2013: La paradoja de la estabilidad. *Revista de ciencia política, 34*(1), 267–292.

Baym, G. (2009). Stephen Colbert's parody of the postmodern. In J. Gray, J. Jones, & E. Thompson (Eds.), *Satire TV: Politics and comedy in the post-network era* (pp. 124–146). New York University Press.

Baym, G., & Jones, J. (Eds.) (2013). *News parody and political satire across the globe*. Routledge.

Boas, T. C. (2005). Television and neopopulism in Latin America: Media effects in Brazil and Peru. *Latin American Research Review, 40*(2), 27–49.

Brad Pitt escupió a Zach Galifianakis por Jennifer Aniston. (2014, October 23). *RPP*. https://rpp.pe/lima/actualidad/brad-pitt-escupio-a-zach-galifianakis-por -jennifer-aniston-noticia-736380

Cadena, M. d. l. (2011). Reconstructing race: Racism, culture and mestizaje in Latin America. *NACLA Report on the Americas, 34*(6), 16–23.

Camacho, G., & Sosa-Villagarcia, P. (2021, July 15). Peru's democracy is at a breaking point. *Foreign Policy*. https://foreignpolicy.com/2021/07/15/peru-democracy

Cameron, M., & Sosa-Villagarcia, P. (2021, May 13). Peru's upcoming presidential election is really a referendum on its troubled constitution. *Washington Post*.

Cánepa, G., & Lossio, F. (Eds.) (2019). *La nación celebrada: marca país y ciudadanía en disputa*. Fondo Editorial Universidad del Pacífico.

Castilla, Ó. (2016, December 1). El poder económico detrás de los medios. *Ojo Público*. https://duenosdelanoticia.ojo-publico.com/articulo/mom-peru-una-base-de -datos-para-conocer-a-los-duenos-de-los-medios/

Cinco retos que enfrenta la educación en el Perú. (2018, October 30). *RPP*. https://rpp .pe/campanas/contenido-patrocinado/5-retos-que-enfrenta-la-educacion-en-el -peru-noticia-1156259

Comisión de la Verdad y Reconciliación. (2004). *Hatun Willakuy: Versión abreviada del Informe Final de la Comisión de la Verdad y Reconciliación*. https://repositorio .pucp.edu.pe/index/handle/123456789/110702

Conaghan, C. M. (2002). Cashing in on authoritarianism: Media collusion in Fujimori's Peru. *Harvard International Journal of Press/Politics, 7*(1), 115–125.

Conaghan, C. M. (2005). *Fujimori's Peru: Deception in the public sphere*. University of Pittsburgh Press.

Cotler, J. (2013). Las paradojas de la democracia peruana. In B. Revesz (Ed.), *Miradas cruzadas: Política públicas y desarrollo regional en Perú* (pp. 55–88). Instituto de Estudios Peruanos.

Crabtree, J. (2010). Democracy without parties? Some lessons from Peru. *Journal of Latin American Studies, 42*(2), 357–382.

Cueva Chacón, L. M. (2021). *Digital News Report 2021: Perú*. Reuters Institute. https://reutersinstitute.politics.ox.ac.uk/es/digital-news-report/2021/peru

Cuevas-Calderón, E. (2016). Peru brand: A nation under construction? *Contratexto, 25*, 95–120.

Dargent, E. (2009). *Demócratas precarios: Élites y debilidad democrática en el Perú y América Latina*. Instituto de Estudios Peruanos.

Degregori, C. I. (2000). *La década de la antipolítica: Auge y huida de Alberto Fujimori y Vladimiro Montesinos*. Instituto de Estudios Peruanos.

Druick, Z. (2009). Dialogic absurdity: TV news parody as a critique of genre. *Television & New Media, 10*(3), 294–308.

En Perú, una mujer es víctima de violencia física cada minuto. (2019, April 25). *RPP*. https://rpp.pe/peru/actualidad/en-peru-una-mujer-es-victima-de-violencia-fisica-cada-minuto-noticia-1193671

Felch, J. (2004). Have Peru's press heroes gone too far? *Columbia Journalism Review, 43*(2), 43–47.

Ferraro, J. (2021, June 1). *El Cacash y Jaime Ferraro en La Liga Electoral (primera vuelta, elecciones Perú 2021)* [Video]. YouTube. https://www.youtube.com/watch?v=EPUzRCqIRgk

Flores Galindo, A. (1994). *Buscando un inca: Identidad y utopía en los Andes*. Horizonte.

Fowks, J. (2000). *Suma y resta de la realidad: Medios de comunicación y elecciones generales 2000 en el Perú*. Friedrich Ebert Stiftung.

Fowks, J. (2017, March 3). La educación sobre igualdad de género divide a Perú. *El Pais*. https://elpais.com/internacional/2017/03/03/america/1488578133_128529.html

Gargurevich, J. (1991). *Historia de la prensa peruana, 1594–1990*. La Voz Ediciones.

Gargurevich, J. (2000). *La prensa sensacionalista en el Perú*. Fondo Editorial PUCP.

Gente Como Uno. (2014a, July 23). *Carla García: "Nunca he masturbado a un perro"* [Video]. Útero.pe. http://gcu.utero.pe/2014/07/23/carla-garcia-nunca

Gente Como Uno. (2014b, September 10). *¿Es Marco Sifuentes el Genaro Delgado Parker de la web?* [Video]. Útero.pe. http://gcu.utero.pe/2014/09/10/video-es-marco

Gente Como Uno. (2014c, September 3). *¿Incitan las mujeres al acoso callejero con sus escotes y sus ganas de buscar novio?* [Video]. Útero.pe. http://gcu.utero.pe/2014/09/03/video-incitan

Gente Como Uno. (2014d, September 24). *Le preguntamos a un diseñador de moda sobre los modelos blancos y su respuesta te hará sentir cholo* [Video]. Útero.pe. http://gcu.utero.pe/2014/09/24/video-le-preguntamos

Gente Como Uno. (2014e, September 17). *Le preguntamos a un rockero peruano sobre el K-pop y su respuesta te hará fumar coca* [Video]. Útero.pe. http://gcu.utero.pe/2014/09/17/video-le-preguntamos

Gente Como Uno. (2014f, August 13). *Le preguntamos a un sociólogo cómo eliminar la cultura chicha y su respuesta te hará bailar cumbia* [Video]. Útero.pe. http://gcu .utero.pe/2014/08/13/video-afecta-la-tigresa

Gente Como Uno. (2014g, July 30). *¿Sería Nadine una buena ama de casa?* [Video]. Útero.pe. http://gcu.utero.pe/2014/07/30/video-seria-nadine

Gente Como Uno. (2014h, August 5). *¿Son los artistas más especiales que usted?* [Video]. Útero.pe. http://gcu.utero.pe/2014/08/05/video-son-los-artistas

Gente Como Uno. (2014i, August 27). *¿Son los Españoles aún mejores que los Peruanos?* [Video]. Útero.pe. http://gcu.utero.pe/2014/08/27/video-son-los-espanoles

Gorriti, G. (1993). Living dangerously: Issues of Peruvian press freedom. *Journal of International Affairs, 47*(1), 223–241.

Gray, J. (2005). Television teaching: Parody, *The Simpsons*, and media literacy. *Critical Studies in Media Communication, 22*(3), 223–238.

Gray, J., Jones, J., & Thompson, E. (Eds.) (2009). *Satire TV: Politics and comedy in the post-network era.* New York University Press.

Higuera, S. (2021, June 15). Exit of journalists during elections threatens the credibility of television channels in Peru. *LatAm Journalism Review.* https://latamjournalismreview.org/articles/exit-of-journalists

Hildebrandt, C. (2008, November 19). La "rata" y el ratón. *Diario La Primera.*

Hirsch, E. (2020). Hidden treasures: Marca Perú (PeruTM) and the recoding of neoliberal indigeneity in the Andes. *Latin American and Caribbean Ethnic Studies, 15*(3), 245–269.

Huerta, A. (2019). *El chongo peruano: Antropología del humor popular.* MITIN.

Hutcheon, L. (1985). *A theory of parody: The teachings of twentieth-century art forms.* Routledge.

Kumar, S. (2012). Transgressing boundaries as the hybrid global: Parody and postcoloniality on Indian television. *Popular Communication, 10*(1–2), 80–93.

Lanzamiento de programa satírico: Gente Como Uno (GCU). (2014, July 22). *Útero.pe.* http://gcu.utero.pe/2014/07/22/lanzamiento

Levitsky, S., & Cameron, M. (2003). Democracy without parties? Political parties and regime change in Fujimori's Peru. *Latin American Politics and Society, 45*(3), 1–33.

Livise, A. (2021, March 9). 8 fake news del canal de Erasmo Wong (que ya es un peligro para la salud pública). *Útero.pe.* http://utero.pe/2021/03/09/8-fake-news

"Los chistosos," 22 años de pasión por el humor. (2015, May 24). *La República.*

Low, B., & Smith, D. (2007). Borat and the problem of parody. *Taboo: The Journal of Culture and Education, 11*(1), 27–39.

Macassi, S. (2001). *Prensa amarilla y cultura política en el proceso electoral.* Asociación de Comunicadores Sociales Calandria.

Mahshie, A. (2005). A media plot against the president or a case of incompetence? *IPI Global Journalist, 11*(2), 18–19.

Matos Mar, J. (2004). *Desborde popular y crisis del Estado: Veinte años después.* Fondo Editorial del Congreso del Perú.

Medina Rivas Plata, A. (2021, January 5). Is political crisis the "new normal" in Peru? *Australian Institute of International Affairs.* https://www.internationalaffairs.org.au/australianoutlook/is-political-crisis-the-new-normal-in-peru/

Mella, R., & Prado, C. (2021, June 9). Purga en América televisión y Canal N. *IDL—Reporteros.* https://www.idl-reporteros.pe/purga-en-america-television-y-canal-n/

Ñaupas, A. (2021, July 19). Las peligrosas mentiras de Willax TV durante la pandemia. *Sudaca.pe.* https://sudaca.pe/noticia/informes/las-peligrosas

Nugent, J. G. (1992). *El laberinto de la choledad.* Fundación Friedrich Ebert.

Pajares, G. (2012, September 14). En corrupción, los presidentes han sido parejos. *Peru 21.* https://peru21.pe/voces/corrupcion-presidentes-han-sido-parejos-45878-noticia/

Pighi, P. (2020, August 28). Coronavirus en Perú: 5 factores que explican por qué es el país con la mayor tasa de mortalidad entre los más afectados por la pandemia. *BBC Mundo.* https://www.bbc.com/mundo/noticias-america-latina-53940042

Pighi, P. (2021, April 20). Pedro Castillo vs Keiko Fujimori: Por qué el antifujimorismo sigue siendo una de las fuerzas políticas más importantes del país. *BBC Mundo.* https://www.bbc.com/mundo/noticias-america-latina-56754234

Polivision Atlanta. (2023, October 23). *Interview with comedian Jaime Ferraro (by Paul Alonso)* [Video]. YouTube. https://www.youtube.com/watch?v=-DbHFVpfBKo

Portocarrero, G. (1993). *Racismo y mestizaje.* Sur.

Roberts, K. M. (1995). Neoliberalism and the transformation of populism in Latin America: The Peruvian case. *World Politics, 48*(1), 82–116.

Salazar, D. (2021, July 14). El show no debe continuar: La prensa peruana tras la campaña electoral. *Washington Post.*

Saunders, R. A. (2008). *The many faces of Sacha Baron Cohen: Politics, parody, and the battle over Borat.* Lexington Books.

Sue, C. A., & Golash-Boza, T. (2013). "It was only a joke": How racial humour fuels colour-blind ideologies in Mexico and Peru. *Ethnic & Racial Studies, 36*(10), 1582–1598.

Taj, M., & Turkewitz, J. (2021, June 6). Left and Right clash in Peru election, with an economic model at stake. *New York Times.*

Tanaka, M., & Vera, S. (2007). Perú: Entre los sobresaltos electorales y la agenda pendiente de la exclusión. *Revista de Ciencia Política, 27(esp.),* 235–247.

Tegel, S. (2021, July 15). Unproven fraud claims delay election result, challenge Peru's fragile democracy. *Washington Post.*

Thorp, R., Caumartin, C., & Gray-Molina, G. (2006). Inequality, ethnicity, political mobilisation and political violence in Latin America: The cases of Bolivia, Guatemala and Peru. *Bulletin of Latin American Research, 25*(4), 453–480.

Thorp, R., & Paredes, M. (2010). *Ethnicity and the persistence of inequality: The case of Peru.* Palgrave Macmillan.

Vargas Llosa, M. (1996). *La utopía arcaica: José María Arguedas y las ficciones del indigenismo.* Fondo de Cultura Económica.

Vergara, A. (2013). *Ciudadanos sin República: ¿Cómo sobrevivir en la jungla política peruana?* Planeta.

Vergara, A. (2021, June 8). Tiempos recios en Perú. *New York Times.*

Vivas Sabroso, F. (1999). No es broma. *Caretas, 1581.*

Weyland, K. (2001). Clarifying a contested concept: Populism in the study of Latin American politics. *Comparative Politics, 34*(1), 1–22.

Weyland, K. (2003). Neopopulism and neoliberalism in Latin America: Unexpected affinities. *Studies in Comparative International Development, 31*(3), 3–31.

Wood, D. (2000). The Peruvian press under recent authoritarian regimes, with special reference to the *autogolpe* of President Fujimori. *Bulletin of Latin American Research, 19*(1), 17–32.

YouTube. (n.d.a). *El Cacash* [Channel]. https://www.youtube.com/c/ELJUAN

YouTube. (n.d.b). *El diario de Curwen* [Channel]. https://www.youtube.com/c/EldiariodeCurwen

YouTube. (n.d.c). *Henry Spencer* [Channel]. https://www.youtube.com/@spencerlandia

Zarate, A., & Casey, N. (2019, October 3). How a political crisis seized Peru: Boom times, corruption and chaos at the top. *New York Times.*

6

Latinx Millennial Digital Humor and Intersectional Identities in the United States

Joanna Hausmann

Before arriving at a house party in what seems to be a Brooklyn neighborhood, three Latinx millennials address Matt, their American friend, to give him a "rundown on the nicknames that we call our friends because that's what we do in our culture." Matt learns that the host of the party is called "El Flaco" (the skinny one), even though he is very large. Other friends at the party include "Disco Rayado" (scratched record), because of his "crippling stutter"; and "Batman," not because of any superhero qualities or inherited wealth, but because "he was orphaned after his parents got into a tragic accident." Matt questions the appropriateness of making fun of physical characteristics or traumas, but the Latinos respond that it's not offensive because they love those friends. When Matt asks about some names they have been calling him in Spanish, they all deflect, tell him they love him, and hurry to the party. This nuanced critique of questionable cultural practices is developed in the satiric video "Explaining (Problematic) Spanish Nicknames to an American" by Joanna Hausmann (2020), a Venezuelan American comedian who has been part of a recent wave of millennial digital humor in the United States. While keeping a critical view of the "problematic" aspects of Latino cultures, her comedy discusses their diversity and complexity, particularly in the sociopolitical context of the election and administration of President Donald Trump, a time that she considers a "chasm" (personal interview, 2023).

Trump's anti-immigration platform, racist and sexist comments, and incendiary rhetoric about Latinos were predominant features of his run for office that exacerbated an already tense and dangerous climate for many Latino communities. Warning about Mexican immigrants "bringing drugs" into the country and being "rapists," Trump played into prevalent stereotypes historically disseminated by the US media. The term *Latino* (now increasingly used in its gender-neutral version, Latinx) encompasses hugely diverse and multicultural communities and represents one of the nation's fastest-growing populations. Traditional Latino/Hispanic media in the United States has conventionally tried to group these communities around ecstatic notions of *latinidad* to reach broader audiences, many times reinforcing the stereotypes disseminated by mainstream US media.

During the past decade, however, a new wave of alternative Latinx media has challenged monolithic notions of Latino identity, embracing its racial, cultural, linguistic, geographic, and generational diversity. This chapter analyzes the case of Joanna Hausmann (host of *Joanna Rants*, a show on Flama, Univision's bilingual digital platform from 2014 to 2016), as a representative of a comedy trend that also includes Pero Like (Buzzfeed's project to create "content that resonates with English speaking Latinxs" [Wang, 2016]) and Mitú (a large multichannel network that describes itself in terms of "the 200%—youth who are 100% American and 100% Latino" [Mitú, n.d.]). Developed by and for a bilingual or English-speaking millennial Latinx generation, these cases show the new ways in which the issue of identity is approached (and contested) by a new generation of Latinx creators who have embraced diversity and intersectionality as a central component of their collective and self-identification. Framing the discussion within the evolution of Latino media, entertainment, and ethnic comedy in the United States, this chapter also illuminates current ideological tensions within Latinx communities and offers insight into a time in which the Latino vote for Trump significantly increased in the 2020 election.

Latino Media, Stereotypes, and Identity

The US Hispanic/Latino population comprised roughly 62.6 million people by 2021, accounting for 19 percent of all Americans, according to the US Census Bureau.[1] They are considered the second-largest ethnic group in the United States, while more than half of the nation's foreign-born population is from Latin America (Lopez et al., 2023). Since 1970, when Latinos made up 5 percent of the US population, they have been one of the fastest-growing groups in the country, which has attracted attention both politically and commercially (Barreto, 2007; Negrón-Muntaner, 2014; Soto-Vásquez, 2020). Between 2010 and 2020, the Latino population grew by 23 percent, and its voting bloc grew by 121 percent from 2000 to 2020

(Lopez et al., 2023). Despite the exponential demographic growth of the past several decades and Latinos' increasing political and economic power, when compared with white Americans, "Latinos earn less, face more barriers to education and health care, and find themselves underrepresented in higher-paid areas of the workforce, as well as in popular culture" (Taladrid, 2021). Furthermore, Latinos have been "perpetually absent in major newsrooms, Hollywood films and other media industries where their portrayals—or lack thereof—could deeply impact how their fellow Americans view them" (Galvan, 2021).

Stereotypical representations of Latinos—"greasy bandidos, fat mamacitas, romantic Latin lovers, lazy peons sleeping under sombreros, short-tempered Mexican spitfires, violent revolutionaries, faithful servants, gang members, and sexy señoritas with low-cut blouses and loose morals" (F. F. Gutiérrez, 2013)—and depictions of them as immigrant, foreign, and criminal have historically dominated the US mediascape (Beltran, 2009; Dixon & Williams, 2015; Mastro & Greenberg, 2000; National Hispanic Media Coalition, 2012; Santa Ana, 2002; Tamborini & Mastro, 2000). During the past few decades, scholars have increasingly worried about how multiple media formats represent Latinos in society (Aldama, 2013; Aparicio & Chavez, 1997; Dávila, 2012; Hernández et al., 2019; Mendible, 2010; Negrón-Muntaner, 2004). Significant academic research has shown that negative characterizations of Latinos damage the viewer's sense of self-worth (Rivadeneyra et al., 2007), and that media portrayals of minority groups influence how the public perceives them and whether other segments of society support policies that positively affect them (Ordway, 2020). Media coverage of minority ethnic and cultural groups has "critical consequences for intergroup relationships and for marginalized group members' self-concept" (Tukachinsky, 2015, p. 186). As a reaction and act of resistance to imposed out-group stereotyping, ethnic media offers platforms for the social, political, and cultural expression of marginalized minority groups.

Since the creation of *El Misisipi*, the first Latino newspaper (founded in New Orleans in 1808), many Latino media outlets have proclaimed "defense of the community" as their mission, "explaining the U.S. to their readers, listeners, and viewers, while also covering news in Latin America" (F. F. Gutiérrez, 2013). In contrast to the Anglo media and its ethnocentric approach when covering other multicultural communities, Latino media in the United States (primarily in Spanish and/or English) has sought to create close cultural connections among a distinctly diverse set of communities with roots in Latin America. Operating as businesses or in association with political parties, religious groups, cultural organizations, and activist movements, Latino media outlets have assumed a variety of sociopolitical and cultural roles, from the defense of Latino populations against the abuse of authorities to the publication of community social news (F. F. Gutiérrez, 2013). By 2019, according to the report *The State of the Latino News Media*, there were 558 Latino news media outlets in the United States. In terms of television, two big players, Univision and Telemundo, have dominated the market (Craig Newmark Graduate School of Journalism, 2019).

The exponential growth of the Hispanic/Latino population during the past two decades has also produced a significant growth of Latino media in the United States (Allen, 2012; Castañeda, 2008; Dabdoub, 2016; Dávila & Rivero, 2014; Piñón & Rojas, 2011; Sinclair, 2003; Wilkinson, 2009), accompanied by an increasing process of media ownership concentration by large transnational conglomerates.[2] Appealing to a potentially wide bicultural audience, these conglomerates have "identified [Latinos] as a profitable commodity" (Gómez, 2016, p. 2812), especially in the television market. In fact, "TV and cable networks sail with the banner of Latino diversity but, in the end, that discourse is constrained by the media market logic of packaging audiences as commodities to advertisers" (Gómez, 2016, p. 2815).

Part of the problem seems to be how *latinidad* (the condition of being Latino/a) has been conceptualized in the United States. Holling and Calafell (2011, p. xvi) have questioned the idea of a homogenous Latino voice, highlighting the multiplicity of identities and experiences shaped by "the weight of history, governmentality, and grassroots organizing that reflect acts of self- and group assertion, thereby producing ideological struggles over how Latin@s are understood socially." While Latinos—with their complex heterogeneity—embody "polycentric multiculturalism" (Shohat & Stam, 1994), they have traditionally been viewed under homogenizing narratives that make invisible their radical differences. In this sense, *latinidad* has become a problematic and overdetermined concept:

> Latinidad appears as a cohesive pan-ethnic unity, binding people. It sits among the great human differences of race, ethnicity, class, gender, sexuality, religion, and nation that have played a key role in determining political, economic, and cultural change in the last five hundred years in the hemisphere. . . . As with any nation of the Amer-

icas, the cultural construction of Latinidad in the US arrives from a particular history of difference. Difference in the US is dominated by race, informed by the colonialism of manifest destiny and its political and economic urgencies, and guided by the logics of a commercial media system serving the ideologies of capital, consumption, and the political status quo. (Del Río, 2017, pp. 9, 15)

In this scenario, the creation and expansion of new media outlets have not necessarily meant more varied representations of Latinos (there is a continued dominance of Mexican and Mexican American media), new opportunities for jobs or access to media markets, or more empowering ways to consume or utilize new media for political aims. Dávila (2014, p. 9) observes that homogenizing narratives of *latinidad* have meant "the casualty of the 'local' in favor of neutral themes and formats that can have greater exportability at the cost of diversity at all levels." Furthermore, "these developments have been accompanied by a rise in anti-immigration discourse and anti-Latino sentiment" (Dávila, 2014, p. 4), as evidenced by the xenophobic zero tolerance policies of the forty-fifth president of the United States, and hate crimes such as the 2019 mass shooting in El Paso, Texas (Hatzipanagos, 2019; Lopez, 2020).[3]

The conceptual ambiguity and contestation of *latinidad* are reflected in the various terms utilized to group diverse communities: Hispanic, Latino/a, and Latin@, as well as identifiers based on ethnicity and regions (Chicano, South American, Central American), nations (Mexican American, Cuban American), or even cities, particularly capital cities versus provinces and rural areas in Latin America. More recently, the label *Latinx*, popularized among millennials, has been used to question the gender binary and the constraints of other socio-ethnic identity terms (Guidotti-Hernández, 2017; Milian, 2017b). Its use has been a "social-media firestorm, social movement, and social divider" (Carrillo, 2016). While for some activists and scholars, *Latinx* reflects "transgressive sexual, gender, and language politics" (De Onís, 2017, p. 79), others argue that it poses pronunciation issues, alienates non-English-speaking migrant communities, and symbolizes linguistic imperialism.[4] As can be seen, the tension between the desire to create a pan-Latino identity and the persistence of radical differences within and among Latin American–descended communities has been a central site for questioning Latino identity politics. The evolution of Latino humor in the United States has reflected this tension, embracing the issue of identity as a central component.

Latino Humor and Media Representations

In the United States, television comedy has allowed for more representation of minority groups (Marc, 1989; Peraccini & Alligood, 2005; Reyes & Rubie, 1994). Since the 1970s, multiculturalism and notions of diversity have become central to popular culture, and many comedians have explored ways to place their own ethnic identity within the larger US multiethnic context (Gillota, 2013). As noted by Avila-Saavedra (2011, p. 271), "because of its obvious humorous intent, comedy can make explicit racial and ethnic references less controversial." Nevertheless, the potential social effects of ethnic comedy are contentious. Some scholars argue that humor serves a social function by destigmatizing social issues, while others think that it normalizes tolerance of discrimination against minorities (Martinez & Ramasubramanian, 2015). Because of this complexity, humor can be seen as a unique "site to investigate the symbolic articulation of ethnic identities and the power of media representation to challenge or reinforce ethnic stereotypes" (Avila-Saavedra, 2011, p. 272). Latino comedy in the United States has reflected these interpretational divergences.

Across most of the twentieth century, in the years after Desi Arnaz played the heavily accented Ricky Ricardo on *I Love Lucy*, only a few Latino comedians achieved prominence in the US mediascape: Freddie Prinze on the sitcom *Chico and the Man* (1974–78), Cheech Marin through his partnership with Tommy Chong in the late 1970s and 1980s, and Paul Rodriguez and John Leguizamo in the 1980s and 1990s (Gillota, 2013). During the last few decades, and in parallel to the Latino demographic expansion, Latino humor in US television has grown and diversified. A wave of recognizable (mainly male) Latino comedians—Carlos Mencia, George Lopez, and Gabriel Iglesias, among others—became nationally prominent, with humor that heavily relied on their ethnic backgrounds. While they did not achieve the level of fame or artistic complexity of the most famous Black comedians—like Richard Pryor, Dave Chappelle, Eddie Murphy, or Chris Rock—they were influenced by African American comedy. Not only have they publicly stated their appreciation for icons like Pryor, but their humor adopts a "just us" aesthetic and is often based on comical comparisons between white and Latino cultures. Frequently exhibiting a homogenous and totalizing view of whiteness, Latino humor has tended to be more conservative (except on topics such as immigration) than African American comedy, which "largely articulates disillusionment with American culture and with such ideological myths as the American Dream" (Gillota, 2013, p.

160). Contrastingly, Latino comedy has tended to "frame the Latino immigrant experience within recurring U.S. mythologies such as the self-made man and overcoming adversity" (Avila-Saavedra, 2011, p. 286).

An important issue for the articulation of Latino identities in contemporary media is the use of the English language instead of Spanish. Most contemporary Latino/a/x comedians in the United States deliver their performances in English, aiming at Latino and non-Latino audiences. Nevertheless, they tend to include Spanish words and cultural references to create a sense of intimacy and authenticity regarding their Hispanic backgrounds and cultural identities (without alienating non-Latino audiences). As noted by Avila-Saavedra (2011, p. 289),

> This strategy rarely isolates the non-Latino members of the audience. In fact, the commercial viability of the Latino comedy in English language television lies in its ability to attract the larger, non-Latino audience. The Spanish used in Latino comedy is never indispensable for comic effect. When understood, these Latino-specific references may increase the appeal of the programs. . . . The use of language and cultural references may increase the perception of authenticity, and therefore the appeal, of Latino television texts in the eyes of mainstream, non-Latino audiences. Furthermore, seeing representations of Latinos who are fluent in English and embrace U.S. values may ease social fears about the purported resistance of U.S. Latinos to culturally assimilate.

Following this conservative path, Latino comedians like Lopez and Mencia have recurrently been accused of reinforcing gender and racial stereotypes through lowbrow humor. Nevertheless, some scholars have seen in their humor an aspiration to articulate a tension between ethnic otherness and a desire for assimilation in the United States while serving a cathartic function among Latino and non-Latino audiences, helping relieve intergroup social tensions (Avila-Saavedra, 2011). Pacheco and Nelson (2015, p. 143) argue that the performances of comedians like Lopez or Mencia, while engaging with stereotypes, seek "to push against negative images [of Latinos] and build towards a more positive identity." To counter the negative stereotypes and the history of exclusion, marginalization, and racialization of Latinos in media, comedians have offered "more positive, celebratory, fair and just representations. . . . as an antidote, but little agreement arises about what might be understood as positive" (Del Río, 2017, p. 16). Instead of a negative/positive approach, Valdivia (2003, 2010) calls for a relational approach that considers "radical hybridity" for evaluating and understanding the quality of Latina/o representation. In a similar vein, Del Río (2017) suggests taking a broader view of articulations of Latinidad through an approach informed by "radical contextuality," in which context becomes the object of study, and Latino/a media becomes the access point. This book connects with these approaches, considering that multilayered context is essential for the analysis of contemporary satire, particularly about the social, political, cultural, national, and global tensions within which it exists. Additionally, an understanding of the changing nature of the mediascape and diverse audiences is indispensable to an understanding of the evolution of media humor and contemporary, millennial Latinx digital comedy.

Latinx Millennials' Digital Media

For more than a decade, native-born Latinos in the United States have increasingly outnumbered their foreign-born counterparts, changing the demographic characteristics and their media use (Samuelson, 2012). Native-born Latinos are younger, more frequently bilingual, more likely to own a smartphone and go online, and more comfortable with (even immersed in) digital media culture than are foreign-born Latinos (Abrajano et al., 2022; Livingston, 2010). This has created a generational chasm because of the cultural differences between a shrinking, older, immigrant, Spanish-speaking population and a younger, US-born, bilingual, and bicultural population, with an impact on their preferred media content (for example, formerly popular telenovelas have not been appealing to younger Latinx viewers [Craig Newmark Graduate School of Journalism, 2019]). While Spanish is still culturally relevant for Latinx people (Mizrahi, 2017), market research also shows that "only about a fifth of U.S. Hispanics now prefer Spanish-language programming on TV. The rest—some 80% of the Latino population—are bilingual or prefer English" (Allen, 2012). In parallel, the internet has increasingly rivaled television as a source of news for US Hispanics, with 74 percent of Hispanics stating in 2016 that they used the internet, including social media and smartphone apps, as a source of daily news, up from 37 percent in 2006 (Flores & Lopez, 2018). At the same time, according to Flores-González (2017), Latinx millennials have become the most racially and culturally diverse generation because of the 1980s migration waves from different Latin American regions; they are also the most politically liberal and economically insecure generation in US history. While they identify with panethnic labels such as Hispanic and Latino/a/x (even more than older generations), they also identify by national origins and other ethnocultural identities affected by gender, education, social class, phenotype, and language, among other sociocultural markers.

Since the early 2010s, a variety of news and entertainment media operations have increasingly sought to become more appealing to this "billennial" (bicultural, bilingual, and millennial) Latinx market (Avilés-Santiago & Báez, 2019; Craig Newmark Graduate School of Journalism, 2019).[5] Mitú, a large digital multichannel network targeting a Latinx audience between the ages of thirteen and thirty-four, was founded in 2012 by a group of media entrepreneurs.[6] The company has described itself as geared toward "the 200%—youth who are 100% American and 100% Latino" (Mitú, n.d.). Congregating a variety of Latinx content creators on YouTube, Facebook, and Vine, Mitú became by 2016 the biggest Latino digital channel, attracting two billion monthly views across its various platforms and more than a hundred million subscribers, drawing millions in advertising and funding from various sources and transnational companies (Kozlowski, 2014; McAlone, 2017; Reyes, 2015). Similarly, Pero Like, Buzzfeed's project to create "content that resonates with English-speaking Latinxs," was launched in 2016. Active primarily on YouTube and Facebook, it sought to "look at the myriad identities under the 'Latinx umbrella'" (Wang, 2016). Showcasing content by Latinx creators of different national backgrounds and ethnicities, Pero Like tried to present appealing popular entertainment to "Blaxicans in LA, Tejanos in Corpus Christi, Cubans in Miami (and their abuelitas), and everyone who's been told they don't 'look Latina'" (Wang, 2016). A. Gutiérrez (2021) analyzed how female millennial Latinx digital video creators on Pero Like and Mitú navigate issues of *latinidad* and negotiate ethnicity, race, generational differences, language practices, and beauty standards. She concludes that,

> They push against homogenized representations of Latinidad by showcasing ethnic specificity while also appealing to a wider panethnic collective. Their content features vocal bodies that center ethnically specific vernacular and bilingualism and dispel the notion that all Latinxs speak Spanish. Their videos also contest Latinidad's hegemonic racial hierarchies by educating audiences on how anti-Blackness and anti-Indigeneity operate within the panethnic col-

lective. In doing so, this SME [social media entertainment] content puts forth representations of ideological panethnicity that challenge Latinidad's flattening of difference. By exposing audiences to the diversity of experiences within Latinidad, these spreadable videos also enable and facilitate experiential panethnicity for Latinx audiences. (A. Gutiérrez, 2021, p. 101)

Nevertheless, these types of millennial Latinx content have also been criticized "for creating monolithic, reductive, and stereotypical depictions of Latinidad. Some have accused [them] of creating tired caricatures, treading the line of cultural exploitation, and reducing Latinidad to tropes such as Hot Cheetos, tacos, pupusas, conchas, cacti, and Selena Quintanilla" (A. Gutiérrez, 2021, p. 102). With an acknowledgment of these limitations, the case of Joanna Hausmann, a Venezuelan American comedian, offers a more complex approach to Latinx identities from a nuanced and politically transnational perspective.

Joanna Hausmann: Complex Hybrid Latinx Identities and Transnational Political Humor

Venezuelan American comedian Joanna Hausmann, born in the United Kingdom and of Jewish descent, initially became known as the host of *Joanna Rants*, a humorous YouTube video series distributed by Flama (Univision's bilingual digital platform in alliance with Bedrocket Media from 2014 to 2016, aimed primarily at millennial audiences interested in Latinx culture), and later on her own YouTube channel (see figure 9). Most of her videos, of around five minutes each, follow the "rant" monologue format, in which the host passionately speaks directly to the camera about a specific topic, but her channel also includes sketch comedy and short video variations such as informal conversations with friends and family members. Her most popular videos, with millions of views, aim at deconstructing stereotypes and monolithic notions of *latinidad* by showcasing the diversity of Latin American experiences and national cultures.

One of Hausmann's frequent access points to the subject of diversity is language or, more specifically, the variety of dialects, accents, and colloquialisms in Latin America and Spain. In videos such as "Types of Spanish Accents" (FLAMA, 2015g), "10 (Accidental) Spanish Curse Words" (FLAMA, 2015c), and "13 Great Latin American Slang Words" (Hausmann, 2017a), she highlights the linguistic differences in the use of Spanish language—

Figure 9. Venezuelan American comedian Joanna Hausmann embraced diversity as a central component of Latinx identities in the context of the Trump presidency. Film still.

arguably the most unifying aspect among Hispanic American cultures— throughout regions and nations. Similarly, in her efforts to highlight diversity, her comedy also devotes attention to alleged traits of national specificity. Videos such as "Signs You're Venezuelan" (FLAMA, 2015e), "Argentinian Intervention" (FLAMA, 2016a), "A Few Words on Chile" (Hausmann, 2017b), "Mexico vs. El Salvador: Taste Test" (FLAMA, 2016e), and "One Fact about EVERY Latin American Country" (Hausmann, 2019a) aim at showcasing and satirizing real and perceived attributes of varied Latin American countries, celebrating their uniqueness, contrasting their cultures, and ridiculing nationalist traits and social vices. Hausmann believes that pointing out differences and contrasting cultures is a productive way of not only rescuing the "specificity of our cultures" but also "unifying us" in a mediascape that tends to rely on statistics to portray Latinos in popular culture (personal interview, 2023). She explains this through a story from her early days at Flama:

> [For] one of the first videos we made, a marketing team came to tell us what Latinos love and who Latinos are. They gave us a sheet and they walked us through it, and they said, "You know, Latinos are majority Mexican. Latinos speak Spanish at home, but English at work or school. Latinos hold their culture very close to their heart, and La-

tinos over-index on zombies, as in they like zombie movies." So, the team was like, "Well, we should make a video with all this stuff. Let's have a Mexican family who speaks English [at work and school] and then Spanish with each other. And there's a zombie apocalypse." And we did that.... It was so bad we had to take it off YouTube. So, that is like trying to create comedy and art through statistics. And I think a lot of people see the word *Latino* almost as a statistic. But art doesn't work like that. (personal interview, 2023)

Acknowledging how limiting it is that in the United States, Latinos are "just put all in one group" ("A comedian," 2016), Hausmann showcases diversity through her comedy in order to debunk Latinx cultural stereotypes reproduced in public discourse. "Contrary to what the media may have you believe, we aren't all maids, cholos, Pitbull fans," Hausmann declares in the video "5 Misconceptions about Latinos" (FLAMA, 2015a). She addresses stereotypes about nationality, religion, ethnicity, language, and personality traits while contextualizing and elucidating multiple dimensions of what unites and differentiates diverse Latin American cultural practices. Through examples, humorous exaggeration, statistics, and cultural descriptions relatable to American audiences, she creates a bridge for intercultural communication. In this vein, she often engages in critical cultural comparisons involving the United States. In the video "Cursing in English vs. Spanish," she not only contrasts different ways of swearing, but also highlights what both idiomatic adaptations have in common: their basis on social taboos, emasculation, and gendered attributes (FLAMA, 2016c). As with the example of the video "Explaining (Problematic) Spanish Nicknames to an American" that opens this chapter (Hausmann, 2020), the comedian engages in cultural comparisons with a critical mind that does not condone prejudice but exposes it as a shared transcultural social problem.

Another example of cultural comparison is her sketch comedy video "Latino vs American Wedding," in which she addresses bicultural stereotypes about the nuptial celebration, a still-predominant social practice beyond borders (Hausmann, 2018). In this video, a couple is meeting with a wedding planner to discuss options for their Long Island–Venezuelan wedding, but there are recurrent misunderstandings. The groom and bride have different views on the number and type of guests attending the celebration. The American groom wants to invite just a small circle of no more than 40 close friends and family, while the Venezuelan bride considers inviting at least 440 guests with divergent levels of connection. Similar disparities in preference are revealed regarding the types of food and eating arrangements (a modest buffet versus constant rotating plates and appetizers), the duration of the party (to end at eleven at night or eleven the next morning), and the type of music for the first dance (Dave Matthews versus salsa). The over-the-top demands of the bride contrast with the restrained preferences of the groom, through which the comedian satirizes stereotypes of Latinx extravagance in contrast with "lame" white American culture. Nevertheless, the couple does agree on a few things. When asked about religion—her family is Jewish and his is Catholic—both agree that it doesn't matter, because neither of them believes in God. After the bride proposes having reggaeton artist Daddy Yankee perform at the wedding, the overall estimated cost becomes absurdly high, so they decide to cancel the ambitious event, get married at city hall, and celebrate with beers in her parents' basement. In this comedic universe, nonreligiousness and financial concerns unite the postmodern, intercultural millennial couple, beyond the stereotypical forms of wedding celebrations.

Hausmann's problematization of stereotypes and prejudices also addresses issues of gender. In "The F Word," she reminds her audience about definitions of feminism, highlighting its core meaning as aiming for gender equality (Hausmann, 2017c). She then responds to a variety of sexist, ignorant, and aggressive online comments—ranging from "feminazi" to "stop victimizing yourself"—by deconstructing the flawed premises underpinning them. In "Sexist YouTube," she analyzes the demeaning online insults that public women receive on social media ("slut," "whore," "ugly," "I wouldn't fuck her"), exposing the preponderance of violence and objectification of the female body in the digital world (FLAMA, 2015d). Similarly, in "Beauty Standards Are B.S." she educates viewers about the long history of artificial and arbitrary women's beauty norms—from corsets and footbinding to liposuction and lip implants—imposed by sexist and objectifying societies, the role that media and celebrities play in the construction and maintenance of unhealthy practices, and the difficulties that Latin American women in particular face today (FLAMA, 2016b). How sexism affects today's Latinas is also highlighted in "5 Sexist Things Abuelitas Say" (FLAMA, 2015b). After explaining that most *abuelitas* (grandmothers) grew up in a time when "women were mainly baby machines," Hausmann recounts sexist things that her grandmother said to her (and not to her brothers), including "a lady never says bad words," "you are never going to find a man if you work all the time," "sírvele" (serve food to a man), and "you look *gordita* [fatty]." Again, Hausmann's comedic strategy is to engage with stereotypes—here, of Latina grandmothers—with empathy, but with a critical eye that does not condone their implicated prejudices.

Hausmann's humorous questioning of stereotypes aims at elucidating their social implications and their ambivalent relationship with existing cultural practices:

> I see people using stereotypes as crutches instead of using them to il-luminate something. Stereotypes are something that, as a comedian, you can, in a certain way, use as a tool to reverse expectations. I think comedy has to come from a very genuine, real place. For instance, my mom is a very stereotypical Latina mom and I celebrate the hell out of her being the way she is. She's not a crutch, I use my stories about her to depict a part of my life that is real. In that way, walking the fine line is easy when you look within yourself and tell a story that's true to you, rather than using a stereotype to get laughs. . . . I've seen a lot of comedy about violence, about having a lot of babies, all those old, overused tropes that aren't celebrating anyone's identity and that's just not useful. I think people laugh when they realize you're not human-izing a stereotype but, rather, using a stereotype to humanize yourself. (quoted in Cepeda, 2015)

These concerns and her awareness about the (problematic) uses of ste-reotypes have their roots in the comedian's own complex cultural identity. Hausmann was born in Warwickshire, England, to first-generation Vene-zuelan immigrant parents. She is Jewish on her father's side; he has Belgian and German origins, and his family escaped the Holocaust. Her mother's side of the family includes Cuban exiles of European and Lebanese descent who escaped the island during the Castro dictatorship. Fleeing the Chávez-Maduro regime, her parents relocated from Venezuela to the United States (where she completed her studies in history and English and became a citizen in 2012). A self-described "Jewtina," she bases her humor on her family's background, defined by immigration, and her relationship with diverse intersectional identities. She explains,

> I grew up explaining who I was . . . as a white Latina with a Jewish last name. That does not make sense in the conceptualization of what a Latina should be. Also, I'm not particularly suave; I'm incredibly awkward. There's something about my identity that does not mesh with what people think the identity should include. . . . I was trained

in explaining my identity in a way that wasn't surface level. And it also opened me up in understanding that people can literally have absolutely any background and what we conceive to be their identity, or their reality, or their background is usually not the case. There's a lot more to unpackage there. (quoted in "A comedian," 2016)

Further, she explains,

Even my astrological sign isn't clear because I was born on a cusp. So, I don't know if I'm Pisces or Aries, like there's nothing about me that's clear. I'm a Jew, but my mom isn't Jewish, so I'm like a muggle Jew. I'm Venezuelan, but I just recently did a show with a Venezuelan comedian, and I couldn't keep up with the Venezuelan pop culture facts. I'm American, but when I traveled to South Carolina, I was like, "What?" I'd be lying if I said it was easy all the time. But discomfort is the best place to create comedy. And [I feel] this discomfort of not really understanding myself and not feeling comfortable ever. This is a very privileged place to make comedy, [because] perspective and point of view are really important in creating comedy. And when you have an intersectional identity, the cons are: you're never fully 100 percent anything, and you'll constantly miss something. The pros are: you have many vantage points from which to see things. (personal interview, 2023)

To unpack the implications of complex Latinx identities, Hausmann constantly seeks to educate audiences about their historical, sociopolitical, and cultural implications. In "Jewish AND Latino?," she uses her heritage as a "Jewtina" to explain the history of Jewish immigration to the Americas, from the beginning of the Spanish conquest to the diverse hybrid cultural practices that it has generated in many Latin American countries (FLAMA, 2016d).[7] In "Things White Latinos Are Sick of Hearing," she addresses the issue of race, recounting a variety of misconceptions and prejudices about white Latinos in the United States (in the voices of ethnically varied characters) while debating how to fill out a government form (as Caucasian or Hispanic/Latina) (FLAMA, 2015f). These concerns and her intention to deconstruct and explicate complex identities take a more holistic approach in her video "What the F*ck Is Identity?" (FLAMA, 2016h). In this video, she explains that "humans want to belong to groups and tend to categorize people, because categories make things simpler," and that in today's global world, "it has become more difficult to categorize people, because they don't belong to just one culture, place, or ethnicity." By describing her background—"I'm Venezuelan, but I was born in England, but I live in the United States, but I have a German last name, but it was originally just Jewish, but I'm Catholic on my mom's side"—she emphasizes the impossibility of categorizing her identity "into one folder." She adds, "you need to put me in at least eight, and that is true for almost everybody." To illustrate her point, she uses examples of figures with Mexican backgrounds—such as federal judge Gonzalo Curiel, actor Salma Hayek, and comedian Louis CK—whose identities are contrastingly defined by dissimilar layers of their cultural upbringings. Her overall conclusion is that we live in the hyphen era, "a time in which a little line allows us to string together all the things that make us unique." These ideas about hybrid, intersectional identities reflect Latinx millennials' rejection of homogenized representations and, at the same time, their constant search for experiential panethnicity. In the case of Hausmann, her quest to portray complex, nontraditional Latinx identities problematizes not only regimented categories but also their political implications.

In the same video about identity, the comedian comments on the political consequences of having a narrow-minded perspective about cultural identities: "there are still assholes that think that the one-folder system still works, and guess what, they are running for president. . . . Trump is putting someone into a folder, into a cabinet, where he keeps his racist stuff. It's a big cabinet" (FLAMA, 2016h). Beginning with the election of Trump in 2016, Hausmann's content engaged more frequently with contextual politics. In the video "What to Do Now That Trump Is President," she navigates the different stages of grief, and—instead of calling Trump voters racists and sexists—decides to say a nice "progressive" thing about each of the pro-Trump states (FLAMA, 2016i). She ends the video with a message about moving on and being kind, observing that "we [immigrants] are not going anywhere."[8] She describes her approach to comedy in the Trump era and how it was affected by the political environment:

> [Trump's election] was a chasm. It was a big chasm for, I think, a lot of comedians. It was such a difficult time because I think very few things made me feel more isolated in the world than that. Because a lot of Venezuelans were pro-Trump. A lot. And I was very much not. I felt like it was impossible to ignore what was happening. It would have been inauthentic for me not to make content around things of political nature. I couldn't. It was worrying me so much, and that

stirred up a lot of discomfort in me, again, and that discomfort needed a vehicle. . . . Things of a political nature hold just so much feeling and hatred. I felt like I was doing the right thing and expressing
what I thought was right and what I thought was wrong. But that also
brought forth a lot of questions of my identity because Venezuelans
were now hating me for standing up for what I thought politically. . . .
It made me realize how toxic the internet space is in the political
conversation. It also made me feel very alone in my intersectionality.
(personal interview, 2023)

Hausmann's political critiques were not only directed at Trump and the
extreme American Right. Her critiques on politics and leaders were transnational, focused on the relations between the United States and Venezuela, her other country. In "Reasons Donald Trump & Hugo Chávez Are
the Same," she compares the authoritarian and clownish traits of the two
political leaders (FLAMA, 2016f). Referring to comments and political actions by Trump and Chávez, she offers several reasons why the comparison
is valid: both were master insulters, both were reality television hosts who
fired people on live television, both believed in conspiracy theories, both
talked about the size of their "dicks," both evidently lacked the respect of
all women save for their own daughters, and both unified people through
hate. Her negative perspective on these authoritarian and outrageous leaders goes beyond their spectacle-oriented performances, politically incorrect discourse, or ideological stands: she focuses on the suffering inflicted
by their decisions. Around the time Trump was elected, the growing socioeconomic crisis in Venezuela became a primary concern for Hausmann,
and she frequently switched from humor to seriousness. In her 2016 video
"Reasons Venezuela Is a Total Disaster," Hausmann briefly explains why
Venezuela, a country with one of the largest oil reserves in the world, is
at the brink of socioeconomic disaster, recounting the political evolution
of the country since Chávez became president, and the ways in which the
situation worsened during Nicolás Maduro's regime (FLAMA, 2016g). She
describes the increasing scarcity of products and services, the hyperinflation, and the exponential rise of crime rates, explaining the failures of a
"socialist revolution" that has heavily censored and controlled the national
media, and forced the exile of millions of Venezuelans.

Even more serious is the 2019 video "What's Happening in Venezuela?
Just the Facts" (Hausmann, 2019b). Hausmann addresses the public protests and demonstrations after Maduro's controversial second inaugura-

tion, which led to a presidential crisis between the regime and the National Assembly president, Juan Guaidó. Without any jokes or humorous punch lines, and including a variety of sources and documentation, she develops the following arguments: "(1) what is happening in Venezuela is not a US-backed coup; (2) this is not a fight between the Venezuelan right wing and left wing, this is a fight of the great majority of Venezuelans to democratically get rid of an illegitimate and punitive dictatorship responsible for countless human rights abuses; (3) the people of Venezuela are seeking fair and democratic elections using the laws written in the Venezuelan constitution; (4) Juan Guaidó did not just declare himself president out of nowhere, he instead took an interim role until democratic elections could be held." Over almost six minutes, Hausmann offers significant sociopolitical and historical context and documentation to support her claims. Her perspectives are based not only on evidence but also on her own family experiences. Her father, economist Ricardo Hausmann, Venezuela's former minister of planning, was exiled during the Chávez regime.[9] Her brother, theater director Michel Hausmann, faced discrimination in his creative work.[10] Her uncle Braulio Jatar, a journalist, was imprisoned, persecuted, and harassed by the Maduro regime for his critical reporting.[11] In the video, Hausmann briefly recounts these and other family experiences, before concluding that the situation in Venezuela goes beyond political leanings or ideological partisanship and is affecting most of the country's people.

Similarly, in a not-comedic op-ed video column for the *New York Times*, "What My Fellow Liberals Don't Get about Venezuela," Hausmann urges liberals to "stop sanitizing a tyrannical dictator" (Hausmann et al., 2019). Arguing that her country "deserves change," she criticizes American leftist figures—Noam Chomsky, Roger Waters, Oliver Stone, Ilhan Omar, Alexandria Ocasio-Cortez, and Bernie Sanders, among others—for protesting America's backing of opposition leader Guaidó and contends that "these people are living on another planet and ignoring a dire humanitarian crisis." While criticizing Trump and his liaisons with tyrannical dictators, she maintains that this is not the case in Venezuela, and that "this time seems like the liberals are siding with the bad one." As with her previous video, she aims at counterbalancing misinformation, offering context and evidence about corruption and human rights violations. She is a progressive, liberal, feminist, anti-Trump woman who criticizes the authoritarian and corrupt "socialist revolution" that led the country into a humanitarian crisis. Sustaining an unpopular opinion among her "fellow liberals," she goes beyond the Left/Right dichotomy to understand a much more complex Latin American reality. This critical approach has caused her rejection from different sociopolitical worlds:

> I feel like the American Left hates me for saying I don't stand for Maduro, even though he's a dictator. The Venezuelan Right hates me because I don't like Trump. I don't belong anywhere. . . . Politics in Venezuela and politics now in the States [have become] almost like religion. People believe something, and that's their identity, and that's their belief system. And challenging it means challenging, basically, God. . . . And there's just a group of people I know who will never like me because I spoke against their God. And I'm not beyond that either. If someone said they loved Trump or loved Maduro, I would have a lot of trouble consuming their work, to be honest with you, because I feel like it stands against my morals, but it's just the reality of the world we live in. And unlike times in the past, we live in a world where we're so interconnected, where I interact with these people every day. (personal interview, 2023)

In this polarized environment, Hausmann's critiques of the American Left and Right have wider implications for US democracy. They also resonate with wider concerns about the increasing Latino vote for Trump in the 2020 election. One-third of Latinos voted for the Republican candidate, despite Trump's racist and xenophobic rhetoric against Latinos, mismanagement of the pandemic, attempts to repeal the Affordable Care Act, and restrictive policies on immigration, among other issues that negatively affected many Hispanic communities (Russonello & Mazzei, 2021). Across nationality, class, and age, the Trump campaign effectively appealed to conservative Latinos (and Latinas) in various areas of the country (not only to conservative Cubans and Venezuelans in Florida) with beliefs about individualism, economic opportunity, and traditional social values. Trump's economy-first message, opposition to abortion rights, warnings about the threat of socialism, and repeated invocation of an intruding federal government resonated with millions of Latinos who felt misunderstood by the liberal establishment (Paz, 2020). Hausmann's political humor addressed these apparent contradictions as well as the ostracizing consequences of questioning opposing ideological configurations of contemporary, multicultural Latinos in polarized environments.

Conclusion

Joanna Hausmann is part of a wave of digital, bilingual (or English-speaking) Latinx millennial comedians who push back against homogenized and stereotypical representations of Latinos in the media and public discourse. Based on her multifaceted identity as a Venezuelan American Jewish woman with a diverse cultural background shaped by immigration and exile, she has sought in her comedy to challenge monolithic notions of *latinidad* and to present its cultural, linguistic, geographic, ethnic, and generational diversity. Embracing hybridity and intersectionality as unifying aspects of a panethnic collective experience, Hausmann's satire aims to deconstruct stereotypes of specific Latin American countries, celebrating their uniqueness, but also mocking their nationalist traits and social vices. In contrast to stereotypical representations of Latinos in ethnocentric Anglo media and a history of conservative Latino comedy in the United States, Hausmann engages in cultural comparisons with a critical mind that does not condone prejudice but exposes it as a shared transcultural social issue.

While exposing prejudice and bigotry, Hausmann constantly seeks to educate her audience about the historical, social, and cultural implications of complex Latinx identities. She problematizes not only regimented identity categories but also their political implications, particularly in the context of the election and government of President Trump. Criticizing the sexist, racist, and xenophobic discourse coming from the White House and from the extreme American Right, Hausmann also takes a transnational approach to politics and leaders, particularly concerning her other home country, Venezuela. As with her approach to Trump, her denunciation of the Venezuelan humanitarian crisis and the Chávez/Maduro regime turns from humor to seriousness. Holding unpopular opinions among "fellow liberals" and conservative Venezuelans alike, she uses her comedy to challenge the Left/Right dichotomy and to understand complex Latinx and Latin American realities, which echo complex intersectional identities. The consequential alienation of rigid ideological audiences and the ostracization of political discourses that do not follow binary narratives reflect the prevalent polarized environment in the United States and Latin America. Humor, nevertheless, as in the case of Hausmann, presents itself as an educational tool to combat ignorance and disinformation beyond partisanship, and as an artistic vehicle for expressing a generational discomfort with superficial and limiting—as opposed to intersectional—realities.

Notes

1 *Hispanic* has long been a contested category or label. US government documents introduced the term in the 1970s, creating complicated debates about identity politics in relation to race and ethnicity. Because of its focus on a shared Spanish culture and language, some hold that the term *Hispanic* privileges the colonizer (Martinez & Hernández, 2017). While others prefer to use *Latino/a/x* to emphasize the Latin American origin or heritage of people living in the United States, many individuals still identify as Hispanic, possibly highlighting unconscious assimilationism (Hernández et al., 2019; Martinez & Hernández, 2017). The 2020 US Census used the label *Hispanic* for those who identified as such (Lopez et al., 2023).

2 For example, Univision—the largest media company targeting the Latino population—was acquired in 2006 by a private equity consortium led by Saban Capital Group. Founded in Texas (under a different name) by a Mexican immigrant in 1955, Univision has long been connected to Televisa, the largest media conglomerate in Mexico, owned by the Azcárraga family. Saban Capital Group bought the network from the Cisneros Group, a Florida-based media group originally from Venezuela. In 2022, Televisa and Univision closed a $4.8 billion media merger deal, becoming TelevisaUnivision, and reaching over a hundred million Spanish speakers daily (Villafañe, 2022).

3 In 2019, a Pew Research Center study found that 58 percent of Hispanic adults said that they had experienced discrimination or been treated unfairly because of their race or ethnicity; and most Americans (65 percent) said that it had become more common for people to express racist (or racially insensitive) views since Trump became president (Horowitz et al., 2019). Additionally, "researchers say victims of racism experience negative health outcomes. Studies have linked Trump's rise to an increase in premature births among Latinas, and others have tied it to increased anxiety and depression in the general Latinx population" (Hatzipanagos, 2019).

4 In a context where undocumented immigrants are often dehumanized, Milian (2017a, p. 128) points out that the indeterminacy of the *X* "does not necessarily present an option for liberation or self-realization."

5 Even Univision departed from its long tradition of safeguarding neutral Spanish to embrace Spanglish and other variations more appealing to "billennials," prompting "a linguistic flexibility that challenges the traditional lineup of neutral, Spanish-only, television, and is more inclusive of Latina/o audiences' language use" (Avilés-Santiago & Báez, 2019, p. 128).

6 Created by Latinx producers Beatriz Acevedo, Doug Greiff, and Roy Burstin, Mitú was initially funded with $3 million by investor Peter Chernin. In 2020, the company was acquired by Latido Networks, a division of GoDigital Media Group. By 2022, the company website described its target audience as between the ages of eighteen and forty-four.

7 Hausmann's celebration of hyphenated and intersectional identities can also be seen as a continuation of Latin American Jews' struggles to be considered as part of na-

tional communities in addition to their ethnic one, a struggle that materializes in the dilemma of "double identities" (Bejarano et al., 2017; Ran and Cahan, 2012). In relation to humor, Hausmann also connects with the Jewish American comedy tradition, from the critical pedagogical rants of Lenny Bruce to the self-deprecatory humor and "receptive Jewish multiculturalism" of comedians such as Sarah Silverman and Larry David, who "engage multiculturalism as a way to 'open up,' redirect, or reclaim Jewishness" (Brook, 2003, p. 155; see also Caplan, 2022; Cohen, 1987; Rosenberg, 2015).

8 This wasn't the only time that Hausmann tackled the issue of immigration in the Trump era. In the video "It's Already Hard to Immigrate to America," she explains the discriminatory immigration reforms proposed by the Trump administration: "As long as you have a PhD, a Nobel Prize, or an Olympic medal, you are almost welcome to join us here," she says, before recounting the already problematic process to immigrate from Latin America to the United States, "a country created by and for immigrants" (Hausmann, 2017d).

9 Ricardo Hausmann was also appointed by opposition leader Juan Guaidó as the country's representative to the Inter-American Development Bank, but he resigned in 2019 to return to his work as director of an economic development center at Harvard University ("Venezuela's Guaido," 2019).

10 In 2009, the Orquesta Sinfónica Gran Mariscal de Ayacucho, a government-funded orchestra, canceled its participation in Michel Hausmann's production of *Fiddler on the Roof*, citing the Chávez government's concerns about the orchestra's association with a "Jewish play." Its refusal made the news. Hausmann hired independent musicians, and many people attended the performances; supporting his work became an "anti-Chavista statement" (Levin, 2021).

11 According to the Committee to Protect Journalists (2021), "Venezuelan intelligence officers first detained Jatar, who manages the news website *Reporte Confidencial*, on September 3, 2016, one day after he covered local residents jeering at President Nicolás Maduro during a visit to Margarita Island. . . . Authorities accused him of money laundering, claiming that he was planning to fund a 'terror attack.' . . . After spending almost three years in detention and house arrest, Jatar was conditionally released on July 8, 2019, but was barred from leaving the country and required to present himself before the court every 15 days." In 2021, a court acquitted him of the charges.

References

Abrajano, M., Garcia, M., Pope, A., Vidigal, R., Tucker, J., & Nagler, J. (2022, November 8). Latinos who use Spanish-language social media get more misinformation. *Washington Post*.

Aldama, F. (Ed.) (2013). *Latinos and narrative media*. Palgrave Macmillan.

Allen, G. (2012, April 3). Media outlets adapt to growing Hispanic audience. *NPR*. https://www.npr.org/2012/04/03/149845056/

Aparicio, F., & Chavez, S. (Eds.) (1997). *Tropicalizations: Transcultural representations of Latinidad.* University of Chicago Press.

Avila-Saavedra, G. (2011). Ethnic otherness versus cultural assimilation: U.S. Latino comedians and the politics of identity. *Mass Communication & Society, 14*(3), 271–291.

Avilés-Santiago, M., & Báez, J. (2019). "Targeting billennials": Billenials, linguistic flexibility, and the new language politics of Univision. *Communication Culture & Critique, 12,* 128–146.

Barreto, M. A. (2007). Sí se puede! Latino candidates and the mobilization of Latino voters. *American Political Science Review, 101*(3), 425–441.

Bejarano, M., Harel, Y., Topel, M., & Yosifon, M. (Eds.) (2017). *Jews and Jewish identity in Latin America: Historical, cultural, and literary perspectives.* Academic Studies Press.

Beltran, M. C. (2009). *Latina/o stars in U.S. eyes: The making and meanings of film and TV stardom.* University of Illinois Press.

Brook, V. (2003). *Something ain't kosher here: The rise of the "Jewish" sitcom.* Rutgers University Press.

Caplan, J. (2022). American Jewish humor. *Religion Compass, 16*(11–12). https://doi.org/10.1111/rec3.12455

Carrillo, S. (2016, August 12). "Latinx is me": How one letter links controversy, community. *Cronkite News.* https://cronkitenews.azpbs.org/2016/08/12/latinx

Castañeda, M. (2008). Rethinking U.S. Spanish-language media market in an era of deregulation. In P. Chakravarty & Y. Zhao (Eds.), *Global communications: Toward a transcultural political economy* (pp. 201–216). Rowman & Littlefield.

Cepeda, E. J. (2015, December 23). What I've learned: Bilingual comedian Joanna Hausmann. *NBC News.* https://www.nbcnews.com/news/latino/what-i-ve-learned-bilingual-comedian-joanna-hausmann-n482091

Cohen, S. B. (Ed.) (1987). *Jewish wry: Essays on Jewish humor.* Indiana University Press.

A comedian "rants" on different Latino cultures (2016, March 5). *NPR Weekend Edition Saturday.* https://www.npr.org/2016/03/05/469211567/

Committee to Protect Journalists. (2021, September 13). *CPJ welcomes acquittal of Venezuelan journalist Braulio Jatar* [Press release]. https://cpj.org/2021/09/cpj-welcomes-acquittal-of-venezuelan-journalist-braulio-jatar/

Craig Newmark Graduate School of Journalism. (2019, June). The industry at a glance. In *The state of the Latino news media.* City University of New York. https://thelatinomediareport.journalism.cuny.edu/the-industry

Dabdoub, A. (2016, November 23). La prensa en español se afianza en EE UU gracias a los migrantes. *El País.* https://elpais.com/internacional/2016/11/24/mexico/1479943379_739298.html

Dávila, A. (2012). *Latinos, Inc: The marketing and making of a people* (updated ed.). University of California Press.

Dávila, A. (2014). Introduction. In A. Dávila & Y. Rivero (Eds.), *Contemporary Latina/o media: Production, circulation, politics* (pp. 1–18). New York University Press.

Dávila, A., & Rivero, Y. (Eds.) (2014). *Contemporary Latina/o media: Production, circulation, politics.* New York University Press.

Del Río, E. (2017). Authenticity, appropriation, articulation: The cultural logic of Latinidad. In M. E. Cepeda & D. I. Casillas (Eds.), *The Routledge companion to Latina/o media* (pp. 9–21). Routledge.

De Onís, C. (2017). What's in an "x"?: An exchange about the politics of "Latinx." *Chiricú Journal: Latina/o Literatures, Arts, and Cultures, 1*(2), 78–91.

Dixon, T., & Williams, C. (2015). The changing representation of race and crime on network and cable news. *Journal of Communication, 65*(1), 24–39.

FLAMA. (2015a, May 30). *5 misconceptions about Latinos – Joanna Rants* [Video]. YouTube. https://www.youtube.com/watch?v=kpeYP8CqTmY

FLAMA. (2015b, August 6). *5 sexist things abuelitas say – Joanna Rants* [Video]. YouTube. https://www.youtube.com/watch?v=JgMDoQsYBlY

FLAMA. (2015c, June 20). *10 (accidental) Spanish curse words – Joanna Rants* [Video]. YouTube. https://www.youtube.com/watch?v=TKKCVctGucA

FLAMA. (2015d, November 12). *Sexist YouTube – Joanna Rants* [Video]. YouTube. https://www.youtube.com/watch?v=MfbCwMNs1F8

FLAMA. (2015e, June 9). *Signs you're Venezuelan* [Video]. YouTube. https://www.youtube.com/watch?v=9RvFMNwGk4Y

FLAMA. (2015f, January 13). *Things white Latinos are sick of hearing* [Video]. YouTube. https://www.youtube.com/watch?v=SdbEMBmzo2U

FLAMA. (2015g, October 1). *Types of Spanish accents – Joanna Rants* [Video]. YouTube. https://www.youtube.com/watch?v=VlK-neOypDM

FLAMA. (2016a, June 12). *Argentinian intervention* [Video]. YouTube. https://www.youtube.com/watch?v=rsHn9VJuTzA

FLAMA. (2016b, June 12). *Beauty standards are B.S. – Joanna Rants* [Video]. YouTube. https://www.youtube.com/watch?v=z7wtQMQvxMw

FLAMA. (2016c, August 4). *Cursing in English vs. Spanish – Joanna Rants* [Video]. YouTube. https://www.youtube.com/watch?v=GeADIfQTeEs

FLAMA. (2016d, March 22). *Jewish AND Latino?* [Video]. YouTube. https://www.youtube.com/watch?v=Snww9a8OoLM

FLAMA. (2016e, December 14). *Mexico vs. El Salvador: Taste test* [Video]. YouTube. https://www.youtube.com/watch?v=hqfqEfrD5fo

FLAMA. (2016f, August 25). *Reasons Donald Trump & Hugo Chavez are the same – Joanna Rants* [Video]. YouTube. https://www.youtube.com/watch?v=Jh7YV4HaBhE

FLAMA. (2016g, June 2). *Reasons Venezuela is a total disaster – Joanna Rants* [Video]. YouTube. https://www.youtube.com/watch?v=XhIFr6e8EBI

FLAMA. (2016h, June 23). *What the f*ck is identity? – Joanna Rants* [Video]. YouTube. https://www.youtube.com/watch?v=ghnknrmResQ

FLAMA. (2016i, November 17). *What to do now that Trump is president – Joanna Rants* [Video]. YouTube. https://www.youtube.com/watch?v=Q59Zyoh9rPU

Flores, A., & Lopez, M. H. (2018, January 11). Among U.S. Latinos, the internet now rivals television as a source for news. *Pew Research Center.* https://www.pewresearch.org/fact-tank/2018/01/11/among-u-s-latinos

Flores-González, N. (2017). *Citizens but not Americans: Race and belonging among Latino millennials*. New York University Press.

Galvan, A. (2021, September 22). Latinos vastly underrepresented in media, new report finds. *PBS News Hour*. https://www.pbs.org/newshour/arts/latinos-vastly

Gillota, D. (2013). *Ethnic humor in multiethnic America*. Rutgers University Press.

Gómez, R. (2016). Latino/a television in the United States and Latin America: Addressing networks, dynamics, and alliances. *International Journal of Communication, 10*, 2811–2830.

Guidotti-Hernández, N. (2017). Affective communities and millennial desires: Latinx, or why my computer won't recognize Latina/o. *Cultural Dynamics, 29*(3), 141–159.

Gutiérrez, A. (2021). Pero Like and Mitú: Latina content creators, social media entertainment, and the politics of Latinx millenniality. *Feminist Media Histories, 7*(4), 80–106.

Gutiérrez, F. F. (2013). More than 200 years of Latino media in the United States. *National Park Service*. https://www.nps.gov/articles/latinothemestudymedia.htm

Hatzipanagos, R. (2019, August 16). Even before the El Paso mass shooting, Latinos said Trump's anti-immigrant rhetoric made them feel unsafe. *Washington Post*.

Hausmann, J. (2017a, May 3). *13 great Latin American slang words – Joanna Rants* [Video]. YouTube. https://www.youtube.com/watch?v=wBgm-9YS74s

Hausmann, J. (2017b, September 15). *A few words on Chile . . .– Joanna Rants* [Video]. YouTube. https://www.youtube.com/watch?v=zJqk0iM96iE

Hausmann, J. (2017c, June 8). *The F word – Joanna Rants* [Video]. YouTube. https://www.youtube.com/watch?v=vfWOyxHQEBY

Hausmann, J. (2017d, August 17). *It's already hard to immigrate to America – Joanna Rants* [Video]. YouTube. https://www.youtube.com/watch?v=eT8Zz0Y23rQ

Hausmann, J. (2018, October 5). *Latino vs American wedding – Joanna Rants* [Video]. YouTube. https://www.youtube.com/watch?v=LCuhJCt0JtI

Hausmann, J. (2019a, March 11). *One fact about EVERY Latin American country – Joanna Rants* [Video]. YouTube. https://www.youtube.com/watch?v=LCd8mgNdLD0

Hausmann, J. (2019b, January 28). *What's happening in Venezuela? Just the facts* [Video]. YouTube. https://www.youtube.com/watch?v=bEvHwiJWgAY

Hausmann, J. (2020, December 22). *Explaining (problematic) Spanish nicknames to an American* [Video]. YouTube. https://www.youtube.com/watch?v=NbbT0FULkN8

Hausmann, J., Varjacques, L., & Knight, K. (2019, April 1). *What my fellow liberals don't get about Venezuela* [Video]. *New York Times*. https://www.nytimes.com/video/opinion/100000006424693/venezuela-us-hands-off-joanna-hausmann.html

Hernández, L. H., Bowen, D., Upton, S.D.L. S., & Martinez, A. (Eds.) (2019). *Latina/o/x communication studies*. Lexington Books.

Holling, M. A., & Calafell, B. (Eds.) (2011). *Latina/o discourse in vernacular spaces: Somos una voz?* Lexington Books.

Horowitz, J. M., Brown, A., & Cox, K. (2019, April 9). Race in America. *Pew Research Center*. https://www.pewresearch.org/social-trends/2019/04/09/race

Kozlowski, L. (2014, June 27). MiTu, a YouTube network changing how Latino content creators and audiences connect. *Forbes*. https://www.forbes .com/ sites/lorikozlowski /2014/06/27/mitu-a-youtube-network-changing-how-latino-content-creators -and-audiences-connect/

Levin, J. (2021, February 24). Michel Hausman [*sic*] is remaking Miami theatre, one controversy at a time. *Forward*. https://forward.com/news/464728/

Livingston, G. (2010, July 28). The Latino digital divide: The native born versus the foreign born. *Pew Research Center*. https://www.pewresearch.org/hispanic/2010/07/ 28/the-latino

Lopez, G. (2020, August 13). Donald Trump's long history of racism, from the 1970s to 2020. *Vox*. https://www.vox.com/2016/7/25/12270880/

Lopez, M. H., Krogstad, J. M., & Passel, J. S. (2023, September 5). Who is Hispanic? *Pew Research Center*. https://www.pewresearch.org/short-reads/2023/09/05/who-is -hispanic/

Marc, D. (1989). *Comic vision: Television comedy and American culture*. Unwin Hyman.

Martinez, A. R., & Hernández, L. H. (2017). Latina/o communication. In M. Allen (Ed.), *The SAGE encyclopedia of communication research methods* (pp. 850–854). Sage.

Martinez, A. R., & Ramasubramanian, S. (2015). Latino audiences, racial/ethnic identification, and responses to stereotypical comedy. *Mass Communication & Society*, *18*(2), 209–229.

Mastro, D., & Greenberg, B. (2000). The portrayal of racial minorities on prime time television. *Journal of Broadcasting & Electronic Media, 44*(4), 690–703.

McAlone, N. (2017, April 11). Media startup Mitú is wildly popular on Facebook, but Snapchat helped it in a much different way. *Business Insider*. https://www .businessinsider.com/mitu-latino-focused-media-startup-profile-from-youtube -to-facebook-to-snapchat-2017-4

Mendible, M. (Ed.) (2010). *From bananas to buttocks: The Latina body in popular film and culture*. University of Texas Press.

Milian, C. (2017a). Extremely Latin, XOXO: Notes on LatinX. *Cultural Dynamics, 29*(3), 121–140.

Milian, C. (Ed.). (2017b). Theorizing Latinx [Special issue]. *Cultural Dynamics, 29*(3).

Mitú. (n.d.) *About Mitú*. https://wearemitu.com/about-mitu/

Mizrahi, I. (2017, April 4). Is marketing in Spanish still relevant to Hispanics? *Forbes*. https://www.forbes.com/sites/onmarketing/2017/04/04/is-marketing-in-spanish -still-relevant-to-hispanics/

National Hispanic Media Coalition (2012, September). The impact of media stereotypes on opinions and attitudes towards Latinos. https://www.nhmc.org/national-poll -impact

Negrón-Muntaner, F. (2004). *Boricua pop: Puerto Ricans and the Latinization of American culture*. New York University Press.

Negrón-Muntaner, F. (2014). *The Latino media gap: A report on the state of Latinos in U.S. media*. National Association of Latino Independent Producers. https://www .nalip.org/latino_gap_study

Ordway, D.-M. (2020, August 8). How the news media portray Latinos in stories and images: 5 studies to know. *Journalist's Resource.* https://journalistsresource.org/race-and-gender/news-media-portray-latinos/

Pacheco, G. J., & Nelson, D. R. (2015). Mex vs. BC: Notions of a perspective by incongruity in Hispanic/Latina/o ethnic humor. *Studies in Popular Culture, 37*(2), 143–161.

Paz, C. (2020, October 29). What liberals don't understand about pro-Trump Latinos. *Atlantic.*

Peraccini, C., & Alligood, D. L. (2005). *Color television: Fifty years of African American and Latino images on primetime television.* Kendall/Hunt.

Piñón, J., & Rojas, V. (2011). Language and cultural identity in the configuration of the US Latino TV industry. *Global Media and Communication, 7*(2), 129–147.

Ran, A., & Cahan, J. (Eds.) (2012). *Returning to Babel: Jewish Latin American experiences, representations, and identity.* Brill.

Reyes, L., & Rubie, P. (1994). *Hispanics in Hollywood: An encyclopedia of film and television.* Garland.

Reyes, R. A. (2015, July 23). Mitú's Beatriz Acevedo wants to be voice of millennial generation. *NBC News.* https://www.nbcnews.com/news/latino/mitus-beatriz-acevedo-wants-be-voice-millennial-generation-n396381

Rivadeneyra, R., Ward, L. M., & Gordon, M. (2007). Distorted reflections: Media exposure and Latino adolescents' conceptions of self. *Media Psychology, 9*(2), 261–290.

Rosenberg, R. (2015). Jewish "diasporic humor" and contemporary Jewish-American identity. *Shofar: An Interdisciplinary Journal of Jewish Studies, 33*(3), 110–138.

Russonello, G., & Mazzei, P. (2021, April 2). Trump's Latino support was more widespread than thought, report finds. *New York Times.*

Samuelson, R. (2012, September/October). No habla español. *Columbia Journalism Review.* https://archives.cjr.org/feature/no_habla_espanol.php

Santa Ana, O. (2002). *Brown tide rising: Metaphors of Latinos in contemporary American public discourse.* University of Texas Press.

Shohat, E., & Stam, R. (1994). *Unthinking Eurocentrism: Multiculturalism and the media.* Routledge.

Sinclair, J. (2003). "The Hollywood of Latin America": Miami as regional center in television trade. *Television & New Media, 4*(3), 211–229.

Soto-Vásquez, A. (2020). *Mobilizing the U.S. Latinx vote.* Routledge.

Taladrid, S. (2021, September 21). The exclusion of Latinos from American media and history books. *New Yorker.*

Tamborini, R., & Mastro, D. (2000). The color of crime and the court: A content analysis of minority representation on television. *Journal of Mass Communication Quarterly, 77*(3), 499–521.

Tukachinsky, R. (2015). Where we have been and where we can go: Looking to the future in research on media, race, and ethnicity. *Journal of Social Issues, 71*(1), 186–199.

Valdivia, A. (2003). Radical hybridity: Latina/os as the paradigmatic transnational post-subculture. In D. Muggleton & R. Weinzierl (Eds.), *The Post-Subcultures Reader* (pp. 151–166). Berg.

Valdivia, A. (2010). *Latina/os and the media.* Polity Press.

Venezuela's Guaido pushes to name new representative to regional lender. (2019, March 4). *Reuters.* https://www.reuters.com/article/us-venezuela-politics-hausmann/venezuelas-guaido-pushes-to-name-new-representative-to-regional-lender-idUSKCN1QL2A6/

Villafañe, V. (2022, January 31). Televisa and Univision close $4.8B media merger. *Forbes.* https://www.forbes.com/sites/veronicavillafane/2022/01/31/televisa-and-univision-close-48b-media-merger/?sh=132756ef7405

Wang, S. (2016, February 12). BuzzFeed launches Pero Like, a distributed project for the "English-speaking Latinx" community. *Nieman Lab.* https://www.niemanlab.org/2016/02/buzzfeed-launches

Wilkinson, K. (2009). Spanish language media in the United States. In A. Albarran (Ed.), *The handbook of Spanish language media* (pp. 3–16). Routledge.

7

Conclusions

Digital Satire as Subversive Cultural Glocalization

The 2010s wave of Latin American and Latinx audiovisual sociopolitical satirists on digital-native platforms coincided with an increasing climate of ideological polarization in the region. Mass protests and state repression in various countries evidenced fundamental challenges to fragile Latin American democracies, as well as to the United States, particularly after the 2016 election of Donald Trump (and the rise of other authoritarian right-wing neopopulist leaders in the region) and the COVID-19 pandemic. Structural problems of corruption, social inequality, violence, and discrimination in terms of race, gender, and social class have been at the center of satire's sociopolitical critiques, alongside the poor democratic performance of the mainstream media, the widespread rise of fake news, and the media's detrimental effects on citizens' lives and public communication.

The digital-native satire cases analyzed in this book responded to specific national sociopolitical crises (that in many cases led to popular protests) and the negative role that a significant segment of traditional and conservative news and entertainment media has taken in support of antidemocratic, polarizing, and reactionary forces. In Mexico, *El Pulso de la República* (*EPR*) was born in the context of the citizens' movement Yo Soy 132, initially created by students calling for the democratization of the national media and the repudiation of the "mediatic imposition" of Enrique Peña Nieto, the Institutional Revolutionary Party (PRI) candidate, as president in 2012. In opposition to the historical alliance between the PRI and Televisa (the country's biggest media conglomerate), *EPR* channeled the dissatisfaction with concentrated media operating as a de facto power in Mexico by offering an alternative to its coverage. In Colombia, reacting to the trauma of the long period of political violence and addressing the debates around the national peace process, *La Pulla* used its coverage

to summarize many of the sociopolitical tensions that led to the polarizing 2016 referendum and later the 2021 mass protests, while *Las Igualadas*
highlighted the gender component of the discussion about violence in the
country, calling for a focus on *periodismo de género* (gender journalism)
in contrast to the predominant patriarchal narratives. Both digital shows
counterbalanced the mainstream media's biased coverage of the armed
conflict and the peace process in a mediascape marked by self-censorship
and violence against journalists. In Argentina, Guille Aquino's *El Sketch*
was launched with the election of the conservative president Mauricio
Macri in 2015 and the intense polarization between Macrism and Kirchnerism, a continuation of the Peronist and anti-Peronist dichotomy that
has historically divided the country. Satirizing the contradictions of the
Right, the Left, and the "apolitical," Aquino's critiques targeted *la grieta*
(the crack or ideological gap) and the role of the media in framing the
public issues that have fueled the conflict and the recurrent crises since
the country's 2001 economic collapse. In post-Fujimori Peru, *Gente Como
Uno* (*GCU*) satirized the mainstream media's conservative, prejudiced, and
ignorant role—inherited from its alliance with the 1990s dictatorship—in
celebrating the macroeconomic growth and superficial branding of a
country that failed to expand social and educational programs, evidencing
huge inequalities across social groups and geographic areas. Similarly, the
character El Cacash addressed the ingrained corruption exhibited in the
context of political instability (with four presidents in office within a year
and most of the presidents of the past three decades incarcerated, dead
by suicide, or sentenced for corruption), the devastating public health crisis with the COVID-19 pandemic, and the controversial presidential election in the 2021 *bicentenario* (the two hundredth anniversary of the independence of the country). Both *GCU* and El Cacash tackled Peru's severe
institutional crisis and polarization, criticizing the mainstream media's
increasingly biased role in supporting right-wing candidates and conservative discourses that legitimized the authoritarian and corrupt legacy of
the Fujimori years. In the United States, Venezuelan American comedian
Joanna Hausmann viscerally reacted to the presidential election and discriminatory discourse of Donald Trump as well as the responsibility of
the Chávez/Maduro regime in the humanitarian crisis in Venezuela. As
part of her critiques, Hausmann repeatedly targeted the role of the media in reproducing negative and homogeneous stereotypes of Latinos/as in
the United States and the partisan framing of the Venezuelan conflict. In

all these contexts of highly ideological polarization, digital-native satiric shows were able to articulate critical, distinctive, and nonpartisan interpretations of reality, filling a gap left by traditional journalism and commercial entertainment, and offering social catharsis by saying what was otherwise unsaid in their national mediascapes during times of sociopolitical crisis. Responding to generational dissatisfaction—particularly from Gen Xers and millennials—with public discourse, these satiric voices increasingly sought to dismantle fake news, elucidate social tensions, and establish new versions of "truth" with in-depth content that went beyond confrontational attacks between opposing ideological or political views.

While digital satire deconstructs traditional media's claims of authority, exposes the media's limitations and contradictions, and suggests new forms to communicate about political and sociocultural issues, it also maintains an ambivalent relationship with those outlets. Not only do many of the hosts and producers sporadically or recurrently participate in commercial media, but their digital satiric shows tend to combine mainstream and alternative characteristics. Created with low-budget, DIY production methods and seeking to offer "different" content than most traditional media outlets, most of them aim at high-quality professional standards in terms of substance, artistry, and reporting. In some cases, their satiric videos were eventually broadcast on television or cable networks (as in the cases of *El Sketch*, Malena Pichot's *Cualca*, *Enchufe.tv*, and Chumel Torres's show on HBO) or were distributed by wider news and entertainment portals (as in the cases of *Joanna Rants*, *La Pulla*, *Las Igualadas*, and *GCU*). In all cases, however, the satiric shows maintained the web as their main independent platform, controlling their own social media accounts. Furthermore, digital satire shows have implemented hybrid business models. While they operate under today's platform capitalism, most of them do not rely on traditional advertising or an affiliation with bigger media conglomerates (arguing that doing so would limit their editorial control). They have found new methods of sustainability—YouTube monetization, crowdfunding, sponsorships, grants, public talks, merchandising, and theater/stand-up shows, among others. The case of *La Pulla* is particularly interesting and exceptional, because its origin and development are tied to *El Espectador*, the oldest newspaper in Colombia. But even in this case, while the show's producers receive mentoring and editorial and legal protection from the newspaper, they fundraise to pay for their own salaries in order to maintain independence and editorial control.

Operating as hybrid alternative media enterprises that engage in the discursive integration of news, politics, and entertainment, digital satire shows challenge hegemonic discourses about their national realities as a result of the global flows of information and communications media. All the cases analyzed in this book were inspired by global satiric formats and internationally popular shows, particularly from the United States—from late-night shows such as *The Daily Show*, *The Colbert Report*, *Saturday Night Live*'s Weekend Update, and *Last Week Tonight with John Oliver* to sitcoms and stand-up comedian projects such as *Seinfeld*, *Girls*, *Da Ali G Show*, *Curb Your Enthusiasm*, *The Office*, and *Between Two Ferns*, among others. Influenced by these internationally popular, irreverent satiric television styles, Latin American satirists adapted those references to their national realities using colloquialism, local popular culture, and national news agendas and themes, while simultaneously establishing a dialogue with their own country's satiric and countercultural history. Chumel Torres has frequently referred to Mexico's Brozo, *el payaso tenebroso* (the shady clown), a subversive, fictional clown created in the 1990s that commented on the news and criticized the political establishment in Mexico. Guille Aquino is artistically indebted to the satiric show *Peter Capusotto y sus videos*, which surrealistically used the lens of rock music culture to tackle Argentine sociocultural tensions. *La Pulla* performs under the shadow of Jaime Garzón, the political satirist of the 1990s who was killed in Colombia by paramilitaries. Contrastingly, Latin American digital satire also reacts to prevalent national traditions of discriminatory entertainment media and comedy, particularly to humor based on simplistic reproductions of sexist, racist, and homophobic jokes. In contrast to the media corporations that adapt noncontroversial global formats to appeal to the (widest possible) local audiences by creating nonalienating homogeneous content, Latin American digital creators of satire combine transgressive global satiric formats with their own irreverent cultural traditions to create new complex, subversive, and unique glocal voices that tap into specific national tensions.

In this sense, the multilayered configuration of Latin American digital satire as subversive cultural glocalization connects with the characteristics of postmodern critical metatainment—a carnivalesque result of and a transgressive reaction to the global process of tabloidization in the media spectacle era—in its aim to "use humor to develop a sociocultural and political critique, while at the same time questioning the role of media in society and deconstructing news and entertainment genres through parody in order to challenge their claims of authority and/or moral consistency" (Alonso, 2018, p. 152). I developed the concept of critical metatainment as negotiated dissent particularly for broadcast and cable television, where satiric shows need to negotiate their ability to transgress within the strict limits of network regulations, interests, and editorial stances coming from the stations' close connections to power. In the case of digital-native satire, however, the internet offers different (arguably looser) parameters, and the limits of dissent are broader. While still conditioned by restrictions deriving from platform capitalism and attempts of co-optation and censorship, online shows are able to articulate the sort of complex sociopolitical critiques rarely seen in Latin American national and cable television. In this sense, digital-native satire as subversive cultural glocalization highlights a more disruptive approach to audiovisual satire than does focusing on television precedents, drawing from foreign and national transgressive cultural traditions and engaging in a more nuanced and multilayered critique of the cultural status quo, the sociopolitical establishment, and hegemonic media practices, including those of the satiric shows' own digital platforms.

Thus, digital-native satire delves into topics otherwise infrequently touched on by Latin American television entertainment, such as a deconstruction of gender and other local and transnational ideological identities related to racial, ethnic, socioeconomic, and political divisions, with an emphasis on intersectionality as a cornerstone to approaching these issues. Often practicing a self-critical attitude toward their own positionality within the realm of identities, online satiric shows negotiate contemporary media sensibilities, creating sophisticated online glocal communities of satiric interpretation, mostly formed by progressive, young, urban, and educated niches, instead of trying to appeal to wider television audiences. The fact that many of these satiric online videos circulate and resonate among many Latin American cities speaks of a regional globalization, in which issues such as gentrification, discrimination, corruption, and violence are perceived as shared social problems with similar characteristics among Latin American societies. Because of this, some online satirists are able to establish a regional voice. For example, Chumel Torres expanded the Mexican political satire of *EPR* by focusing on broader Latin American issues with his late-night show on HBO, which targeted a regional audience. Malena Pichot, whose feminist videos were already famous in various Latin American cities, has recurrently promoted her humorous work through shows in Spain and even released a stand-up comedy special on Netflix. This internationalization marks an interesting stage in their relationship with cultural globalization: while the cases first adapt international referents and create a distinct voice at the local/national level, they then adapt this voice to reach wider regional or geolinguistic audiences, creating a new layer in the hybrid process.

While all the digital-native satiric shows analyzed in this book were created by late Gen Xers and millennials, not all of them have successfully adapted to more recent social media platforms. Many early YouTubers who also became prominent on Facebook or Twitter (now X) have avoided transitioning to TikTok or Snapchat, arguing time constraints, lack of resources/interest, or the difficulty of translating their content to shorter formats. Further comparative research would need to contrast satiric content across digital platforms in order to understand new transmedia logics, cross-national and intergenerational changes in the production and consumption of political satire, and the evolution of memetic communication and artificial intelligence (AI) into new forms of audiovisual humor. A limitation of this book remains the lack of audience research in the region. While this study examined representative digital satire shows in terms of their content, production conditions, and sociopolitical contexts, there is scarce knowledge about their reception, how are they being interpreted by Latin American multicultural audiences. In chapter 5, I propose the notion of satiric literacy, which can be considered part of a wider conceptualization of media literacy, to begin a conversation about how to evaluate Latin American audiences' ability to access, analyze, and interpret polysemous, ironic, and metareferential satiric texts. Future qualitative audience research should consider differences of gender, race, social class, age, geographic area, and access to education and global sources of information, among other variables such as digital divides, to further understand satiric literacy in a context marked by ideological polarization and disinformation. Furthermore, future studies should carefully consider how the increasing fundamental challenges to Western democracies affect the role of satire in the postpandemic/Trump world, when certain types of satiric media have become part of the mainstream (sometimes repetitive and stagnant) offerings of political communication in the United States, and when multimedia right-wing entertainment and cynical irony have taken a central place in the exercise of power and the rise of extreme (anti) political movements.

* * *

On May 29, 2023, I participated in a timely roundtable under the title "Reexamining Political Satire in an Age of Broken Politics," held at the International Communication Association conference in Toronto, Canada. Chaired by Dr. Geoffrey Baym, a professor at Temple University and a pioneer academic on contemporary political television satire in the United States, the event gathered a variety of international scholars to discuss the state of the genre. The brief description, included in the program of the conference, was as follows:

> Some decade and a half ago, a range of scholars argued that emerging forms of political satire could help to bring about a new kind of political conversation, characterised by humour, civility, and engagement with popular citizenship. Now, with deliberative democracy under assault, a public sphere flooded with disinformation, and traditional outlets for civic communication struggling to be heard among a deluge of different voices, what has happened to, and what *is happening with*, political satire? (International Communication Association, 2023)

Contributions ranged from elaborations on the disappearance or fragmentation of a shared (satiric) public sphere and satire's decreasing "surprise effect" to the rise of right-wing comedy, the potential of "participatory satire," and reduced audiences for meaningful political conversation.[1] Speaking from a Latin American perspective, I warned about US-centric assumptions that broken politics and deliberative democracy under assault are recent phenomena. I argued that at least in Latin America, satiric media has long operated under systems of fragile or broken politics in which deliberative democracy has been under assault, whether from US-backed military dictatorships or from the imposition of corrupt neoliberal democracies, authoritarian populism, and narco-states. In these scenarios, contemporary (and particularly digital) political satire remains an essential barometer of freedom of expression in Latin American countries. It frequently establishes the limits of dissent within national mediascapes, dealing with recurring attempts of censorship and co-optation, and navigating a world in which populist leaders appropriate the symbolic impact of transgression with their outrageous behavior or cynically use political correctness to "cancel" dissident voices. Moreover, satire's configuration as a discursive object of complex meanings still ignites furious backlash—from violent attacks and online harassment to cancel culture—among both progressives and conservatives. Concerns about safe spaces for comedy have increased in the United States, and satire remains a front-runner in negotiating the limits of transgressive dissent in today's mediascapes and public discourse as well as in shaping its motivations, morals, and potential effects. As Chilean writer Roberto Bolaño (2007, p. 295), who considered humor to be "something similar to happiness, revolution and love," once wrote, "sharp humor . . . threatens the fragile stability of imbeciles who, when they read, have an uncontrollable desire to hang the author in the town square. I can't think of a higher honor for a writer." And this honor has been frequently served in many platforms. From Diogenes of Sinope to Dave Chappelle, from Jonathan Swift to digital humorists all over the world harassed by armies of trolls, the ancient genre of satire has resisted attacks, survived technological revolutions, and always been able to reinvent itself. Artificial intelligence will only become a central threat to humans when it becomes able to create original subversive humor that condenses our deepest fears and anxieties. And makes us laugh.

Note

1 The complete list of presentations included in the program: "The Satiric Cross-Roads: How to Critique When No One Is Listening" (Amber Day, Bryant University); "The Success That Proved a Failure: The Post-Stewart Satiric Community" (Jonathan Gray, University of Wisconsin–Madison); "The Pitfalls and Possibilities for Future Satire Investigations" (Mark Boukes, University of Amsterdam); "Online Satire during Pandemic Lockdowns in China" (Guobin Yang, University of Pennsylvania); "Satire on the Right" (Matt Sienkiewicz, Boston College, and Nick Marx, Colorado State University); "Tilting at Windmills: The Problem(s) with Jon Stewart" (Geoffrey Baym, Temple University); "Sociopolitical Satire in Times of Polarization and the Pandemic Global Crisis" (Paul Alonso, Georgia Institute of Technology); "'Birds Aren't Real': Participatory Satire in an Age of Participatory Disinformation" (Stephen Harrington and Phoebe Matich, Queensland University of Technology); "Populist Appropriations of Satire and Parody in India" (Sangeet Kumar, Denison University); "The Values of Right-Wing and Left-Wing Political Memes: A Critical Examination" (Limor Shifman, Hebrew University of Jerusalem); and "Satire Hunger Games: Can Political Satire Survive?" (Heather LaMarre, Temple University) (International Communication Association, 2023).

References

Alonso, P. (2018). *Satiric TV in the Americas: Critical metatainment as negotiated dissent.* Oxford University Press.

Bolaño, R. (2007). Horacio Castellanos Moya. In S. Schnee, A. S. Mason, & D. Felman (Eds.), *Words without borders: The world through the eyes of writers* (pp. 295–296). Anchor Books.

International Communication Association. (2023). *73rd annual ICA conference: Conference program.* https://www.icahdq.org/mpage/ICA23-Program

INDEX

Paul Alonso, associate professor at the Georgia Institute of Technology, is the author of *Satiric TV in the Americas* and *Thirty Years of Entertainment and Politics in Peru*. His research has appeared in a variety of prestigious Latin American studies and communication journals and been included in edited collections. He has published journalism in diverse international newspapers, magazines, and international outlets and is the author of four books of fiction. He has also hosted interview shows in Peru, as well as the satiric digital show *Gente Como Uno*.

Reframing Media, Technology, and Culture in Latin/o America

Edited by Héctor Fernández L'Hoeste and Juan Carlos Rodríguez

Reframing Media, Technology, and Culture in Latin/o America explores how Latin American and Latino audiovisual (film, television, digital), musical (radio, recordings, live performances, dancing), and graphic (comics, photography, advertising) cultural practices reframe and reconfigure social, economic, and political discourses at a local, national, and global level. In addition, it looks at how information networks reshape public and private policies, and the enactment of new identities in civil society. The series also covers how different technologies have allowed and continue to allow for the construction of new ethnic spaces. It not only contemplates the interaction between new and old technologies but also how the development of brand-new technologies redefines cultural production.

Telling Migrant Stories: Latin American Diaspora in Documentary Film, edited by Esteban E. Loustaunau and Lauren E. Shaw (2018; paperback edition, 2021)

Mestizo Modernity: Race, Technology, and the Body in Postrevolutionary Mexico, by David S. Dalton (2018; first paperback edition, 2021)

The Insubordination of Photography: Documentary Practices under Chile's Dictatorship, by Ángeles Donoso Macaya (2020; first paperback edition, 2023)

Digital Humanities in Latin America, edited by Héctor Fernández L'Hoeste and Juan Carlos Rodríguez (2020; first paperback edition, 2023)

Pablo Escobar and Colombian Narcoculture, by Aldona Bialowas Pobutsky (2020; first paperback edition 2024)

The New Brazilian Mediascape: Television Production in the Digital Streaming Age, by Eli Lee Carter (2020; first paperback edition, 2024)

Univision, Telemundo, and the Rise of Spanish-Language Television in the United States, by Craig Allen (2020; first paperback edition, 2023)

Cuba's Digital Revolution: Citizen Innovation and State Policy, edited by Ted A. Henken and Sara Garcia Santamaria (2021; first paperback edition, 2022)

Afro-Latinx Digital Connections, edited by Eduard Arriaga and Andrés Villar (2021)

The Lost Cinema of Mexico: From Lucha Libre to Cine Familiar and Other Churros, edited by Olivia Cosentino and Brian Price (2022)

Neo-Authoritarian Masculinity in Brazilian Crime Film, by Jeremy Lehnen (2022)

The Rise of Central American Film in the Twenty-First Century, edited by Mauricio Espinoza and Jared List (2023)

Internet, Humor, and Nation in Latin America, edited by Héctor Fernández L'Hoeste and Juan Poblete (2024)

Tropical Time Machines: Science Fiction in the Contemporary Hispanic Caribbean, by Emily A. Maguire (2024)

Digital Satire in Latin America: Online Video Humor as Hybrid Alternative Media, by Paul Alonso (2024)

www.ingramcontent.com/pod-product-compliance
Lightning Source LLC
Chambersburg PA
CBHW031134270326
41929CB00011B/1617